The Pragmatics of Fiction

Edinburgh Textbooks on the English Language – Advanced

General Editor
Heinz Giegerich, Professor of English Linguistics, University of Edinburgh

Editorial Board
Heinz Giegerich, University of Edinburgh – General Editor
Laurie Bauer (University of Wellington)
Olga Fischer (University of Amsterdam)
Willem Hollmann (Lancaster University)
Marianne Hundt (University of Zurich)
Rochelle Lieber (University of New Hampshire)
Bettelou Los (University of Edinburgh)
Robert McColl Millar (University of Aberdeen)
Donka Minkova (UCLA)
Edgar Schneider (University of Regensburg)
Graeme Trousdale (University of Edinburgh)

Titles in the series include:

Construction Grammar and its Application to English, 2nd edition
Martin Hilpert

Pragmatics
Chris Cummins

Corpus Linguistics and the Description of English, 2nd edition
Hans Lindquist and Magnus Levin

Modern Scots: An Analytical Survey
Robert McColl Millar

Contemporary Stylistics: Language, Cognition, Interpretation
Alison Gibbons and Sara Whiteley

A Critical Account of English Syntax: Grammar, Meaning, Text
Keith Brown and Jim Miller

English Historical Semantics
Christian Kay and Kathryn Allan

A Historical Syntax of English
Bettelou Los

Morphological Theory and the Morphology of English
Jan Don

Construction Grammar and its Application to English
Martin Hilpert

A Historical Phonology of English
Donka Minkova

English Historical Pragmatics
Andreas H. Jucker and Irma Taavitsainen

English Historical Sociolinguistics
Robert McColl Millar

Corpus Linguistics and the Description of English
Hans Lindquist

English Syntax: A Minimalist Account of Structure and Variation
Elspeth Edelstein

The Pragmatics of Fiction: Literature, Stage and Screen Discourse
Miriam A. Locher and Andreas H. Jucker

Visit the Edinburgh Textbooks in the English Language website at
https://edinburghuniversitypress.com/series-edinburgh-textbooks-on-the-english-language-advanced.html

The Pragmatics of Fiction
Literature, Stage and Screen Discourse

Miriam A. Locher and Andreas H. Jucker

EDINBURGH
University Press

Edinburgh University Press is one of the leading university presses in the UK. We publish academic books and journals in our selected subject areas across the humanities and social sciences, combining cutting-edge scholarship with high editorial and production values to produce academic works of lasting importance. For more information visit our website: edinburghuniversitypress.com

© Miriam A. Locher and Andreas H. Jucker, 2021

Edinburgh University Press Ltd
The Tun – Holyrood Road, 12(2f) Jackson's Entry, Edinburgh EH8 8PJ

Typeset in Janson MT by
Servis Filmsetting Ltd, Stockport, Cheshire,
and printed and bound in Great Britain.

A CIP record for this book is available from the British Library

ISBN 978 1 4744 4793 5 (hardback)
ISBN 978 1 4744 4795 9 (webready PDF)
ISBN 978 1 4744 4794 2 (paperback)
ISBN 978 1 4744 4796 6 (epub)

The right of Miriam A. Locher and Andreas H. Jucker to be identified as the authors of this work has been asserted in accordance with the Copyright, Designs and Patents Act 1988, and the Copyright and Related Rights Regulations 2003 (SI No. 2498).

Grateful acknowledgement is made to sources for permission to reproduce material previously published elsewhere. Every effort has been made to trace the copyright holders, but if any have been inadvertently overlooked, the publisher will be pleased to make the necessary arrangements at the first opportunity.

Contents

List of figures and tables ix
To readers xi
Acknowledgements xiii
Transcription conventions xv

Part I: The pragmatics of fiction as communication

1 Fiction and pragmatics 3
   1.1 Introduction 3
   1.2 The scope of fiction 4
   1.3 The scope of pragmatics 6
   1.4 The levels of communication in fiction 8
   1.5 Fictional data for pragmatic research 10
   1.6 The aims of this textbook 11
   Key concepts 13
   Exercises 13
   Further reading 13

2 Fiction and non-fiction 15
   2.1 Introduction 15
   2.2 Fictional utterances as 'non-serious' speech acts 17
   2.3 Literary models of fiction 19
   2.4 A pragmatic model of fiction 22
   2.5 Fictitious worlds and their extensions 27
   2.6 Conclusions 33
   Key concepts 34
   Exercises 34
   Further reading 35

3 Literature as communication 36
   3.1 Introduction 36

	3.2	Communicating literature	37
	3.3	Participation structure: the recipients	41
	3.4	Participation structure: the creators	49
	3.5	The complexities of performed fiction	51
	3.6	The audience talking back	55
	3.7	Conclusions	56
	Key concepts		56
	Exercises		57
	Further reading		58

Part II: The pragmatics of story worlds

4	Genres of fiction		61
	4.1	Introduction	61
	4.2	Structures of expectation in face-to-face communication	61
	4.3	Structures of expectation in written communication	64
	4.4	Structures of expectation in fiction	65
	4.5	Frames within frames: intradiegetic and extradiegetic	71
	4.6	Conclusions	73
	Key concepts		74
	Exercises		74
	Further reading		75

5	The narrative core		77
	5.1	Introduction	77
	5.2	Stories as fundamental meaning making units in discourse	78
	5.3	Stories in fiction: from starting point to intertextuality	84
	5.4	Stories in fiction: story world and narratorial voice	88
	5.5	Conclusions	95
	Key concepts		96
	Exercises		96
	Further reading		97

6	Character creation		98
	6.1	Introduction	98
	6.2	Multimodal cues in character creation	99
	6.3	Contrasts: regional, social and ethnic variation in past and present	103

6.4	Multilingualism in fictional character creation	112
6.5	Alienation effects: past and future	116
6.6	Translation challenges for character positioning	118
6.7	Conclusions	118
	Key concepts	119
	Exercises	119
	Further reading	121

Part III: Themes in the pragmatics of fiction

7	The performance of fiction	125
7.1	Introduction	125
7.2	The role of dialogue in fiction	127
7.3	Planning, production and interaction	135
7.4	Features of orality	139
7.5	Conclusions	146
	Key concepts	147
	Exercises	148
	Further reading	149

8	Relational work and (im/politeness) ideologies	150
8.1	Introduction	150
8.2	Relational work and (character) identity construction	153
8.3	Relational work in fiction	158
8.4	Fiction as locus for discursive im/politeness ideologies	162
8.5	Censuring and manufacturing	166
8.6	Conclusions	170
	Key concepts	171
	Exercises	171
	Further reading	172

9	The language of emotion	173
9.1	Introduction	173
9.2	The nature of emotions	175
9.3	Two modes of presenting emotions in fiction	177
9.4	Emotion cues in fiction	180
9.5	The paradox of fiction: real and fake emotions	189
9.6	Conclusions	192
	Key concepts	194
	Exercises	194
	Further reading	195

10	Poetic language	196
	10.1 Introduction	196
	10.2 Poetic effects	197
	10.3 Metaphors	207
	10.4 Irony	214
	10.5 Conclusions	220
	Key concepts	221
	Exercises	221
	Further reading	222
11	Fiction, pragmatics and future research	224
	11.1 Introduction	224
	11.2 Fact, fiction and the fictional contract	226
	11.3 Distinctive pragmatic features of fiction	230
	11.4 Outlook and future research	235
	Exercises	237
	Further reading	238

Glossary — 239
Bibliography — 257
   Literary sources — 257
   Movies and television series — 258
   Dictionaries and corpora — 259
   Websites — 259
   References — 259

Index — 271

Figures and tables

Figures

1.1	Three types of fiction	5
1.2	Layering of language use	9
2.1	A pragmatic model of fiction: genres plotted according to levels of fictitiousness and reader/viewer expectations concerning fictionality	23
2.2	Dynamic reader/viewer expectations concerning fictionality of genres and specific texts	25
3.1	Recipient roles in the speech situation	43
3.2	Recipient roles in extradiegetic fictional discourse	44
3.3	A simple model of communication	51
3.4	A model of communication for fiction in general	52
3.5	A model of communication for performed fiction	53
5.1	Structural conventions for personal experience storytelling	81
5.2	Extract of *Tristram Shandy*	87
7.1	Orality in spontaneous interaction, performed fiction and written fiction	136
8.1	PhD Comics by Jorge Cham (2008). 'Average time spent composing one e-mail'	172
9.1	Two modes of presenting emotions in fiction	179
9.2	CALVIN AND HOBBES	181
9.3	Screenshots (details) from *My Life Without Me* (2002)	186

Tables

4.1	The relation between text functions and text features	65
5.1	Core elements of narratives of personal experience	80
5.2	Levels of focalisation	93
6.1	Explicit, implicit and authorial cues	102

6.2	Reasons for variation	104
6.3	A taxonomy of multilingualism in fictional texts	113
7.1	The roles of dialogue in fiction (overlap possible)	128
7.2	Examples of features of orality	140
8.1	An open list of potential factors influencing the choice of relational work strategies with respect to the imposition of a particular speech act in its socio-cultural context	155
9.1	Overview of emotion cues	183
9.2	Five levels of emotional connection with fiction	192
10.1	Three pragmatic accounts of metaphors	213

To readers

The authors of this book have both been trained in English philology in the Swiss educational system. This means that we studied anglophone literatures and cultures as well as English linguistics. We have always perceived this merging of disciplines as beneficial for our own understanding of the use of English in its many different cultural contexts. While we specialised in English linguistics and in particular in pragmatics and discourse studies over the course of our careers, we have retained our love for fiction in all its many forms from poems, plays, novels, mangas, cartoons and graphic novels to telecinematic artefacts. They are an integral part of our lives and an indispensable source of inspiration, emotion, information and discovery. For this book, we have joined forces to write up our ideas on how to approach fiction from a pragmatic angle.

Our background in English studies and linguistics means that our target audience for this book is, on the one hand, our own students of English. For this reason, we have drawn almost exclusively on fictional sources in English. Our choice of texts follows our own preferences of reading and watching, inspired also by our students. There is no hidden agenda as to what texts we included but we are aware that some of the texts are part of the canon in English studies while others may be less so. We invite all readers to find different examples from the abundance of fiction in English to illustrate the issues we raise on a pragmatic level. On the other hand, we have conceptualised this textbook such that any student interested in fiction and pragmatics in general can benefit from it and add their own examples from fiction in other languages.

Each chapter builds on the next. This means that the later chapters draw on the key issues and concepts introduced in previous chapters. For those readers who prefer reading chapters out of sequence, we have added pointers to the chapters where key concepts are introduced earlier. In addition, each chapter introduces a number of key issues in text boxes and lists key concepts. At the end of the book you will find a glossary of these concepts in alphabetical order. This should allow students to easily review and navigate. It is followed by a bibliography of the sources used in this book and an index. Below, just before Part I, you will find an explanation of the transcription conventions that we have used for extracts from telecinematic artefacts.

As the book is written as an introductory text and not an academic study, we have quoted fewer sources and have mentioned fewer studies than we would in our research publications. Each chapter is therefore completed with pointers to further scholarly literature for the benefit of those readers who want to deepen their understanding of the issues raised. In particular, we refer our readers to the handbook *Pragmatics of Fiction*, which we edited in 2017, and which contains many valuable overview chapters written by experts in the field.

Finally, being passionate about fiction as well as linguistics, we hope that our observations and introductions to pragmatic approaches to fiction will change the ways in which our readers appreciate fiction in the future. We therefore invite our readers to develop a keen eye and ear for the issues raised in the book when engaging with fiction in their own time.

Acknowledgements

From Miriam

This textbook has had a long gestation time and bears the marks of many people who influenced me over the years. My first thanks go to Gunnel Tottie, who always included fictional sources in her linguistics lectures and courses and taught me in a seminar on language in the movies. Thanks to her, I was made aware not only of the possibility of merging approaches but also of fiction as relevant and fascinating data in its own right. Heidi Hamilton opened my eyes to narratives in general during my research stay at Georgetown University and her teaching has inspired me. Over the years, this interest has led me to teach lectures and seminars on the pragmatics of fiction. With their feedback, my students helped develop the courses on which the ideas for the handbook *Pragmatics of Fiction* and this textbook (both with Andreas Jucker) are based. Thanks go in particular to Susann Scheich for alerting us to the movie *My Life Without Me* and to Andrea Wüst for initial transcription of some of the movie scenes for a lecture that has now made it into this book and to Denise Kaufmann for endnote support. Thanks also go to Hikyoung Lee, who kindly hosted me during two sabbaticals at Korea University, where I found optimal writing conditions to concentrate on this project. I dedicate this book to my grandmother, whose undying love for literature was passed on to all her sons and grandchildren, and to my parents, who never ever questioned the need to buy yet another set of new books and whom I have never seen without a pile of them at their bedside.

From Andreas

When I decided to study English at the University of Zurich, my main motivation was my love for reading and my wish to immerse myself in a foreign culture. My love for books and reading never abated but in the course of my studies I discovered that at that point in my life, linguistics was even more exciting and therefore embarked on a career in a field that at that time had little contact with literature. It was only through the discovery of historical pragmatics and my cooperation with Irma Taavitsainen that my scholarly work increasingly made use of fictional data. So, my thanks go to Irma for her close cooperation spanning several decades. My work on politeness in the history of English also forced me to turn to fictional data. When the opportunity offered itself to cooperate with Miriam Locher on a handbook of fiction, I could combine the two fields more systematically, for which I am very grateful. I am also grateful to my colleagues at the University of Zurich for always generously allowing me to extend the narrow definition of my professorship and offer courses on the history of English and on the pragmatics of fiction. And my thanks go to my students who responded with enthusiasm to these choices and who keep challenging me with their insights and erudition.

From both

We both wish to thank the Basel beta-readers Dominick Andrew Boyle, Arthur Eberhardt and Joelle Loew for their honest and constructive feedback from the point of view of students. Equal thanks go to Martin Mühlheim and Rahel Oppliger from Zurich, who helped us with their expertise in literary and cultural studies. We also thank the reviewers for constructive and helpful feedback.

Writing this book together has been an absolute pleasure. It is rare to find someone who not only shares the same linguistic approach, has the same work ethics and even labels files in the same way, but our discussions and honest critical input on each other's writings has shaped this book and turned it into something that we could not have written on our own in this way.

Seoul/Zurich, March 2020

Transcription conventions

The following conventions are based on Du Bois et al. (1992) with some adaptations and have been presented in this way in Locher (2004: vii–x):

.	:	A period is used to indicate a falling intonation with a conclusion point.
,	:	A comma expresses a continuing intonation.
?	:	A question mark indicates an appeal which is achieved by 'a marked high rise in pitch at the end of the intonation unit' (Du Bois et al. 1992: 30).
^word	:	A caret marks a word which carries the primary accent in an intonation unit.
'word	:	A raised stroke indicates a minor or secondary accent.
=	:	In order to show lengthening of sounds, an equals sign is used. Alternatively, it is used to indicate run-on lines (see illustration below).
-	:	A single hyphen is used to indicate an unfinished word.
--	:	Two hyphens show that a whole intonation unit was left unfinished.
..	:	Two periods indicate a short pause (according to the author's judgement).
...	:	Three periods or more are used to indicate a medium or very long pause.
[...]	:	Square brackets indicate speech overlap. Double or triple square brackets are used to distinguish this overlap from previous ones.
{ ... }	:	Curly brackets are used to indicate overlap within overlap or help to make complicated passages with much overlap easier to read.
@	:	This symbol is used to represent laughter in syllables.
X	:	The letter X is used to indicate either a speaker whose identity is unclear or an unintelligible syllable or word.

*	: An asterisk points to further background information given in double parentheses.

The following combinations indicate that the words enclosed by the angle brackets have the quality of the additional symbol(s):

<X...X>	: Utterances marked by this are unintelligible. The words given are the best guess the transcriber was able to make.
<A...A>	: allegro, rapid speech
<P...P>	: piano, soft
<Q...Q>	: quotation quality
<@...@>	: laughter quality
<I...I>	: imitating
<W...W>	: whispering
<PRC...PRC>	: pronounced
((GULP))	: Double parentheses are used to accommodate the transcriber's comments.
→	: The arrow points to the phenomenon under discussion.
335	: Line numbers help to locate the points of interest.

The transcriptions are based on intonation units. This means that every line represents one unit of talk, which is either terminated by a final intonation (.), a questioning intonation (?), an intonation which implies that the speaker wishes to continue (,); or the intonation unit is left unfinished (--). Primary (^) and secondary (') stresses are given in every unit.

If the intonation unit is too long to fit on one line, it continues on the next with an equals sign indicating the latch, as can be seen in lines 345–347:

342	Roy:	but the ^premise of the study is that you 'control,
343		'everything you can ^control for,
344		'because,
345		we're not ^allowed to do 'experiments on identical twins in=
346		=which we bring them up in absolutely ^identical and ^control=
347		=everything.
348		we ^do that with 'with uh,

When the conversation splits into two or more parties who talk at the same time, the dialogues are written down next to each other, as exemplified in lines 95–99:

92	Kate:	Roy I think you're putting [a lot in your mouth.]		
93	Anne:	[it should be ^both.]		
94	Miriam /Kate:	[@@@]		
95	Anne:	it should be-	Roy:	<X XX XX. X>
96		it should be ^both.	Kate:	<@ and you're talking at=
97		if you are straight A and poor,		= the same time. @>
98		you should have more ^money.	Roy:	right.
99			Kate:	poor ^you.
100	Anne:	... if you are straight A uhm,		
101		.. if you are C and ^no money,		

Part I

The pragmatics of fiction as communication

Part 1

1 Fiction and pragmatics

1.1 Introduction

Imagine the following situation: together with some friends you have just watched the most recent instalment of your favourite TV series and now you talk about the events that you have just witnessed. Perhaps you share your excitement or frustration about some turn of events, perhaps you feel happy or sorry for one of your heroes, perhaps you were even a little scared by some unexpected dangers afflicting one of the characters. But at the same time, you realise that what you have just witnessed were not real events. They were performed by actors who pretended to be in love or in agony or in danger or all of them at the same time. The actors talked to each other, chatted, shouted, whispered, interrogated other characters, made promises, declared their never-ending love and so on. Occasionally we may be drawn in and believe that we are witnessing real people interacting with each other, while at the same time it is clear that we are witnessing actors performing dialogues that somebody else has written for them in order to perform a storyline. Nevertheless, we are regularly moved by events that are only fictitious and sometimes even more so than by the real events with which we are confronted every day in the news media, and this is at least part of the reason why fiction in its many forms and guises is so enjoyable for many of us.

When we think of fiction, we immediately think of novels, theatre plays and movies, but there are also poems, short stories, fairy tales, soap operas, fan fiction and many, many more ways of narrating stories. It is tempting to say that what they all have in common is the fact that they all present characters and events in a story world that are invented by the imagination of an author and, therefore, are in an important sense not real or not factual. But needless to say, things are more complicated than they seem as we will show in some detail in Chapter 2. The boundaries between fiction and non-fiction are notoriously fuzzy. Historical novels, autobiographies and even documentaries – to take just three obvious examples – may consist of a complex mix of actual and fictitious characters, events and incidental details.

However, what all these forms of fiction also have in common is the fact that they are rather complex forms of communication, and it is this aspect that we are going to focus on in this book. Novels, plays, movie scripts and all the other forms of fiction are written by authors, sometimes teams of authors, for an audience. The authors create a text through which they communicate with the audience. This communication differs considerably from the prototypical communication between two people who engage in a face-to-face interaction. In the typical case, the author and the audience never meet directly. The author may even have lived many centuries ago, and the audience generally does not have a chance to communicate back, except in the form of silent approval expressed through purchasing copies of the book or watching the play or movie and so on. By and large, all these forms of fiction are – or at least appear to be at first sight – a kind of one-way communication.

Fictional texts also have in common that they generally depict – among other things – communicative events. It is difficult to imagine a play, a novel or a short story, for instance, without some form of interaction between characters. Radio plays typically rely almost entirely on dialogues between characters unless they use a narrator or a significant amount of sound effects. Perhaps some poems come to mind that depict a scene without the intervention of any communicating characters but even in such cases literary scholars talk of a 'lyrical I' communicating to a 'lyrical thou', which should be distinguished clearly from the actual author and the actual reader.

1.2 The scope of fiction

In this book we adopt a broad and inclusive notion of what fiction is with a fuzzy boundary between fiction and non-fiction. We will explore the nature of this boundary in more detail in Chapter 2. At this point, we want to delimit the scope of fiction by listing some examples and by introducing a distinction between written fiction, performed fiction and spontaneously produced fiction (see Figure 1.1). Under the heading of 'written fiction', we subsume such prototypical literary genres as novels, novellas, short stories and poems, which are texts written by an author, or sometimes by multiple authors, for a large audience who will consume them by actually reading them. Under this heading, we also include graphic novels and stories for children with more drawings than written text. Picture stories without any text at all cannot really be

Figure 1.1 Three types of fiction

called 'written' any more, but these, too, are fictions that are generally consumed directly without the intervention of orators or actors and would, therefore, also be subsumed under our general label of 'written fiction'.

Under the heading 'performed fiction', we subsume theatre plays, movies for the cinema or television, television serials, soap operas and the like, which generally rely on actors who perform what an author, or a team of authors, has written for an audience of spectators rather than readers. This also includes music theatre in the form of operas or musicals. It might even include dance theatre and ballet which, in a way, also narrate stories for an audience. Such forms are particularly interesting because they communicate in highly complex and fascinating ways but as they do not involve language in the traditional sense, we will not cover such art forms in this book. The boundary between written fiction and performed fiction is porous, too. An orator, perhaps even the author, may read out parts of a novel and turn it into an audiobook and thus the written fiction becomes performed fiction. In contrast, plays, which are meant to be the basis of performed fiction, are often read silently and thus turn into written fiction.

In addition to written and performed fiction, we recognise what might be called 'spontaneous fiction'. In a wide sense, this term applies to all forms of daydreaming or collaborative conversational creations of imaginary worlds in which we imagine 'what would happen if...'. We might spend our coffee break, for instance, in fantasising what we would do if we had won the lottery and didn't have to come back to work tomorrow, or if we had the power of witchcraft and could turn the bleak coffee-room facilities into a dream holiday destination. Children often create such fantasy worlds in their play. They take on roles of explorers, racing car drivers, astronauts, nurses, teachers or whatever else takes their fantasy. Or they might use dolls, stuffed animals, play figures or even everyday objects to enact these roles or to furnish their fantasy world with the appropriate artefacts. A stick turns into a magic wand, a stone into a car, or a piece of paper into an aeroplane.

Spontaneously created fiction also includes the art form of improvisation theatre, often called improv theatre. Most of what the actors perform is unplanned and unscripted. It is created and invented during the performance, often in collaborative interaction with the audience, which may make suggestions for specific scenes to be improvised by the actors, for continuations of unfinished scenes, for words or phrases that the actors should try to integrate into their dialogues and so on. And again, the boundaries are not hard and fast. The performance of a given play may include ad lib passages, for instance, thus blurring the boundary between spontaneous and performed fiction. And children's fantasy worlds may be closely modelled on an existing fairy tale, blurring the boundary between spontaneous and written fiction. In this textbook, however, our main focus will be on written and performed fiction, with only occasional references to the pragmatic peculiarities of spontaneously created fiction.

1.3 The scope of pragmatics

In order to disentangle these communicative complexities, we are going to use the tools of pragmatics because pragmatics is the linguistic discipline that focuses on the communicative aspects of language. It studies the many different ways in which we use language in actual everyday situations. As a discipline in its own right it started in the sixties and seventies of the last century. Initially it was the philosophers of language, John Austin and John Searle, who pointed out the performative aspect of language. When we use language, we perform actions; we ask questions, we apologise, we greet each other, or we assert something. From this point of view, it was no longer the way in which words or sentences are constructed that was at the centre of interest but what sentences achieve in the real world when they are used in actual conversations. In the following decades, pragmatics as a field of study grew and diversified at a remarkable rate to become one of the dominant fields in linguistics with a large number of dedicated and specialised conferences, journals, textbooks and handbooks.

From very early on, two strands of pragmatics could be distinguished, and to some extent they still exist today and manifest themselves in a somewhat different range of topics that is included in the respective textbooks and handbooks. They are called 'Anglo-American pragmatics' and 'Continental European pragmatics' respectively (e.g. by Huang 2014: 4), or 'theoretical pragmatics' and 'social pragmatics' (e.g. by Chapman 2011: 5; see text box). The names reflect the fact that one strand, the more theoretical one, seems to be the preferred option for researchers with an Anglo-American background, while the other strand, the more social one, is preferred by researchers with a Continental European background.

> **Anglo-American pragmatics** is the more theoretical branch of pragmatics which focuses on utterance interpretation in all its complexity. It studies the principles of language use that account for meaning in context, and it often has a cognitive dimension, that is to say it asks questions about the way in which speakers and listeners cognitively process language. **Continental European pragmatics** studies the use of language in its broader social and cultural context. It focuses on the ways in which people interact with each other, including societal ideologies of what appears to be polite or impolite in a particular culture.

Textbooks and handbooks in the Anglo-American tradition focus on the theoretical aspects of utterance interpretation. In the tradition of the language philosophers, they ask questions about how we perform actions by using language. What does it mean to make a promise, to apologise or to ask a question? They ask questions about implicit meanings and investigate the ways in which we understand not only what is explicitly said by our interlocutors but also what is implied by this. Or they ask questions about the precise workings of so-called deictic elements such as *here, now, yesterday* and so on, which rely on a specific context to be interpretable. Researchers in this tradition often work with invented data and rely on philosophical methods of theoretical argumentation.

Textbooks and handbooks in the Continental European tradition, on the other hand, generally have a somewhat broader perspective and crucially also ask questions about the social and cultural embedding of the use of language. Their tools of the trade go back to methods originally developed by sociologists and anthropologists, and they generally prefer richly contextualised conversational data, for instance in the form of carefully transcribed and annotated everyday interactions of groups of speakers. Some researchers in this tradition also use experimental methods, such as role plays for instance, to isolate specific aspects of social interaction in the controlled environment of a laboratory, or they investigate the linguistic manifestations of how people are being polite or impolite to each other. While theoretical pragmatics focuses mainly on the interpretation of utterances, social pragmatics today focuses more and more on the interaction between interlocutors. Some relevant examples are listed in the 'Further reading' section at the end of this chapter.

The distinction between the two traditions has, of course, never been entirely clear-cut but even today it can be seen, at least in vestiges, in the way that textbooks and handbooks aiming to cover all of pragmatics sketch out the field and by what they include and exclude in their scope. But it is probably fair to say that the Anglo-American tradition has now also opened up its scope to some extent.

The pragmatics of fiction is clearly rooted in the wider tradition of social pragmatics. It relies on empirical investigations of how communication works in specific situations. However, in view of the multi-layered communicative complexities of fiction, we have to ask ourselves whether the existing tools of pragmatics are sufficient to describe and analyse what is going on in fiction. Pragmatics has shown how complex even the seemingly straightforward communicative situation of a face-to-face conversation is. The communicative nature of fiction differs from this situation on many different levels, and it is these complexities that we are going to explore from a pragmatic perspective in this book.

1.4 The levels of communication in fiction

At the beginning of this chapter, we briefly referred to the different levels of fictional communication, the communication between the creator and the recipient of a piece of fiction. We use the terms 'extradiegetic' and 'intradiegetic' for these two levels (see text box). In his book *Using Language*, the sociolinguist Herbert Clark (1996: chapter 12) talks of layering to describe these two levels. He first illustrates the concept of layering with the example of two children who in their play world pretend to be gold diggers in the gold rush of 1876 in Dakota. He visualises these layers with Figure 1.2.

On layer 1, the children are playing in a back yard in San Francisco, and on this level their actions are serious. When their mother calls them in, they have to go home. Layer 2 is like a theatrical stage that is set on top of layer 1. On this level, the children are gold diggers who pan for

> The terms **extradiegetic** and **intradiegetic** derive from the noun **diegesis**, which has a Greek origin and, according to the *Oxford English Dictionary* (diegesis, *n.*), means '[t]he narrative presented by a cinematographic film or literary work; the fictional time, place, characters, and events which constitute the universe of the narrative.' The definition suggests that 'intradiegetic' refers to aspects within the fictional text, and 'intradiegetic communication' refers to communication between the characters depicted in the movie or the novel or some other work of fiction. The adjective 'extradiegetic', accordingly, refers to the outside of the fictional text, such as its author and audience, who communicate on an extradiegetic level. Literary scholars often use the terms in a slightly different way and reserve the term 'extradiegetic' for the fictitious narrative level outside of the main story world, i.e. for a narrator who tells the main story.

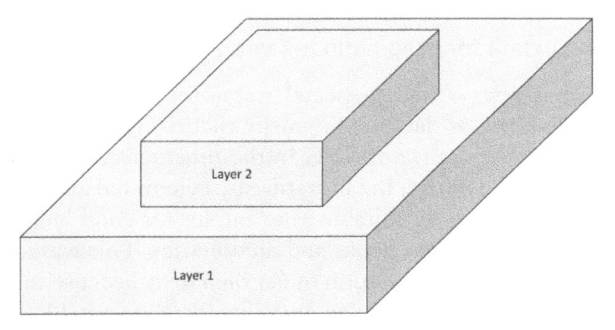

Figure 1.2 Layering of language use (Clark 1996: 354)

gold and strike lucky, but their actions are non-serious because they are not really gold diggers and they do not live in the Dakota of the 1870s.

On layer 1, they find a pebble in the dirt, which, on layer 2, is a nugget of gold. The patio of the back yard and its picnic table (layer 1) become a saloon with a poker table (layer 2), where they play a few hands with an invisible deck of cards and so on. At layer 1, the children jointly pretend that their actions at layer 2 are real. Clark, then, extends this concept of layering to fiction writing. On layer 1, what we have called the extradiegetic level, the author of a novel and his or her readers jointly pretend that the actions on layer 2, the intradiegetic level, are real. Clark points out that authors often use more than just two levels because their stories may contain characters who tell stories or engage in some pretence activity that adds further levels.

Clark uses the example of Herman Melville's novel *Moby Dick* to illustrate this layering in the case of literature. The first chapter of the novel starts with the sentence 'Call me Ishmael.' According to Clark, this is Melville's invitation to his readers to join him in the pretence that these are the words of a man called Ishmael talking to certain 'landsmen' in the early or mid 1800s. On layer 1, Melville and his readers jointly pretend that what happens on layer 2 is real, and on layer 2, Ishmael asks his intradiegetic audience to call him Ishmael. Additional layers are added when Ishmael quotes the speech of other characters. Literary critics also talk about the level of the implied author and the implied reader. In stage plays, in movies and in TV series, the complexity multiplies because of the intervention not only of actors who enact the characters and perform the events but also of production crews and perhaps even live studio audiences who are also part of the communicative events. In Chapter 3 we will come back to these issues and develop a model of participation structure that separates all these communicative layers.

1.5 Fictional data for pragmatic research

Literature has always had a special status for linguists, but opinions about its suitability as data for linguistic theorising have changed very considerably in the course of time. In the nineteenth century and well into the twentieth century, the literature by celebrated authors was considered to be particularly suitable as examples for good language usage to be depicted in grammar books and dictionaries. This was followed by a period of almost entire rejection of fictional texts because they came to be seen as artificial and contrived and, therefore, unsuitable for the linguists' endeavours. The theoretical linguists tried to capture the native speaker's intuitive knowledge of the language system. They did not rely on what they saw as the limited scope of actual language data. The empirical linguists, who were interested in actual language usage, i.e. the sociolinguists and pragmaticists, were interested mainly in everyday communication. For them, literary language seemed particularly unsuitable because it was so far removed from what they were interested in.

However, there were always some linguists whose interests differed from the mainstream, be it theoretical or empirical, and, therefore, also ventured into using fictional texts as data for their work. This was particularly common among historical linguists who became increasingly interested in the everyday use of language in earlier periods. They could not rely on native-speaker intuition and they could not use speech recordings of earlier periods. Such recordings only became available in the course of the twentieth century. Therefore, they turned to texts that could be argued to be closer to natural spoken language than other types of texts, such as personal letters, court records and, in particular, plays and dialogues in novels. But they generally felt that they had to justify their choice of data and that they had to apologise for it on the grounds that nothing else was available for the period they wanted to investigate. Or they argued that the most celebrated dramatists, e.g. William Shakespeare, would have been particularly skilful at capturing the authentic version of everyday speech of their time (see Jucker and Locher 2017: 8–11 for an extended presentation and critique of these argumentations).

This is not the view that we take in this book because we do not treat the language of fiction as an imperfect substitute for everyday language. There can be no doubt about Shakespeare's skill of writing dialogues for his characters, but it is very unlikely, to put it mildly, that anybody in Elizabethan or Jacobean England would have used iambic pentameters, Shakespeare's preferred verse form, in their everyday interactions. In this book, we want to suggest that the language of fiction is of sufficient interest in itself to warrant pragmatic analyses. Its highly complex nature of extradiegetic and intradiegetic communication requires a pragmatic perspective, and it challenges pragmatics to extend, adapt and adjust the available tools of analysis. And even if the analysis at a certain point focuses exclusively on the intradiegetic level, i.e. on the communicative behaviour of the fictitious characters, the analysis must always be understood as being concerned with the ways in which a particular author chose to depict communicative behaviour. We cannot assume that a pragmatic analysis of Shakespeare's characters gives us a direct insight into the language behaviour of Shakespeare's contemporaries. And we cannot assume that the characters of a popular US sitcom, like *The Big Bang Theory*, for instance, gives us a direct representation of everyday interactions of young American academics and professionals. This may seem to be a serious limitation of such investigations. However, if we study fictional texts in their own right, we can explore how language is used to create pragmatic effects that create story worlds and characters for readers and viewers. As a consequence, we see no need to apologise for the use of fictional data.

1.6 The aims of this textbook

The aims of this textbook are twofold. First, it wants to raise awareness of the complexity of fictional data for pragmatic analyses. And second, it wants to demonstrate how fictional texts can be studied from a pragmatic perspective. By combining these two aims, we treat the language of fiction as one important source of data for pragmatic theorising. For a long time, pragmatics confined itself to a description of everyday face-to-face interaction. However, in order to make progress, pragmatics has to reach out to all kinds of complex communicative situations. In this textbook we want to demonstrate how this can be done in the case of the communication of fiction, which, we believe, is a particularly challenging and fascinating one. This means that we do not pursue the traditional way of treating fictional language from a linguistic perspective in which linguistics, or pragmatics, is merely seen as a toolbox that provides fresh insights for the interpretation of literature. Instead, we believe that fictional language is important enough to warrant fresh pragmatic theorising. And at the same time, we want to show how pragmatic investigations can provide fresh insights from a stylistic or literary point of view. We draw on a large range of fictional examples from poems and songs to novels, plays, movies, cartoons and fan fiction. For reasons that have to do both with convenience and with our own background, we rely on texts in English (see also 'To readers'). We use these texts as illustrative samples for our pragmatic theorising. Questions of quality do not figure prominently in this endeavour, except perhaps for Chapter 10, where we talk about one possible way in which we evaluate the depth and richness of fiction.

The three chapters of Part I deal with the basics of literature as communication and literature as data for pragmatic theorising, in which fiction is not seen as a substitute for other forms of language use, such as everyday face-to-face interaction, but as an interesting form of communication in itself. We explore the fuzzy boundary between fictional and non-fictional uses of language, e.g. in the form of historical novels which combine historically attested people and events with fictitious ones or in the form of everyday interactions with all their fictional and semi-fictional anecdotes, funny stories and jokes. And we give an outline of the complex participation structure of literary communication.

Part II expands these themes and adds a number of other dimensions connected to story worlds created in fictional texts. Chapter 4 explores the extent to which genre expectations guide our understanding of fictional texts, while Chapter 5 provides a pragmatic approach to narrative and plot. Story worlds are populated by characters who are created through multimodal means, crucially including language. The power of linguistic features to index a range of regional, social and ethnic markers and their link to ideologies are discussed in Chapter 6.

Part III zooms in on a number of important pragmatic themes. It starts with a close analysis of the pragmatics of performance in Chapter 7, including a discussion of the various functions of dialogue in fiction, which range from representation of speech exchanges with plot consequences to presentation of narrative context. Fictional language both in its written form and when it is performed in plays or movies contains features of orality that differ significantly from such features in everyday spoken language. In this sense, fictional language performs orality among other things. Chapter 8 explores the ways in which societal ideologies permeate fictional texts and focuses in particular on relationship creation in connection with im/politeness and gender norms, and Chapter 9 looks at the language of emotion both on the level of the emotions evoked in the audience and the depicted emotions of the characters. Chapter 10 focuses on a range of specific literary devices, such as metaphors and irony, and proposes a relevance theory inspired pragmatic analysis that shows them to be far from unique to literary language but analysable by the same principles in non-fictional contexts. The last chapter, finally, draws together the different strands of argumentation of this book and indicates some possible future areas to explore within the pragmatics of fiction.

Key Concepts

Anglo-American pragmatics, Continental European pragmatics, diegesis, extradiegetic, fiction, intradiegetic, performed fiction, pragmatics, spontaneous fiction, written fiction

Exercises

1. Keep a diary for three days and note all cases of fiction that you engaged with throughout the day. Do not forget to include small or less obvious items, such as song lyrics, newspaper cartoons, jokes or advertising testimonials. Classify them into cases of written, performed and spontaneously created fiction.
2. When telling your friends a story about what happened during the day, how do you ensure that your story is not considered fictional? Think back to past experience and keep a diary for several days with notes on how you and your friends create this effect.
3. In the next chapter, we are going to explore the fuzzy boundary between fiction and non-fiction. Think of an autobiography and decide on what basis it might be classified as fiction or as non-fiction.

Further reading

The handbook *Pragmatics of Fiction* (Locher and Jucker 2017) provides a backdrop for much of what we have to say in this textbook. The handbook covers more or less all aspects treated in this textbook. The handbook articles are generally more technical and more comprehensive. They also offer detailed overviews of the relevant literature on each topic. This textbook aims at succinct and approachable introductions. Whenever more details and additional references are needed, the handbook may offer an obvious first port of call.

The volume edited by Chapman and Clark (2014) is entitled *Pragmatic Literary Stylistics*. It contains a range of interesting papers that cover similar approaches and interests as the ones of this textbook. Individual chapters can be read as inspirations for further research projects in the field of pragmatics of fiction.

There are many good textbook introductions to pragmatics on the market, but it is not easy to choose between them because they tend to carve out the field of pragmatics in different ways. Chapman (2011), Huang (2014) and Cummins (2019) are recent textbooks in the relatively theoretical Anglo-American delimitation of pragmatics. They all include chapters on the classical areas of pragmatics, such as implicature, presupposition, deixis, reference and speech acts. But they differ in the way in which they present this, and they all have their own unique specialities. Huang (2014) is particularly strong on the interfaces of pragmatics, e.g. semantics and syntax, while Chapman (2011) includes a few pages on politeness and on literature, and thus extends the Anglo-American tradition.

Culpeper and Haugh (2014) and Senft (2014) are textbooks that use a broader approach and give more room to interpersonal and social aspects. Culpeper and Haugh (2014) are particularly strong on interpersonal pragmatics and metapragmatics whereas Senft (2014) includes chapters on sociology and politics.

2 Fiction and non-fiction

2.1 Introduction

The word 'fiction' derives ultimately from the Latin word *fingĕre*, meaning 'to fashion or form', and is related to the word 'feign', which means 'pretence or deceit'. In the English language, the word 'fiction' is first attested at about the time of Shakespeare, and many of the early examples that are listed in the *Oxford English Dictionary* have meanings circling around fashioning and imitating but also feigning, counterfeiting and pretence. But even at that time, it is already attested in the meaning 'species of literature which is concerned with the narration of imaginary events and the portraiture of imaginary characters' (OED, fiction, *n.*, sense 4.a).

Today the word is still used with several different meanings. It is, for instance, applied to suppositions that are known to be untrue but are still maintained by some people who prefer to accept them as true. Extracts (2.1) and (2.2) are taken from the Corpus of Contemporary American English (COCA). They record everyday interactions in which speakers use the term 'fiction'.

(2.1) But why can't they [Google and Facebook] do a better job of policing their own content? Is it because they cling to this fiction that they're not really media companies when in fact they are among the most powerful media companies on earth? (COCA, Spoken, 2017)

(2.2) I would add this, let's dispel with this fiction that Barack Obama doesn't know what he's doing. He knows exactly what he's doing. He is trying to change this country. (COCA, Spoken, 2016)

In Extract (2.1), the speaker talks about the supposition that Google and Facebook are not really media companies, and in Extract (2.2) about the supposition that Barack Obama, the then President of the United States, does not know what he is doing. Both these suppositions are called fictions. The speaker takes them to be at variance with the facts even if some other people apparently take them to be true.

This meaning of the word 'fiction' is distinct but closely related to the meaning that we are concerned with here. In our sense, it refers to a particular type of texts, such as novels, short stories and so on, which are concerned with the narration of imaginary events and the depiction of imaginary characters. However, this is not yet good enough as a definition for what we mean when we talk of fiction in this book. Works of fiction often contain references to characters, places and events that are not imaginary, for instance in a novel set in the present-day United States with references to the actual president or other real people and to places, such as Los Angeles, San Francisco or Miami. And at the same time, we would not want to call everything that contains references to imaginary events works of fiction. This would include not only outright lies and fake news which are meant to deceive the audience but also, for instance, newspaper commentaries in which an expert speculates about the possible effects of some political decisions. Such speculations regularly include descriptions of imaginary scenarios and events that will develop if some decisions are taken or not taken. But this does not turn such texts into fictional texts in our sense. Even research papers in linguistics construe imaginary speakers and hearers to talk about some details of communication – and we indeed do it in this textbook – and again we would not want to talk about such texts, or our textbook, as instances of fiction.

This chapter, therefore, looks more closely into possible ways of distinguishing in a systematic way between fictional and non-fictional texts. This does not mean that we want to draw a sharp line between the two but it means that we want to have clear criteria that account not only for the prototypical cases of fictional texts, in which more or less every detail is the product of the author's imagination, and for prototypical cases of non-fictional texts, which report nothing but attested facts, but also for a large range of intermediate cases. We argue that the key notion in this endeavour is the fictional contract, i.e. a silent agreement between the author of a novel, for instance, and its readers that this text is to be treated as a piece of fiction (see definition in Section 2.3). As we will show in some detail, this contract is fundamentally pragmatic in nature in that it is not concerned with merely the properties of the text itself, but it is concerned with the communicative interaction and with the intentions and expectations that the communicators bring to this interaction.

2.2 Fictional utterances as 'non-serious' speech acts

In an important paper published in 1975, John Searle reflected on the special status of fictional utterances. In earlier work, he had developed John Austin's concept of a speech act, which was to have a profound impact on the field of pragmatics. When we speak or write, we make statements, we ask questions, give orders, make promises, apologise, give our thanks and so on. But in the context of fictional writing, Searle noticed, these speech acts seem to have a different force. If writers make an assertion in the context of a newspaper article, they commit themselves to the truth of what they are writing, and, if asked to do so, they must be able to provide some evidence or a reason for the truth of what they have asserted. In the context of fiction, these rules do not apply. To give an example from performed fiction: if two characters in a play get married, they are not married to each other in legal terms outside of the fictional artefact. In some sense, fictional utterances are 'non-serious'; not in the sense that they are unimportant, but in the sense that they do not have the usual force of utterances in non-fictional contexts. They do not, according to Searle, commit the author in the same way that newspaper journalists are committed to the truth of their sentences.

Before Searle embarks on a justification of this, he introduces some crucial distinctions. First, he makes a useful distinction between literature and fiction. He maintains that most, but not all, works of literature are fictional, and many works of fiction are not literature (1975: 319). As examples, he mentions outstanding books of history writing, which may well be considered to be works of literature without being fictional, and comic books and jokes which are fictional but not works of literature. Thus, according to Searle, the designation of a text as 'literature' is a value judgement, and there is no sharp boundary between the literary and the non-literary because it is ultimately up to the readers to decide whether they consider a text to be worthy of the designation 'literature' or not. For example, many scholars nowadays would not hesitate to consider graphic novels part of literature. The distinction between fiction and non-fiction, on the other hand, is marked by a much clearer boundary because it is connected to the writers' commitment to the truth – or 'seriousness' – of what they are writing.

In Section 2.4 below, we are going to present our own model of fiction in which we challenge Searle's view of a hard boundary between fictional and non-fictional texts. In our model, it is not so much the writer who decides on the status of a text as fictional or not but a combination of how the writer frames his or her text and the expectations that this creates for the readers. We agree with Searle that the distinction between the literary and the non-literary depends on subjective value judgements, but for us the distinction between fictional and non-fictional texts depends on reader expectations about the veracity of the depicted worlds.

As an illustration, Searle contrasts a short passage of a text from the *New York Times* written by the journalist Eileen Shanahan with a passage from a novel written by the novelist Iris Murdoch. He argues that both extracts make assertions about certain people and the events in which they were involved, but only Eileen Shanahan can be held accountable for the truth of what she asserts. The same rules do not apply to the text written by Iris Murdoch. Should we now conclude from this that Murdoch's sentences do not constitute assertions but some different type of speech act, such as writing a story? Such a view would necessarily imply that words in fiction do not have their normal meanings, and readers would have to learn an entirely new set of meanings of words and all other elements of language in order to be able to understand fictional language. This is implausible. Searle suggests instead that Murdoch is pretending to make an assertion. She is pretending not in the sense of deceiving but in the sense of performing a role. With this move, Searle puts the crucial deciding criterion of whether a text is fictional or not squarely on the intention of the speaker or writer. Fiction writing in contrast to newspaper writing, therefore, is a form of pretence. And this means that for fiction to be possible, we need a set of extralinguistic conventions which break the usual connection between words and their effect. These conventions 'enable the speaker to use words with their literal meanings without undertaking the commitments that are normally required by those meanings' (Searle 1975: 326).

This helps to distinguish fictional utterances from lying. For fictional utterances there is a set of conventions that suspends them from the normal conditions of utterances, such as committing the speaker to the truth of an assertion. A fiction writer invokes this extra set of conventions and cannot be held responsible for the veracity of his or her statements. For lying, no such set of conventions exists. Someone who lies simply breaks the rules by saying something which they know not to be true. In Section 2.4, we will argue that this is the point at which the reader becomes important because it is the reader who is either prepared or not to accept this extra set of conventions and to treat a text as fictional writing or as a mere lie.

2.3 Literary models of fiction

For literary theorists, it has always been an important question how fiction can be distinguished reliably from non-fiction. What exactly is the difference between the two? Many different theories have been proposed on this question, and in the following we are going to give a brief outline of the different types of theories that have been proposed and assess their values for our specific purposes. But first, it is useful to make a clear terminological distinction between 'fictional' and 'fictitious' (see text boxes).

The terminological distinction helps us to talk about fictional texts that include not only fictitious but also historically attested characters and events, and – in contrast – about non-fictional, i.e. factual, texts that may include fictitious characters. But the boundary between fictional and non-fictional still remains fuzzy because of the many genres, such as autobiographies, historical novels or docudramas, that may send out conflicting expectations about the fictitiousness or non-fictitiousness of the depicted characters, events and scenes.

> The term **fictitious** is applied to characters, events and other entities that do not exist in our real world. Hamlet, for instance, is a fictitious character in a play by Shakespeare, who is confronted with fictitious events within a world which is mostly fictitious in spite of the fact that it includes some real place names (Denmark or Wittenberg) and in many respects seems to function like the real world at the time (in terms of physical laws, social relations, cultural contexts and so on) (see Klauk and Köppe 2014).

> The term **fictional** describes texts, literary genres or media which typically depict fictitious characters and fictitious events. Thus, movies and plays are fictional. They can be distinguished from non-fictional, or factual, genres, such as newspaper articles or academic research papers. Notice that a newspaper article is a factual genre even if in some cases not everything is true that is being reported in them. In this sense, a factual text can also assert falsehoods (see Klauk and Köppe 2014).

The characters in Charlotte Brontë's novel *Jane Eyre*, for instance, are fictitious characters. The eponymous heroine of the novel, Jane Eyre, Mr Rochester, Thornfield Hall and the events that unfold in the novel have no existence in the real world, and they never existed as real people, actual locations or events. They are part of the fictitious world, created by Brontë, even if many aspects of this world, such as perhaps the means of travel, social distinctions or aspects of education or religion, are closely shaped according to the actual world of England at the beginning of the nineteenth century. The fictional novel *Jane Eyre*, on the other hand, has a reality in the real world. It came into existence through Brontë's act of writing it, and it can still be purchased in the form of a hardcover book, a paperback, or indeed an e-book, or in adapted form as an audiobook or a movie on a DVD or an online streaming platform. These distinctions are important for theories of fiction, which try to find systematic relations between fictional genres and the fictitious worlds that they depict. Generally, such theories distinguish between different genres, that is to say they are interested in the conventional expectations readers have about specific types of text and not about the way in which individual readers deal with individual texts.[1] In our own model we will try to extend this in order to make the model applicable not only to the default expectations but also to individual deviations from the default.

According to Klauk and Köppe (2014), literary models of fiction can be grouped into several types on the basis of how they distinguish between fictional and non-fictional texts.[2] They distinguish between theories that focus mainly on the text itself, its linguistic structure and its relation to the world; theories that focus on the author of the text and his or her intentions; and theories that focus on the reader or recipient of the text.

Text-based theories recognise fictional texts on the basis of specific textual elements, such as, for instance, typical phrases (e.g. 'once upon a time'), typical styles (e.g. free indirect speech), or typical choices of specific lexical elements (like proper names that do not have any correspondence in the real world). Or they may argue that texts are fictional if they contain statements that are not true and expressions that do not refer to anything in real life. Such theories have the advantage that – at least theoretically – they can be applied objectively without any speculation about the writer's intentions or the reader's expectations. It would be enough to inspect the linguistic properties of a text in order to classify it as either fictional or non-fictional. But it seems

---

[1] Here we use the term 'genre' not only for different styles or categories of literature, but in its more general sense that also covers varieties of everyday language, such as newspaper articles, personal letters or WhatsApp messages. We will have a more careful look at this notion in Chapter 4.

[2] Our presentation of the different literary models of fiction is indebted to Klauk and Köppe (2014: 15–19).

clear that this is not possible. There do not seem to be any linguistic peculiarities whose mere presence or whose sufficient frequency would reliably mark a text as either fictional or non-fictional. It is probably fair to say that such theories are usually proposed in combination with other types of theories. Ultimately it appears that fictionality cannot be reliably identified on the textual level alone.

The second group of theories argues on the basis of the intentions of the author. Such production-based theories of fictionality often take Searle's article presented in the previous section as their starting point, but Searle's focus was on the distinction between what he called serious and non-serious uses of speech acts. He did not develop the distinction into a theory of fictional and non-fictional genres, and in fact it seems difficult to imagine how a distinction can be made merely on the basis of speaker or writer intentions without any recourse to the way in which the text is received by the readers.

Which leads us to the reception-based theories. What makes a text a text of fiction is not so much its linguistic structure and not just the writer's or speaker's intentions but above all the way in which it is approached by the reader. The readers pick up the hints given by the context, or paratext, in which the text appears and treat the text accordingly. The book covers of novels generally look different from those of scholarly treatises, their titles and their framing are different. When we watch TV, we are generally aware whether we are watching an item in a news bulletin or an episode of a soap opera. And it is this awareness of the context which makes the reader or viewer treat a certain text as fictional or non-fictional. In his *Biographia Literaria* (1817), Samuel Taylor Coleridge famously described 'poetic faith' as a 'willing suspension of disbelief', that is to say readers know that what they are reading is not literally true but for the sake of the reading experience ignore this knowledge and pretend that it is, in fact, true. Coleridge's catchphrase captures the important insight that a crucial element of the nature of fictional texts is the way they are treated by their readers, even if we may be reluctant to claim that readers must pretend somehow to believe what they are reading.

Ultimately it appears that for any form of fiction, whether written, performed or indeed spontaneous, there is a kind of silent agreement – also known as fictional contract – between everybody involved that the depicted world is to be treated as fictitious (see text box, p. 22). Thus, most current theories of fictionality appear to focus on the interaction between the author and the reader, and in this sense are fundamentally pragmatic in nature. We will come back to the fictional contract in Chapters 4 and 5.

> We use the term **fictional contract** to refer to the silent agreement between the author of a book or the producers of a film and the readers and audiences that this particular artefact is to be taken as a piece of fiction. Depicted characters, locations and events should generally be expected to be fictitious even if some aspects of the depicted world may well correspond to our real world. In contrast to Coleridge's dictum of the 'willing suspension of disbelief', such a contract does not require the audience to 'suspend disbelief' but merely to understand and accept the fictitious basis of the depicted worlds.

2.4 A pragmatic model of fiction

The types of model that we introduced very briefly in the previous section classify different genres in general as either fictional or non-fictional, with possibly some fuzzy area between the two. They are generally not meant to account for individual texts. Our model, however, allows both for the prototypical expectations created by a genre and for deviations from the prototype in specific instances. Such deviations may occur in the form of a movie that proclaims to be 'based on a true story' where viewers might have expected fictitious characters and events, or in the form of individual readers who are particularly gullible and take the events depicted in a book at face value.

We have seen that both the distinction between fictitious worlds and non-fictitious worlds, and the distinction between fictional texts and non-fictional texts are somewhat fuzzy. We therefore describe both of them as scales. Figure 2.1 shows in a preliminary way how the two are prototypically related. Later in this section, will turn this into a dynamic model in Figure 2.2.

The horizontal axis shows the cline from non-fictionality to fictionality, while the vertical axis shows the cline from non-fictitiousness to fictitiousness. Typically, readers are aware of what they have to expect, and their expectations tend to coincide with what they encounter in the text. The diagonal line in Figure 2.1 shows the kinds of texts that meet reader expectations, that is to say reader expectations actually correspond to the empirical status of the depicted worlds. We have placed a selection of non-fiction and fiction genres according to their typical expectations for readers/viewers within this grid to show how these elements can be combined. On the bottom left, there are texts that the reader or viewer expects to be faithful accounts of the physical world we live in, depicting only people and events with an existence in the real world, while on the top right

FICTION AND NON-FICTION

```
Fictitiousness (veracity of characters and events)
more ↑
                                            Fantasy
                                    Science fiction
                            Real people fiction
                    Novels in realistic settings
                True crime fiction
            Docudrama
        Diary blogs
    Memoirs
  Documentaries
 Newspaper reports
less →
        less        Fictionality        more
              (reader/viewer expectations)
```

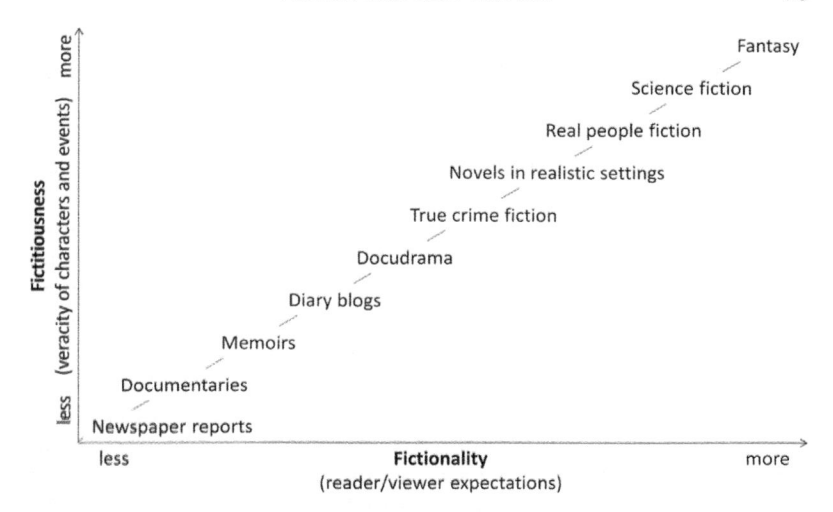

Figure 2.1 A pragmatic model of fiction: genres plotted according to levels of fictitiousness and reader/viewer expectations concerning fictionality

there are texts that the reader or viewer expects to be largely or even entirely fictitious.

Newspaper reports are – or at least claim to be – accurate representations of facts. They are non-fictional and allege that what they report is non-fictitious, i.e. factual. They depict what we would like to call the 'real world'. In a documentary, such expectations are probably equally high but in diary blogs or in memoirs, we may expect some liberties with the selection and presentation of facts. In some cases, for instance, the narrative may be enhanced by an anecdote that is simplified or modified a little to suit the narrative as long as it fits the overall story. But not everybody might share exactly these expectations. Many would perhaps prefer the four genres given in the lower left part of the diagram to be very close together at the very bottom left of the diagram. The model does not claim that there are accurate measurements for the placement of text types on these scales, but merely some relative placements by comparing different genres. Docudrama and true crime fiction can be set somewhere in the middle of the diagonal scale. Docudrama uses the frame of a documentary but includes elements that are presented in a dramatised version. Key scenes are re-enacted to transport the viewers into the events, and viewers who are familiar with the genre will have appropriate expectations about the non-fictitiousness or fictitiousness of the depicted events. True crime fiction is a genre that uses a fictional format but presents characters and events that are modelled on real cases.

Higher up on the scale and further to the right, we find genres that are more clearly fictional. The reader or viewer expects them to be the result of somebody's imagination. Here some distinctions are necessary. First, there are what we want to call realistic worlds which are closely modelled on our real world. They may be inhabited by fictitious characters, but these characters live in worlds that to a large extent work like the real world in a particular geographic location at a specific point in time. Charlotte Brontë's *Jane Eyre*, for instance, is set in England sometime in the early nineteenth century, when people travelled by horse-drawn carriages. They communicated over long distances by writing letters that took several days to arrive, and people were clearly separated into different social classes. At a roughly similar level we can identify what has come to be known as 'real people fiction', a form of writing that is similar to fan fiction (see Section 2.5) but is based on celebrities or other real people who are used as characters in fictitious worlds where they experience fictitious events. Websites such as Archive of Our Own,[3] for instance, store thousands of fictional texts on a large range of celebrities. They explore, for example, what would happen if a specific celebrity were a zombie, a mafia boss or the I-narrator's romantic partner. Real people are cast into anything from very realistic to highly fantastic but clearly fictitious worlds. In this context, Shakespeare's history plays come to mind which also depict real people in somewhat fictionalised contexts. Richard II or Henry V, for instance, were historical kings, but in Shakespeare's plays, they are shown in contexts that are only loosely based on historical events.

Science fiction novels depict worlds that in some respects do not work like the real one. They are no longer realistic. Let us call them futuristic worlds. They depict worlds that do not exist now but may exist sometime in the future, when flying cars and interstellar travel, for instance, might be everyday occurrences. *2001: A Space Odyssey*, *Star Trek* or *Star Wars* would be relevant examples. What happens is often explained in terms of natural science and technology even if it goes far beyond today's science and technology. The literary genres of utopia and dystopia also depict futuristic worlds, either highly desirable or highly undesirable ones, but worlds that one day might become real.

At the far end of the diagonal scale in Figure 2.1, finally, we are talking about fantasy worlds that are inhabited by mythical creatures, dragons, talking animals or fairies. Sorcery and witchcraft are regularly part of them. Obvious examples would be the *Harry Potter* books, *The Chronicles of Narnia*, *The Lord of the Rings*, or *A Game of Thrones*, which

---

[3] <https://archiveofourown.org> (last accessed 2 October 2020).

all belong to the literary genre of fantasy. Fairy tales also depict such fantasy worlds. But even they may, of course, have many resemblances to our real world, for instance in the way in which human characters need to eat and sleep like real humans, in the way they have emotions, in the way that the laws of physics such as gravity apply, or in the way they share features of our physical reality (e.g. London in the *Harry Potter* novels, or the medieval set-up in *A Game of Thrones* and *Lord of the Rings*). Eco (1990: 74) uses the term 'small worlds' for fictional worlds. They are incomplete and semantically heterogeneous (cf. Doležel 1989: 233–235): 'It seems that fictional worlds are parasitical worlds because, if alternative properties are not spelled out, we take for granted the properties holding in the real world' (Eco 1990: 75).

Figure 2.2 shows the same two axes of expectations of more/less fictitiousness versus more/less fictionality. This time, however, we have plotted areas of violated or atypical expectations, either because the author abuses a format and misleads the audience or because a reader or viewer, for whatever reasons, has mistaken assumptions about the default nature of a text type. In the upper left area, we can place fake news, that is to say newspaper reports that are taken to be non-fictional but turn out to report fictitious events. The actual text has moved up on the vertical line because the depicted world is more fictitious than the text type suggests. But here in the upper left, we also find instances of science fiction which some particularly gullible reader takes to be true

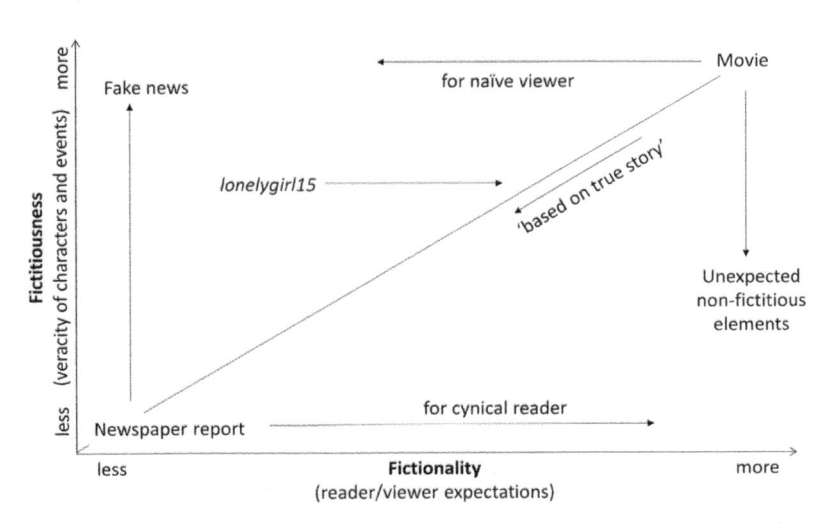

Figure 2.2 Dynamic reader/viewer expectations concerning fictionality of genres and specific texts

facts. In this case, the text, for this particular reader, moves left on the scale of fictionality.

In the lower right area of Figure 2.2, we can imagine novels for which the author used real-life characters but the reader takes them to be fictitious. The text would have moved down on the vertical line. Or a particularly cynical reader might expect nothing but lies in a factual newspaper article. For this reader, the text moves to the right on the horizontal line and has to be placed in the lower right area of Figure 2.2.

When a movie claims to be 'based on a true story' or 'inspired by true events', it makes a claim that it should move some distance along the diagonal line from the upper right to the lower left, i.e. in the direction of a smaller amount of fictitious characters, events and surroundings (down on the scale of fictitiousness), and viewers' expectations should be adjusted accordingly (left on the scale of fictionality). Some viewers, however, will probably be reluctant to go along with the claim. They will still treat pretty much everything as fictitious, while others might prefer to take almost everything at face value. While some people may be touched deeply by films that state, 'based on a true story', others may actually dislike them. It is interesting to muse on the reasons for this like or dislike. Does it matter for the quality of a storyline whether it is based to some extent on actual events or whether everything is the product of the author's imagination? What kind of message does it transmit to the audience beyond the claim for veracity and the acknowledgement that the story is not due to the genius of a writer? For some the depicted emotions may be more sincere if they are replications of real-life emotions (see Chapter 9) while others may prefer the artistic 'truth' of a piece of fiction to the journalistic 'truth' of real-world reporting, or they prefer the safe knowledge that the events depicted in the film are truly fictitious and, therefore, are somewhat less emotionally loaded than real-life events.

Our model of fictionality also helps to analyse the effects of deliberate deviations and manipulations of reader expectations as, for instance, in the case of *lonelygirl15*.[4] In the early days of YouTube video channels, a video blog, or vlog, by a teenage girl, who called herself Bree, started to attract an ever-growing audience. She posted videos from her bedroom by talking directly into the camera and telling the audience about her rather lonely life as a home-schooled sixteen-year-old who spent too much time in front of the computer, about her parents and their

---

[4] Many different accounts of the story of *lonelygirl15* can be found on the internet. Our account is based on Kuhn (2014) and Cresci (2016).

involvement in a mysterious religion and about her best friend Daniel. With the growing audience there also came a growing suspicion among many members of the audience about the true identity of *lonelygirl15* until a newspaper journalist uncovered her identity, and it was revealed that the roles of the lonely teenager and her friend were being played by actors and the videos were scripted and produced by a small team of writers. The uncovering of *lonelygirl15* received a lot of media attention and the video blogs continued for a considerable time with an even wider audience as a result of the publicity. In the process, however, viewer expectations clearly shifted. The depicted world still consisted of fictitious figures played by actors but after the unveiling, the audience took it for what it was, a fictitious world. The video blogs had moved from the upper left area of mistaken assumptions to where they actually belong on the diagonal of appropriate reader and viewer expectations (see Figure 2.2).

Notice that this model is not meant to capture the full extent of the nature of fiction. It just focuses on our expectations that relate to the fictitiousness of the depicted characters, events and surroundings. It does not include our expectations about the aesthetic values of fiction or the emotional dimensions. As pointed out above, the difference between fictional texts that are aesthetically and artistically pleasing and those that are not is a value judgement of the literary quality of a text. This should be distinguished from the expectations that an audience has about the veracity or fictitiousness of the depicted world. The emotional involvement that we experience as a result of reading a text or watching a film would be unlikely to distinguish reliably between instances of fiction and non-fiction. We may, on occasion, be emotionally just as deeply moved by events that we know to be fictitious as by real events or perhaps even more so. This is a topic that we will analyse in more detail in Chapter 9.

2.5 Fictitious worlds and their extensions

So far, we have contrasted the actual world populated by real people who experience non-fictitious events in real time with fictitious worlds in which fictitious characters experience fictitious events. We have considered how individual texts mix the non-fictitious with the fictitious and how audiences bring their specific expectations to specific texts or movies. Fictitious worlds, we have assumed, are the result of the imagination of an author who is responsible for the imaginary world or universe that he or she has created. However, sometimes fictitious characters adopt a life of their own and escape from the fictitious world for which they were created. Or in other words, an author/producer/composer appropriates fictitious characters or events invented by another author and extends their fictitious lives. This can lead to rewritings of classics such as the Greek play *Medea* into an opera or the figure *Cassandra* from Greek mythology into a novel. Shakespeare's and Austen's works have been turned into teen movies in modern settings; well-loved movies can lead to remakes in new settings and with new actors. Fictitious characters and events can also lead to fan fiction and spin-offs. In fact, whenever a reader or viewer contemplates possible different endings to a storyline, possible histories of individual characters not actually depicted in what he or she is reading or viewing and so on, he or she might be considered to be creating a form of fan fiction.

In the following, we want to have a closer look at fan fiction and spin-offs as two particularly interesting forms of the appropriation of fictitious characters and events into new fictional contexts. The term 'fan fiction' is used to refer to fiction created by fans of an original piece of fiction using some of its characters, events or aspects of its story world. As such, it is, of course, a very fuzzy concept because many literary texts draw in one way or another on earlier fictional texts. The term is also used in a wider sense, e.g. for fiction based on real-life celebrities. Such forms of fiction are not new. Before the internet they were often published and circulated in fanzines with small print runs, but the internet has given fan fiction an entirely new dimension with a worldwide forum even for amateur writers. Dedicated websites for fan fiction have been around for a long time, like, for instance, Archive of Our Own,[5] which is a large website with fan fiction based on literature, celebrities, bands and many more, or FanFiction,[6] which also combines a large amount of fan fiction on a very wide selection of originals or 'canons'. A search for fan fiction on *Harry Potter*, for instance, retrieves roughly 240,000 texts on Archive of Our Own and over 800,000 texts on FanFiction. Most of them are no longer than a few hundred words or perhaps a few thousand. But some reach more or less the length of a book in their own right with close to 100,000 words. It appears that contemporary books and media attract the largest number of fan fiction writers, but older texts also regularly inspire fan fiction and spin-offs. It is also true to say that today fan fiction is less stigmatised than it used to be. It is clearly a mass phenomenon, and, while in many cases there may be a quality difference between commercially published fictional texts and fan fiction published on dedicated websites, it is also clear that

---

[5] <https://archiveofourown.org> (last accessed 2 October 2020).
[6] <https://www.fanfiction.net/> (last accessed 2 October 2020).

quality cannot be the deciding criterion to distinguish between one and the other.

Let us take *Jane Eyre* as an example. When it was originally published in 1847, it had the subtitle, 'An Autobiography', which may have created the expectation among Brontë's readers that they were reading about a non-fictitious Jane Eyre. However, the characters, events and all the places that are central to the events depicted in the novel are fictitious, such as Gateshead, where Jane spends her childhood with the heartless Mrs Reed and her children; Lowood, where she spends eight years of her life first as a pupil and then as a teacher; or Thornfield Hall, where the main events of the novel unfold. But there are also references to existing places, such as London, England, France, Paris, or the West Indies. Some critics have searched the novel for real-world clues to find out the exact time frame in which the novel is set, such as technical innovations, e.g. steamboats. Others have tried to find non-fictitious parallels for some of the fictitious figures in the novel. Helen Burns, for instance, Jane's best friend at the Lowood institute, who dies of typhus, is said to be based on Charlotte Brontë's sister Mary, who suffered the same fate in real life. Whatever the precise status of such allusions and parallels, the text, in spite of its fictitiousness, does have a foundation or a frame of reference to the real world. It depicts a realistic world, even if at one point towards the end of the novel, Jane and Mr Rochester have what must appear, at least for a modern reader, to be a supernatural encounter. They believe they hear each other's voices in spite of the fact that at this point they are separated by hundreds of miles.

Charlotte Brontë's novel has been very popular with a large audience ever since its appearance. In fact, in 2003 the BBC carried out a survey on the most popular books in the United Kingdom. Three quarters of a million votes were received, and *Jane Eyre* reached tenth place on the list of the best-loved novels of all time.[7] It is no wonder, therefore, that it has given rise not only to a vast amount of literary criticism but also to countless radio, stage and movie adaptations, spin-offs and to fan fiction. There is no very clear line between spin-offs and fan fiction but often the former term is used for commercially published extensions of an original piece of fiction while the latter term is used for non-commercially published texts.

Let us have a look at two spin-offs created on the basis of Charlotte Brontë's *Jane Eyre*. Jean Rhys's *Wide Sargasso Sea*, first published in 1966, is a prequel to Brontë's novel. It tells the story of Mr Rochester's first

---

[7] The Big Read Top 21. BBC. <https://www.bbc.co.uk/arts/bigread/vote/> (archived website, last accessed 4 July 2019).

wife, Bertha Mason, the violently insane madwoman in the attic of Thornfield Hall. Rhys takes a marginalised and demonised figure from the original novel and puts her in an entirely different light. In Rhys's novel, she is a Creole heiress, Antoinette Cosway, born in the British West Indies shortly after slavery had been abolished there in 1833. She is married to the young Mr Rochester, who as a second-born son could not inherit his father's wealth and therefore agreed to this marriage in order to obtain the fortune of her dowry. But when he hears pernicious rumours about her past, he turns against her and eventually drives her to madness. He takes her back to England and hides her in the attic of Thornfield Hall. Rhys's novel ends with the events of the original that lead to the burning down of the hall and Bertha's fall from the battlements but in this version, they are narrated from her perspective, and the reader takes away a very different understanding of the 'madwoman in the attic'. Her madness culminating in her tragic death is here seen as a result of her past and in particular of the way in which she was treated by Mr Rochester and the world around her.

Jasper Fforde's 2001 novel *The Eyre Affair* takes this even further. Thursday Next, the protagonist of the novel, is a literary detective who pursues Hades, a master criminal, in a world in which time travel is possible and in which a Prose Portal invented by her uncle Mycroft allows people to enter works of fiction. Hades steals the original manuscript of *Jane Eyre* and kidnaps the heroine, which causes the text of all copies of the book to stop about half-way through because without the I-narrator the book cannot continue, but Thursday Next manages to return Jane to the novel and chase Hades, who has withdrawn into the novel in the pursuit of his crimes. As the novel starts to rewrite itself after the return of its I-narrator, the intruders influence the events there to such an extent that the novel supposedly receives a new ending (the one that we are familiar with). Thursday manages to kill Hades but, in the process, Thornfield Hall is set on fire and destroyed, Mr Rochester's mad wife Bertha falls to her death, and Rochester is grievously injured. In order to stop Jane from accompanying her cousin, St. John, in his missionary work in India (the supposed ending of the fictitious *Jane Eyre* in *The Eyre Affair*), Thursday Next impersonates Rochester and calls out to Jane, who is about to leave for India. This matches the situation in the original *Jane Eyre*, where Jane believes she hears Rochester calling out to her from hundreds of miles away. Thursday also discovers that all the characters in *Jane Eyre* must continuously relive the events of the novel whenever a reader turns to the relevant page in the full knowledge of how they will turn out but without the ability to change any of them.

Many fan fiction texts proceed from the question, 'What if?' In the case of the *Jane Eyre* fan fiction, for instance, they ask: what would have happened if Jane had agreed to St. John's marriage proposal? How would the story have developed if it had taken place in a different time frame, for instance today? How would the story have turned out if it had taken a different turn at a particular point in the narrative? Or even, how would the story have developed if the author of the fan fiction himself or herself had played a role in the fictitious events of the novel?

An author with the name poppy.rider (2012), for instance, retells the entire novel in an abbreviated fashion (6,564 words, less than 4 per cent of the original novel) in a modern present-day setting. Jane Eyre, the novel's protagonist, turns into Milan Mary, who is brought up by an uncaring and abusive aunt because her parents died in a plane crash in Marrakech. Edward Rochester, the master of Thornfield Hall, turns into a wealthy Iraqi oil sheikh, Mohammad Abaza, who spends his time on a yacht round the Greek islands, and Thornfield Hall turns into Whittington Manor in the Scottish Highlands. St. John is now Angus McDonald. He and his two sisters are friendly hippies who want to convert Milan to Buddhism and take her along to Kathmandu. But Milan, like her original Jane, prefers to go back to the man of her dreams. In this case, Milan has to fly to Mohammad Abaza's holiday home in French Polynesia, where he has spent his time after his lunatic first wife set fire to Whittington Manor and died in the blast.

Other authors of fan fiction prefer to stick to the original setting and perhaps even try – more or less successfully – to imitate Charlotte Brontë's style of writing and to change only part of the entire story, for instance the ending, by picking up at a certain point towards the end of the original story and then developing it in a different direction. The author named AceGray, for instance, picks up the story when Jane returns to Thornfield Hall for the last time and lets her get involved in a violent fight with the madwoman Bertha, Rochester's first wife:

> The madwoman raised her saber high overhead and brought it crashing down onto the poker, which I had raised just in time. The force of the blow sent me to my knees; Bertha towered over me. The conflagration flashed no more dangerously than the eyes of the maniac, and, at that moment, I knew with utmost certainty that she would deliver the killing blow.
>
> Suddenly, from behind, who should leap but Mr. Rochester! With all of his might he swept the sword from Bertha's grasp and wrestled her to the ground. (AceGray 2007: n.p.)

At this point it takes the author only a few more lines to let everyone die, but not before Jane and Rochester are reunited in their everlasting love for each other.

Cross-overs are fan fiction texts that combine more than one canon. The author WolfsCub (2013), for instance, casts Hermione Granger from *Harry Potter* in the setting of *Jane Eyre*. A curse sends her back in time into the body of Jane Eyre, where she is forced to temporarily endure a life in the nineteenth century. Occasionally she uses some magic in order to ease the discomforts of travelling in a chaise, to quench the fire in Rochester's room or to find out what goes on in the attic. And in the end, she disappears back into her own world, leaving Rochester back in the nineteenth century.

Such texts are pragmatically interesting extensions of original works of fiction because they throw a new light on what might otherwise have been seen as a relatively simple dichotomy between real-world people in non-fictional texts and fictitious characters in fictional texts. Fictitious characters can be viewed as very real in the sense that many original authors are protective about them and do not wish them to be appropriated by their fans. Mayer-Schönberger and Wong (2013: 10) quote Orson Scott Card, the author of a popular science fiction series, who responds to an interview question by Yoda Patta:

> Fan fiction, while flattering, is also an attack on my means of livelihood. It is also a poor substitute for the writers' inventing their own characters and situations. It does not help them as writers; it can easily harm me; and those who care about my stories and characters know that what I write is 'real' and has authority, and what fans write is not and does not. (Patta 1997: n.p.)

This is a strong statement for the 'reality' of fictitious characters. For this author at least, they can take on a life of their own which needs to be protected from infelicitous appropriations by other authors. And indeed, there have been cases of legal disputes over the extent to which copyright protections are infringed by fan fiction. To what extent is it legally and ethically permissible, for instance, to use fictitious characters that somebody else invented for your own piece of fiction? Are the characters the unique property of the original author who alone may use them? Or can they be used by fan fiction writers as long as they acknowledge the original source? Mayer-Schönberger and Wong (2013) draw a parallel with academic publishing, in which authors have no control over the ways in which other academics may use their ideas as long as they reference them properly. A new method or a new insight may immediately be picked up, adapted, changed, set into a new context and so on, as long as the original author is adequately referenced.

Whatever our assessment of the legal implications of spin-offs and fan fiction, such texts have communicative consequences for the original text, which is no longer seen as a small, self-contained world but as part of a larger reality with which new fictional texts may interact in many different ways. Prequels like *Wide Sargasso Sea* leave the original story intact but change its reading because some figures may be seen in a different light on a new reading of the original novel. Sequels extend the storyline after its original ending. Embellishments add more details to some of the events or extend the description of some of the figures. Alternate endings pick up the storyline at a certain point in the narrative and take it in a different direction. Or, as in the case of *The Eyre Affair*, we get an account in which an alternate ending to *Jane Eyre* is excised in order to give the novel the ending that it actually has.

2.6 Conclusions

In this chapter we have shown that it is important to carefully distinguish between the fictionality of genres and specific texts and the fictitiousness of characters, places and events. The fictionality of a text describes the expectations of readers or viewers about the fictitiousness of the depicted events, i.e. the terms of the fictional contract. This contract, which is fundamentally pragmatic because it is concerned with communicative interaction between the text and its readers, can be viewed as a silent agreement between the author and the readers or viewers about the level of veracity that can be expected in a novel, a movie or another piece of fiction. The distinction makes it possible to talk more systematically about the different levels of expectations in different genres, ranging from newspaper reports to docudrama and novels in realistic settings to fantasy fiction. And it also makes it possible to talk systematically about various types of mismatches between reader or viewer expectations and actual texts, ranging from gullible viewers who take movies as facts to authors who purposely mislead their audience by framing their product as something different from what it actually is, as in the case of *lonelygirl15*.

We have also shown that the complexity increases even further if we consider the various extensions of fictitious worlds in adaptations, spin-offs and fan fiction. Through these extensions and the imagination of the authors, the characters, places and events of the original text, for instance *Jane Eyre*, appear to receive an independent level of reality in spite of their fictitious characters. Some readers may object to spin-offs and fan fiction, for instance, on the grounds that they do not respect the integrity of the original characters. On the other hand, fictional material that can stand the test of time has always served as a source for adaptations and reinterpretations, which prolongs the lives of the fictional characters and events.

Key Concepts

Fan fiction, fictional, fictional contract, fictitious, spin-offs

Exercises

1. Think about one of Shakespeare's history plays, which include both fictitious and non-fictitious characters and settings. Does the distinction matter, and why or why not? Alternatively, think about Quentin Tarantino's *Inglourious Basterds* (2009), Christopher Nolan's *Dunkirk* (2017), Sam Mendes's *1917* (2019) or some other war movie and consider the specific mixture of fictitious and non-fictitious elements that they depict.
2. Find a brief newspaper article and rewrite it as a piece of fiction. Why did you choose this particular text and what changes did you make?
3. Consider the following quotation:

   > This is the midday news on Monday, 6th May 1985, and this is Alexandria Belfridge reading it. The Crimean peninsula [...] has again come under scrutiny this week as the United Nations passed resolution PN17296, insisting that England and the Imperial Russian Government open negotiations concerning sovereignty. As the Crimean War enters its one hundred and thirty-first year, pressure groups both at home and abroad are pushing for a peaceful end to hostilities.

   Consider the status of this text as a piece of factual or fictional reporting. Which elements suggest that it reports facts? And which elements, if any, suggest otherwise? In fact, it occurs in Jasper Fforde's novel, *The Eyre Affair: Thursday Next Book 1* (Loc 181 of 5226) published in 2001. How is your interpretation influenced by this piece of information?
4. Find a short story and rewrite it as a news item with an appropriate headline. Why did you choose this particular story and what changes did you make to adapt it to the news genre?
5. Think about the ways in which the American fantasy drama television series *Game of Thrones* (or any other science fiction or fantasy literature of your choice) creates fictitious worlds/places/innovations/etc.

> **Further reading**

Our distinction between fictionality and fictitiousness is based on a paper written in German by Klauk and Köppe (2014). We have also discussed the distinction in Jucker and Locher (2017). *The Fan Fiction Studies Reader* edited by Hellekson and Busse (2014) contains a range of classic articles in the field of fan fiction studies. Their introduction provides a good overview of the field and they justify their focus on a rather narrow definition of the field which focuses on rewritings of shared media, in particular TV texts. Mayer-Schönberger and Wong (2013) discuss the status of authorship and the fight for control over characters in fan fiction.

3 Literature as communication

3.1 Introduction

In the first chapter, we briefly introduced the difference between the intradiegetic level and the extradiegetic level of works of fiction. The intradiegetic level concerns the fictional story world itself and everything that happens within this world while the extradiegetic level concerns the outside of the fictional world, that is to say the author who created this world and the audience who reads it or views it.[1] But this is very much a simplified picture of what is going on, especially if we consider not only novels or other written fictional texts but also performed fiction on the theatre stage or the movie screen. In this chapter, we now want to have a much closer look, from a pragmatic perspective, at the different levels of communication and in particular at the different participants involved in communication. Who exactly communicates with whom and on what levels? In the next section, we start out with the relatively simple case of an author who writes a poem which then is read by an audience. But even in this simple case, additional people are usually involved, such as the people concerned with the actual production of the book in which the poem appears or the website on which it is posted. There might even be literary critics who play a role in the communication between authors and their audiences. In the following sections, we increase the complexity and consider the more intricate cases of theatre plays and telecinematic discourse. In these cases, there are actors who enact the fictional text, and there are teams, perhaps even very large teams, who are involved in the production of the plays, including directors, camera operators, stagehands, costume designers and many more.

---

[1] As pointed out in Section 1.4 above, literary theorists often use these terms in slightly different ways.

3.2 Communicating literature

We want to start with what might appear to be the relatively simple case of a poem. This involves an author who writes the poem, and an audience, which may be very large or very small, who reads the poem. On the surface, this looks very similar to an everyday interaction between a speaker and a hearer, or perhaps better between a writer, for instance a writer of a short text message, and a reader. The writer jots down, or carefully composes, a few lines of text, and after some time, these lines are read by one or several readers. Of course, there are some obvious differences between the short text message and the poem. We might want to point out, for instance, that short text messages are often trivial in content, they mostly concern the everyday world of the sender and the recipient, and they are read very shortly after having been written, while poems are usually assumed to have deeper and more profound meanings. They are often read long after having been written, perhaps even centuries later. Literary theorists would point to the qualitative and aesthetic differences between a well-crafted poem rich in implied meanings and a short text message with their often banal exchanges of trivialities. A pragmaticist would certainly not deny these differences, but from a communicative perspective the differences are not very significant. There are no real limits to how profound a short text message can be with multi-layered meanings, innuendos, ambiguities, allusions and perhaps even some poetic devices such as metaphors or alliteration. Both a short text message and a poem are cases of asynchronous communication, that is to say the processes of producing the message and of receiving it do not happen at the same time but one after the other (see text box, p. 38). Short text messages are sometimes exchanged in what is called a quasi-synchronous manner, i.e. with only very little time between production and reception, but even in this case, production and reception are not entirely synchronous. There is still a difference from everyday spoken interaction, in which the two processes happen synchronously.

So, how then do authors of poems, and by implication larger works of fiction, communicate with their audiences? And how can pragmatics describe this type of communication? As an example, let us take a poem by Jennifer Wong, a writer and poet from Hong Kong, who now lives in London. The poem is taken from her second collection entitled *Goldfish*, published in 2013.

> Interactions are described as **synchronous** if the addressee receives a message at the very same time that it is being produced. This typically applies to face-to-face communication or telephone conversations, but it also applies to written communication if the recipient can read a message keystroke-by-keystroke while it is being produced. Interactions are described as **asynchronous** if there is a time lag between the production of a message and its reception, which is typically the case for email messages, newspaper articles or books. The term **quasi-synchronous** is used for situations in which people exchange written messages in quick succession, for instance via computer or mobile phone. In these situations, the communicators take part in the conversation at the same time (as in synchronous interactions) but they can only read a message from their interlocutor once it has been finished and sent off (as in asynchronous interactions).

(3.1) 'Itinerary', Jennifer Wong, 2013

1   I don't mind the ring roads
2   or the strange intersections,

3   filled in with radio music   tarmac
4   skirting streetlight and   the dissolving   moon.

5   Wing mirrors tell
6   of running trees.

7   My heart races
8   in the heave of the wind.

9   In the pivot of glass everything
10 is so small and manageable.

11 I think of an old song,
12 of purple cows in far fields,

13 I wonder what it'd take
14 to cover miles and miles
15 with no maps or destination.

16 It is not easy anymore
17 to forget or be free of the bear
18 that roams the place where I come from.

Source: Jennifer Wong, 'Itinerary' from *Goldfish*. Copyright © 2013 by Jennifer Wong. (<https://www.poetryfoundation.org/poems/146990/itinerary>, last accessed 18 February 2020. Reproduced with permission)

In the previous chapter, we briefly introduced Searle's (1975) paper on the logical status of fictional discourse, in which he describes fiction as 'non-serious' in the sense that the writer does not have to commit himself or herself to the truth of what he or she is asserting. In the context of this poem, this would probably mean that the author, Jennifer Wong, might actually hate the ring roads and the strange intersections in spite of the first two lines of the poem which deny this. But that would obviously miss the point. The poem communicates by construing what literary theorists call a lyrical I who communicates with a lyrical thou. The reader of the poem is not the direct addressee, for instance, of the assertion 'I don't mind the ring roads or the strange intersections' (lines 1 and 2). This and all other assertions of the poem are, on the surface or explicitly, addressed to a lyrical thou, but also, tacitly, to an implied reader, who may be very different from the lyrical thou described in the poem.

Thus, it is the poem as a whole that the poet communicates to her readers. It is a complex communicative act (see text box) which requires some effort from the reader, and in this sense differs from a simple communicative act, such as the short text message 'See you in 5 minutes at the exit!'. However, both the reader of Wong's poem and the reader of this fabricated short text message have to go through a process of utterance interpretation. The reader of the poem must reflect, for instance, on what kind of intersections are meant in the second line of the poem, and why they are described as strange. Without context, the term 'intersections' (line 2) can be understood in a geometrical sense as a point that is common to two lines crossing each other or a line that is common to two surfaces that intersect. But the context of the first line of the poem, which mentions ring roads, suggests that the intersections of the second line are actually traffic intersections. In the same way, the reader of the short text message must use contextual knowledge to figure out at what point the five minutes will have elapsed and which exit is being referred to. In contrast to the reader of the poem, the reader of the short text message has a rich extralinguistic context. He or she knows when and by whom

> We use the term **communicative act** as a cover term for units of communication that are exchanged between interlocutors. Such units range from the very simple and short to the highly complex and very long. It includes one-word utterances, such as, 'Hi!', as well as long letters, status updates on social media and artistic productions, such as poems, plays or even novels with hundreds of pages (see Jucker and Dürscheid 2012).

the message was written, where the writer is likely to be at this moment and which exit is the most likely one that the writer could have referred to, and in cases of doubt there is the possibility of initiating a repair sequence, i.e. asking for details.

In both cases, a pragmatic interpretation process is necessary to guide the reader in the search for the meaning potential of the communicative act. In both cases, we assume that the result of the interpretation process will be no more than an approximation that is good enough for current purposes. In the case of the short text message, this will be relatively trivial and unproblematic, but as we all know, even in the case of such short and straightforward texts, misunderstandings can and do occur. In the case of the poem, the interpretation process might be more difficult. It offers different readings. There are allusions and ambiguities which might not be resolved with certainty. For one reader, the poem might resonate with rich images and deep meanings while for another reader the meanings may remain relatively obscure. For one reader, the poem might be about the journey of life of the lyrical I, who perhaps grew up in a place where bears had their natural habitat and now lives in a big metropolis with ring roads, and for another reader the poem might describe a more literal journey on a specific occasion. We will come back to such interpretation processes in Chapter 10.

Let us now turn to the communicative act as a whole. The fabricated text message 'See you in 5 minutes at the exit!' can be described as a speech act but without further contextual knowledge it is not clear what kind of speech act it might actually be. Is it an unmitigated directive by a concerned parent who wants to pick up a teenager from a party? Is it a hostile warning by a football fan to a football fan of a rival team? Is it an invitation or

> The **illocutionary force** of a speech act describes the conventional value a speech act has, such as a question, an apology or a promise. It is sufficient that the addressee recognises the speaker's intention for the speech act to have this force whether or not he or she is prepared to answer the question, accept the apology or believe in the promise. The **perlocutionary effect**, on the other hand, describes the effect the speech act has on the addressee, which may or may not have been intended by the speaker and which may differ for different addressees. One and the same utterance may have the effect of insulting an addressee or complimenting him or her. The speaker is normally aware of the potential of being misunderstood and will try to adapt her language accordingly but ultimately, he or she has only partial control over such effects.

a promise from one potential romantic partner to another? Or is it just a piece of information from one friend to another who have lost each other in a crowd of spectators leaving a concert? The reader will use his or her contextual knowledge to figure out what is technically known as the illocution – or illocutionary force – of this speech act (see text box).

But can we describe the poem in a similar way as a speech act whose most likely illocutionary force can be worked out in the interpretation process? Can it be described in terms of a specific speaker intention to produce something like an assertion, a question, a confession, a promise, a warning or something similar? And if so, what is its perlocutionary effect on the reader (see text box)? Can it be described as an act of enlightening, convincing, inspiring or persuading the reader?

The main problem with such an extension lies in the fact that a work of fiction regularly includes what appear to be speech acts in their own right. As a solution, van Dijk (1976: 36) proposed a distinction between macro speech acts comprising the whole discourse, such as an entire piece of fiction, and micro speech acts consisting of single utterances. In this sense, macro speech acts can contain micro speech acts, and we can talk about illocutions and perlocutions on both levels. On a macro speech act level, Wong's poem, for instance, can be read as a lament for a lost home, a narration of a road trip, or musings on the passing of time to mention just a few. Some of these readings are more plausible, others perhaps less so. They depend on the ways in which individual readers connect the ideas expressed in the poem on a micro speech act level with the wider context. In the case of the simple short text message, the relevant context consisted primarily in the situational context. In the case of the poem, it consists more generally in the reader's familiarity with similar poems and his or her personal response to the images conjured up by this specific poem. However, in both cases we are dealing with a communicative act whose details can be described by pragmatic tools, and in the following sections of this chapter we are going to have a more detailed look at the intricacies of this interaction both in everyday exchanges and in different types of fiction.

3.3 Participation structure: the recipients

So far, we have implicitly relied on a very simple, and in fact simplistic, model of communication. An author, such as a poet, writes a text which is then read by a reader. To this extent, as we have seen in the previous section, this kind of communication is, in spite of all the differences, comparable to the communication between the writer of a short text message and its recipient. We are now going to extend this simple model and make it more explicit. In this section, we will focus mainly on the recipient side of communication while in the following section we turn to the complexities of the production side before we put this together in Section 3.5 for the complexities of plays and telecinematic discourse.

In an early paper, Goffman (1979) drew attention to the inadequacy of the canonical model of conversation in which a single speaker talks to a single hearer without any other people being involved, even if the model allows for the two to swap roles at regular intervals so that the speaker becomes the hearer and vice versa. Everyday situations regularly involve additional people. In addition to the person to whom an utterance is directly addressed, there may be others also belonging to the party of conversationalists and some bystanders who accidentally hear what is being said.

Imagine four people sitting in a restaurant, where they have just been served dinner, and one speaker turns to the approaching waiter in order to complain about the quality of the food. In this situation, the waiter is the addressee of the communicative act, the one who is supposed to respond and react to the complaint. The other three diners are the auditors. Both the addressee and the auditors are ratified by the speaker, that is to say they are in some sense approved by the speaker to be official listeners to what he or she says directly to the waiter. The speaker may be aware that people at a neighbouring table are listening in to what is going on. These people are not ratified in the same way as the speaker's fellow diners, but they are known and accepted to be there. These are the overhearers. But it is also conceivable that even more people listen in to the conversation, without the speaker being aware of them. These are the eavesdroppers.[2]

Figure 3.1 gives an overview of the different recipient roles. It is based on Bell (1991: 91), who applied Goffman's insight into different recipient roles to the situation of mass media communication. Bell pointed out that the concentric circles of increasing distance from the centre visualise the diminishing influence that the different recipients have on the speaker's communicative behaviour, and he called this 'audience design' (see text box). The addressee has the most immediate influence. Imagine that the four diners are native speakers of

---

[2] Note that these terminologies are not used consistently in the relevant literature. Some researchers use the term 'third party' for what we are calling 'auditors', and 'overhearer' as a cover term for 'bystanders' (known to be there but not ratified) and 'eavesdroppers' (not known to be there and not ratified) (e.g. Dynel 2011). Other conceptualisations also exist.

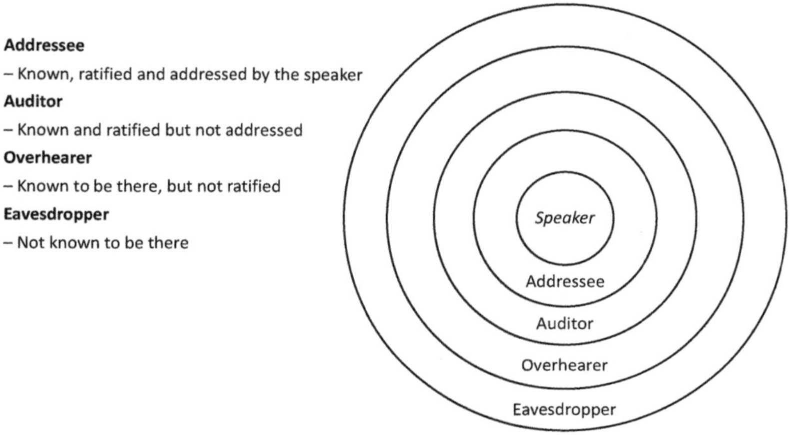

Addressee
– Known, ratified and addressed by the speaker
Auditor
– Known and ratified but not addressed
Overhearer
– Known to be there, but not ratified
Eavesdropper
– Not known to be there

Figure 3.1 Recipient roles in the speech situation (based on Bell 1991: 91)

> 'In **audience design**, speakers accommodate primarily to their addressee. Third persons – auditors and overhearers – affect style to a lesser but regular degree. Audience design also accounts for bilingual or bidialectal code choices.' (Bell 1984: 145, bold added)

English, but they are in a restaurant in Italy. If the speaker realises that the waiter does not understand the complaint in English, he or she might use more gestures and a few simple words rather than complex sentences, or, if possible, switch to Italian. The auditors will also have some influence. Depending on their personalities and their relationship to the speaker, the speaker might want to impress them with his or her audacity by being a little rude, or not to offend them by toning down the complaint into a politer formulation. The overhearers could have a similar effect but presumably less directly than the auditors. The eavesdroppers, finally, cannot, by definition, have any influence on the speaker's communicative behaviour because the speaker does not know that they are there at all. For example, the chef of the restaurant might overhear the conversation from behind the kitchen door.

How do these roles apply to fictional communication? It is again necessary to distinguish carefully between the extradiegetic level and the intradiegetic level. On the extradiegetic level, readers or viewers of fiction are the recipients of a piece of fiction produced by a single author or by an entire production crew including directors, script writers, actors,

Core recipients
– Known, ratified and addressed
  Addressee recipients
  – Regular viewers
  Meta recipients
  – Critics and academics
Incidental recipients
– Irregular and chance viewers
– Known to be there, but not ratified
Accidental recipients
– Not known to be there

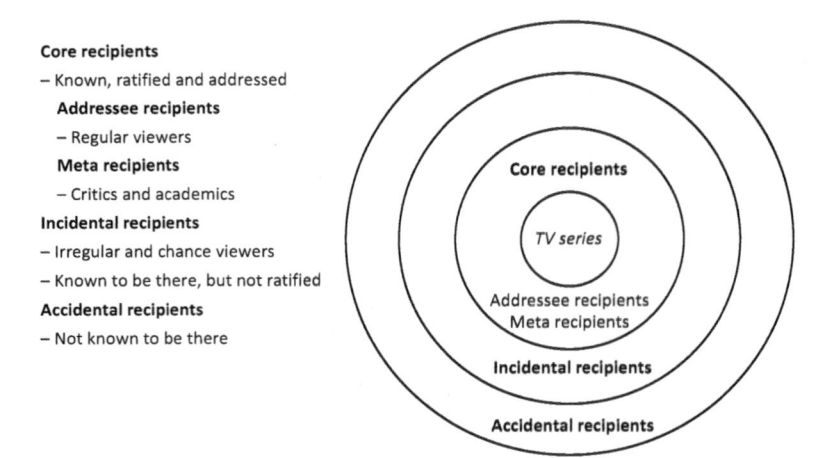

Figure 3.2 Recipient roles in extradiegetic fictional discourse

camera operators and so on. They can be separated into different types: the core recipients, incidental recipients and accidental recipients. The core recipients are those recipients that are directly addressed. They include addressee recipients and the meta recipients (this last term is adopted from Dynel 2011). Let us take a television series as an example (see Figure 3.2).

Television series are always targeted at a specific audience in terms of the viewers' ages, their genders, and perhaps even their social classes. Such targeting may be relatively narrow, or it may be very broad, but it is important not least for commercial reasons. Television series are regularly surrounded and often interrupted by advertisements that are directed at the target audience of the series. Obviously, not all viewers will belong to this kind of target audience, but the addressee recipients are those viewers who watch the series regularly and who are targeted by the producers of the series. They know the characters of the series, they are familiar with previous episodes and so on. The production crew will make sure that for these viewers the characters are sufficiently consistent, that allusions to earlier events in the series are understandable and so on. The meta recipients are critics and academics who analyse the series with professional skill and thoroughness. In *House MD* (2004–2012), an American medical drama series, for instance, the production team makes sure to get all the medical details right in the medical cases that are part of the depicted events. Such details might be lost on a large majority of even regular viewers, but they are not lost on sceptical critics who analyse the series for consistency and medical accuracy. Both the addressee recipients and the meta recipients, therefore, are ratified viewers and, therefore, called core recipients in Figure 3.2.

There will also be incidental recipients who may have missed an episode, or one-off viewers who are entirely unfamiliar with the format of the show and who do not know any of the characters and how they relate to each other. This group of viewers corresponds to the auditors in Figure 3.1. They are known to be there, but they are not ratified. The production crew may occasionally or regularly make some allowances for them, too, by providing sufficient contextual background or by summarising previous episodes.

And finally, there may be accidental recipients who should not even be there at all, such as children watching a movie suitable only for adults (see Section 8.5). They correspond to the eavesdroppers in Figure 3.1 above, and no allowance is made for such viewers, except of course for warnings at the beginning of the movie or television series that it is unsuitable for a certain type of audience. For a similar adaptation of Bell's audience design model, see Watts and Andres Morrissey (2019: 270), who use it in the context of folk singer performances.

Extract (3.2) gives the opening lines of *House MD*, whose main character, Dr Gregory House, is an unconventional and misanthropic medical genius. In this scene, we see a man who is later identified as a 71-year-old cancer research specialist in a laboratory environment dissecting a rat. First, he speaks to the rat and then he spells out the protocol of what he is doing into an autopsy recorder. The transcription conventions for telecinematic examples can be found just before Part I.

(3.2) *House MD*, 2006, Season 3, Episode 3, at 0.12. (Transcription adapted from <https://clinic-duty.livejournal.com/13589.html>, last accessed 2 October 2020, transcription slightly modified)

1 Doctor: ((to the lab rat he's just plucked from a cage))
2 you're 'not gonna make this ^easy 'are you?
((he picks up a syringe))
3 unfortunately as 'much as I admire your ^spirit je ne sais rien.
((he puts the rat to sleep, starts autopsy recorder))
4 subject 'anesthetised with .5 cc of ^sodium pentobarbital,
5 'transfected with human hepatic ^cancer cells,
6 underwent six rounds of intra-abdominal treatment with DS-22,
((he uses scalpel to start cutting))
7 vertical ^incision through the 'rectus sheath,
8 opens the abdominal ^cavity,
9 incision ^extended into ((coughs)) 'thorax,

10		((coughs again, loosens collar, appears to be having trouble breathing))
11		liver appears 'normal in colour,
12		no apparent scarring or, ((coughs as he turns liver over))
13		^damn it.
14		cancerous ^tumor is still 'present on the right lobe,
15		1.12 cm in diameter,
16		no ^reduction ...

On the intradiegetic level, the depicted researcher talks to the rat, and he takes notes of what he is doing by talking into a recorder, but here we are interested in the extradiegetic level and ask ourselves why it is important for the audience to be given the precise details of the sedative injected into the rat and the previous treatment the rat had received in the course of the scientific experiment. It is probable that many viewers would not grasp the details of the researcher's voice protocol and that they would not be able to assess whether the given measurements are plausible or not. For the average viewer without special medical or chemical expertise, the technical vocabulary is sufficient to conjure up a laboratory context. It immediately identifies the elderly man as a serious and highly knowledgeable scientist, and it makes clear that the rat is dissected in the interest of scientific research. However, there will also be meta recipients, i.e. viewers who will easily be able to assess the plausibility of the researcher's protocol and the indicated levels of the sedative and the intra-abdominal treatment. The producers of this series appear to take great care that the medical details hold up to the critical scrutiny of such experts.

The scene continues with the researcher picking up a second rat but before he is able to dissect it, the coughing gets worse, he starts gasping, falls down and passes out. The rat that is now freed from his grasp climbs onto the unconscious researcher and starts nibbling on his lower lip when the scene cuts and the opening credits start to roll in. Immediately after the opening credits the scene opens on the conference room in which a team of doctors is gathered when House enters.

(3.3) *House MD*, 2006, Season 3, Episode 3, at 2.38. (Transcription adapted from <https://clinic-duty.livejournal.com/13589.html>, last accessed 2 October 2020, transcription slightly modified)
((Scene opens on the conference room in the morning. House pushes door open with his cane. The medical team looks at him puzzled that he is using the cane again.))

1	House:	71 year old ^cancer research specialist,
2		minor 'tremors localised 'melanoma removed two ^years ago,
3		cataracts, and he can't ^breathe ..

4		also 'disregard the facial ^lacerations,
5		they're 'creepy but unfortunately ^irrelevant.
6		((he winks))
7		don't you wanna know ^why?
8	Cameron:	you .. have your ^cane.
9	House:	no . why the lacerations are ^creepy.
10		he was about to 'dissect one of his lab rats when he ^collapsed,
11		the little vermin seized the ^day so to speak,
12		and went medieval on his ^ass.
		((the members of the team stare at him with frowns))
13		what my ^fly open?
14	Foreman:	so the .. the ^pain's returned.
15	House:	there ^was no pain,
16		he was ^unconscious.
17		I'm 'guessing because he wasn't able to ^breathe.
18	Cameron:	we're talking about ^you.
19	House:	^obviously.
20		I'm obviously ^not.
21		what is it with ^you people?
22		I ^don't use the cane you're shocked,
23		I ^use the cane . . .

House does not waste time greeting anybody. He starts by listing the main facts of the new case – age and previous medical complaints – before he makes a reference to the wounds caused by the nibbling rat. But his intradiegetic audience apparently does not listen to what he says. The members of the team gathered in the conference room are baffled by the fact that he uses his cane, which leads to some grotesque cross communication. House talks about the new case, everybody else talks about his cane and the assumed return of his pain. To the extradiegetic audience, the regular viewers – or addressee recipients, as we call them – the team's reaction makes immediate sense. Aficionados of the series are aware that House normally uses a cane because of severe pain in his right leg caused by an infarction which he treats by problematic levels of pain medication. They also know that House had given up using his cane and – to their surprise – is now using it again. Irregular or chance viewers – our incidental recipients – will have to infer what has been going on. Enough details are given so that they can guess about the previous importance of either using or not using the cane.

Accidental viewers, the last category in Figure 3.2, are more difficult to illustrate in these two extracts. They are the eavesdroppers who are not even known to be there and for whom the production team does not make any specific allowances, perhaps viewers who take offence at being shown in a close-up how a rat is dissected by the researcher's scalpel cutting open its abdominal cavity or at the second rat's nibbling at the unconscious researcher's lower lip.

Thus, the model can be used to distinguish the different ways in which the production team of a television series adapts to different segments of the extradiegetic audience watching a particular episode, from the core recipients with the addressee recipients and the meta recipients who are directly addressed, to the incidental viewers who are ratified to the extent that the episode makes allowances for irregular viewers to catch up on missed content, and finally to accidental viewers whose presence is perhaps accepted but – by and large – ignored for this particular production.

This model can also be applied to other forms of fiction, such as novels or poems. It may be more difficult to distinguish with conviction between the core recipients, incidental recipients and accidental recipients. But it makes sense to also distinguish between a ratified audience and an overhearer audience. In the first instance, the ratified core recipients consist of those readers who are able to pick up the references and allusions in a text.

While it may seem a given that authors write in 'their' language, this language choice is actually the first selection criterion for reducing the potentially global readership. Writers in English can only reach readers/viewers who understand English (until the moment that their work is translated). This observation might seem banal at first sight, but there are authors who have several languages at their disposal and choose according to whom they want to reach. The Russian-born American author Vladimir Nabokov, for instance, wrote both in Russian and in English, and the Irish writer Samuel Beckett, who spent most of his adult life in Paris, wrote both in English and in French. Furthermore, the author might have, consciously or unconsciously, a very narrow audience in mind and use many regionalisms and other peculiarities that are easily understandable to only a small audience. The author may also be thinking of literary critics or academics. But there might also be other readers who lack some of the necessary background knowledge. Annotated editions of older books come to mind in which an editor provides explanations for literary allusions, obsolete word meanings and references to people and places that might be obscure to an average reader in the twenty-first century.

Extract (3.4) is the first stanza of John Keats's (1795–1821) poem 'To Hope'. It does not appear to be unduly obscure but the editor, Miriam Allott (1970: 12), provides almost a full page of explanatory notes.

(3.4) 'To Hope', John Keats, 1815
1 When by my solitary hearth I sit,
2 And hateful thoughts enwrap my soul in gloom,
3 When no fair dreams before my 'mind's eye' flit,
4 And the bare heath of life presents no bloom,
5 Sweet Hope, ethereal balm upon me shed,
6 And wave thy silver pinions o'er my head.

The notes point out how some of these lines echo the works of Shakespeare and other authors, how some of the details in the lines, e.g. the solitary hearth, relate to Keats's personal biography and the places where he had lived, and they provide a lengthy explanation of the term 'ethereal', meaning 'heavenly' (line 5). To the extent that we have to rely on such editorial help, we are accidental readers not intended and ratified as an audience by the original author. It is impossible to know for certain how many of the allusions and references identified by Miriam Allott were intended by Keats to be transparent to the readers of his poem whom he might have had in mind when writing it. But it is clear that some readers may feel – or perhaps are – more directly addressed than others who may find themselves to be located in one of the circles further out in Figure 3.2. A more extreme case than a poem by Keats may be found in Old English poetry, written in a variety of English that is no longer transparent to speakers of Present-day English without appropriate training or a translation. Or – to take a different example – popular novels in Present-day English are sometimes published in the form of easy readers for audiences with a limited command of the English language. In all these cases, the intervention of an editor or translator makes a piece of fiction more approachable for an audience outside of its original core recipients.

3.4 Participation structure: the creators

We now turn to the creators of a communicative act. Here, too, Goffman (1979: 17) proposed a disentangling of different aspects. He distinguishes between the roles of 'animator', 'author' and 'principal'. The animator utters the actual words of a communicative act. The author is the one who selects the words and their arrangement. And the principal is the one whose ideas and sentiments are being expressed by the communicative act. In everyday interaction, a speaker typically incorporates all three roles. But in many situations, it makes sense to distinguish them. Someone who reads out a passage from a newspaper to a friend, for instance, is an animator but neither the author nor the principal of the words that he or she reads out. If an office worker passes on an oral message from the boss to a co-worker, he or she is the animator of the communicative act and perhaps also the author but not the principal of the message.

These distinctions are particularly useful when thinking about mass media communication. A newsreader is the animator of words authored by a journalist on behalf of the principal, which in this case is the TV or radio station. A spokesperson for a government minister is both the animator and the author of words written on behalf of the government minister as principal. The government minister in turn may deliver a speech that expresses his or her own ideas and convictions but was written by a member of staff. In this case, the minister is both the animator and the principal but not the author of the words that are being delivered. A text that is being read silently has both an author and a principal but no animator.

Let us now adapt these distinctions to fictional communication. Jennifer Wong, the author of the poem 'Itinerary' quoted in Section 3.2, is both the author and the principal of her poem, and whenever she reads out the poem herself for an audience, she is also the animator. Similar things can be said about authors of short stories, novels and other fictional texts. But even in these relatively simple cases, there are usually people who turn the words authored by the poet or novelist into a book or integrate them into a webpage. We call them producers. In the case of plays or movies, the producers regularly consist of large crews, including a director, actors, script writers, camera operators, technicians, sound and light engineers and many more. In this model, they are all subsumed under the heading of the producer.[3] The actual writing of the text may be distributed in different ways between the principal and the producers. In a conventional theatre play, the actors recite the words originally written by the author of the play with little or no intervention of other writers. In the case of a literary adaptation, a script writer turns the original work into the dialogues that can be performed on stage or in front of a movie camera. And there are cases in which script writers have no more than perhaps some plot lines to work on and turn these into the story and the dialogues to be performed in the movie. In Goffman's terminology, the script writer would be the author but in our model, this conflicts with the original author. We therefore deviate from his terminology while retaining the original insight that the three

---

[3] Our use of the term 'producer' is more encompassing and differs from the definition of a movie producer, who is a person who oversees whole teams involved in movie productions.

aspects of production (speaking the words, writing the words and being responsible for the ideas expressed by the words) need to be carefully distinguished.

3.5 The complexities of performed fiction

Let us now combine the insights from the previous sections into one model that captures at least some of the complexities of fiction and in particular performed fiction in the form of theatre plays, TV series or movies. We take a very simple model of communication, as given in Figure 3.3, as our starting point.

The model consists of the three elements sender, communicative act and recipient, which intuitively may seem very plausible, but is too simple in at least three ways. First, it suggests that what the sender puts into the communicative act – or encodes into it – is exactly what the recipient receives or decodes. This is too simple. As we will show in some detail in Chapter 10, even relatively simple communicative acts, such as an everyday short text message, require a complex inferential process on the part of the recipient in order to figure out what the sender wanted to communicate. Such inferential processes become even more complex in the case of allusive communicative acts, such as poems, which regularly give no more than hints at what the sender might want to communicate, or in the case of very extended communicative acts, such as entire novels, plays or movies. Second, the model depicts only a small extract of what goes on in communication. It completely ignores the fact that the sender and the recipient regularly change roles and that the sender's communicative act depends on the linguistic and non-linguistic feedback he or she continuously receives from the recipient, e.g. in the form of his or her gestures and facial expressions. We will briefly focus on this aspect in Section 3.6. And third, in the case of fiction, and in particular performed fiction, all three elements have intricate internal structures themselves as we have seen in the previous sections of the chapter. This is what we are going to disentangle in this section.

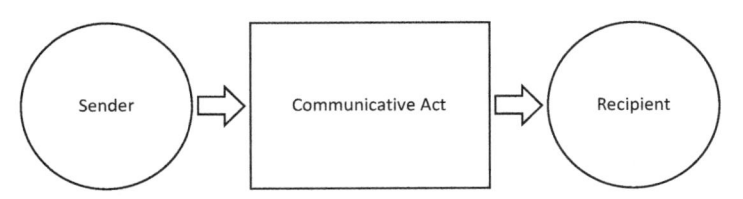

Figure 3.3 A simple model of communication

52   THE PRAGMATICS OF FICTION

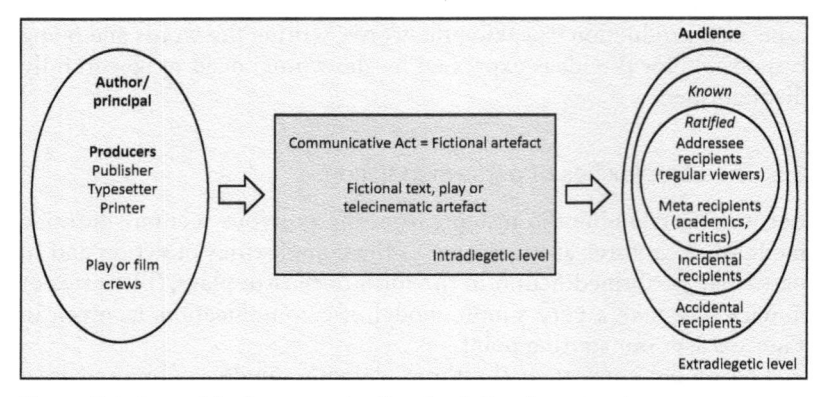

Figure 3.4 A model of communication for fiction in general

[Figure 3.4: Diagram showing three grouped elements connected by arrows. Left oval labelled "Author/principal", "Producers: Publisher, Typesetter, Printer", "Play or film crews". Middle box labelled "Communicative Act = Fictional artefact / Fictional text, play or telecinematic artefact / Intradiegetic level". Right nested ovals labelled "Audience", "Known", "Ratified", "Addressee recipients (regular viewers)", "Meta recipients (academics, critics)", "Incidental recipients", "Accidental recipients", "Extradiegetic level".]

Figure 3.4 is an adaptation of our simple model of communication to the extradiegetic level of communication of a piece of fiction. The sender here consists of the author (or possibly authors), who is (are) also the principal in Goffman's sense, and the producers. Together they create the communicative act, i.e. a piece of fiction, a novel, a play or a movie, which is then received by the recipient, which is made up of the different layers of the audience.

As pointed out in Section 3.4 above, the producers, who turn the author's creation into a shape that can be disseminated to the audience, include the publishers, typesetters and printers of written fiction; the readers and sound recorders of audiobooks; the directors, actors, light technicians of stage productions and so on. And, as pointed out in Section 3.3, the audience consists of the ratified addressees, the incidental recipients and perhaps the accidental recipients.

Let us now turn to the intradiegetic level in the case of performed fiction (see Figure 3.5). Here, we find the characters of a play or movie interacting with each other. As in everyday interactions, other characters might be listening to this interaction as auditors, overhearers or eavesdroppers, depending on whether they are known and ratified, known but not ratified or not even known by the communicating character within the fictitious world presented by them. Television discourse, e.g. in soap operas or sitcoms, often includes a studio audience. Such an audience may be real in the sense that the shooting of the film happens in a setting with a live audience which responds with laughter and clapping, perhaps spontaneously but perhaps also by being prompted to do so. Or the studio audience may be fake and consist only of pre-recorded laughter – so-called canned laughter – that is added to the soundtrack of

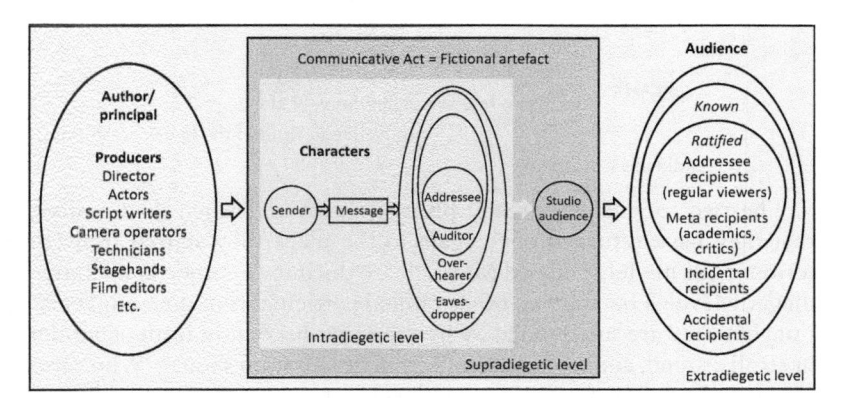

Figure 3.5 A model of communication for performed fiction

the film. Such laughter, whether by a live audience or by pre-recordings, is always meant to be external to the intradiegetic level of what happens on the stage. It constitutes what we call the supradiegetic level and is part of the product that is communicated to the screen audience.

Let us illustrate the levels of Figure 3.5 with a brief segment from the American sitcom *How I Met Your Mother* (season 7, 2011). Ted, Marshall and Marshall's wife Lily are attending a concert, and Ted and Marshall have left the auditorium to get some nachos for Lily, but they seem to be unable to find the place where they can purchase them. They go round in circles and keep joining the queue for the ladies' washroom by mistake.

(3.5) *How I Met Your Mother*, 2011, Season 7, Episode 10, at 12.26

1	Ted:	we just went 'all the way around ^again.	((exasperated))
2	Audience:	@@@@@	
3	Marshall:	where the 'hell are these ^nachos?	
4	Ted:	who ^cares about 'nachos.	
5		((three bystanders in the background, unnoticed by Ted or	
6		Marshall, put up their hands))	
7	Bystander 1:	^I do.	
8	Bystander 2:	I ^love nachos 'man.	
9	Audience:	@@@@	
10	Ted:	you gotta ^relax man ..	
11		you keep 'worrying about stuff like ^nachos,	
12		you're gonna give yourself a ^heart attack ..	
13		I'm going back 'in.	
14	Marshall:	^fine ..	

15		^ha ..
16		^joke's on 'you.
17		the nacho line was right ^here all along.
18		((joins line in front of the ladies' washroom))
19	Audience:	@@@@

The two friends are already pretty exasperated when Ted realises that they have returned once again to the place they started from. In terms of our model, Ted and Marshall are the interlocutors on the intradiegetic level. There are no other ratified participants in their conversation, but they are surrounded by bystanders who wait in front of a toilet or stroll around, and in fact when Ted in desperation shouts, 'Who cares about nachos' (line 4), three bystanders react to his question and put up their hands. Two of them also answer verbally and indicate that they do indeed care about nachos. Neither Ted nor Marshall takes any notice of them. The bystanders are clearly not ratified by Ted and Marshall. They do not even seem to be aware of them. They are eavesdroppers on the intradiegetic level in Figure 3.5.

On the supradiegetic level, audience laughter can be heard at several points in the interaction. The audience laughs at the situation comedy of the two friends who return to the same place in their fruitless search for nachos and who keep joining the queue for the ladies' toilets without realising it, and there is a hint of laughter when the bystanders respond to Ted's rhetorical question, 'Who cares about nachos?' (lines 7 and 8). The humour is, of course, completely lost on Ted and Marshall. They do not find the situation funny at all but are getting increasingly desperate at their own inability to locate the place where they can get nachos and the uncanny way in which they keep ending up near their own entrance back into the auditorium.

On the extradiegetic level, it is the whole package of the intradiegetic interaction between Ted and Marshall including the bystanders together with the laughter of the invisible audience on the supradiegetic level that is communicated to the television viewers. And on this level, we can again distinguish between the ratified audience of regular viewers and aficionados of the series and the incidental viewers who first have to figure out how the characters in this episode are related to each other and who need the explicit hints that are given prior to the above extract that Lily and Marshall are expecting their first child.

3.6 The audience talking back

Our model of communication of performed fiction represented in Figure 3.5 suggests that the communication on all the represented levels is unidirectional, from a sender to a receiver. In this respect, there are some significant differences between the three levels. On the intradiegetic level, the model works largely as in everyday face-to-face communication. Interlocutors take turns at being sender and recipient. Addressees talk back to the speaker. They become speakers themselves and thereby turn the previous speaker into a recipient. Marshall and Ted in our example take turns at speaking, as in real life, except that they follow a script.

On the supradiegetic level, we have the studio audience (whether real or fake), which reacts to the ongoing scene with laughter. If it is a real audience, it is, of course, possible that the actors react somehow to the laughter. They might pause very briefly to let the laughter subside, or they might feel encouraged to continue or emphasise whatever caused the laughter in the first place. However, if the producers used canned laughter, the studio audience does not 'talk back' to the actors. In this case it is clear that the laughter is part of what is communicated, together with the intradiegetic interactions, to the extradiegetic audience.

On the extradiegetic level, the communication may indeed appear to be unidirectional. The audience cannot talk back to the author(s) and producers of the fictional product, except by choosing to consume it or by refusing to do so. A book may sell thousands or even millions of copies or none at all. A play may be performed before a sold-out house night after night or it might have to stop after a single performance. And a movie might be a huge financial success or incur considerable losses for its producers.

In the case of live-theatre audiences, however, there are more ways of communicating back to the actors on stage, for instance by laughter or applause or on a more subtle level by being enthralled or bored by the unfolding events on the stage. Or the actors may even interact with the audience in more direct ways and perhaps pick out somebody sitting in the first row to ask him or her a question. This kind of interaction is not possible in the case of movies, except for the very special cases of test screenings. In addition, popular television series often have blogs and forums where viewers comment and hypothesise about the artefact, complain and make suggestions, and in some cases, producers of these television series pick up some of the suggestions and let them influence the further development of the series.

3.7 Conclusions

In this chapter, we have argued that the communication of fiction is not fundamentally different from everyday communication even though it is often more complex, and this is why pragmatics provides appropriate tools for describing it. Both in everyday communication and in the communication of fiction, we have to distinguish between different roles on the part of both the recipients and the creators of a communicative act. As in everyday conversations, we distinguish between different layers of the audience, depending on their status of being directly addressed and ratified, known by the speaker to be there or concealed. In the case of the communication of fiction, we have proposed the terms 'addressee recipients' and 'meta recipients' for those members of the audience who are both directly addressed and ratified; 'incidental recipients' for those who are acknowledged to be there and for whom some extra information may be provided to fill in possible contextual gaps; and 'accidental recipients' who perhaps should not even be there because the content is deemed to be unsuitable for them.

In addition, it is necessary to distinguish clearly between different levels in the case of the communication of fiction. In particular, we need to distinguish between the extradiegetic level of the communication between the creator(s) of a piece of fiction and its audience; the supradiegetic level, which typically includes a studio audience, either fake or real; and the intradiegetic level of the communication between the depicted characters. This makes it possible to distinguish more systematically between the different types of audiences on the different levels. Thus, the viewers of a television series are not some kind of eavesdroppers who listen in to the conversations of the fictional characters. They are directly addressed. Not on the intradiegetic level, but on the extradiegetic level. Or, in the words of Dynel (2011: 1642), '[c]haracters may not talk to us, but they certainly talk for us.'

Key Concepts

Accidental recipients, addressee recipients, asynchronous, audience design, communicative act, core recipients, incidental recipients, illocutionary force, meta recipients, participation structure, perlocutionary effect, quasi-synchronous, supradiegetic, synchronous

Exercises

1. The American computer-animated comedy film *Inside Out* (2015) tells the story of five personified emotions (Joy, Sadness, Anger, Fear and Disgust) in the mind of a young girl called Riley, who finds it difficult to adjust to a new environment when she and her family move from Minnesota to San Francisco. It clearly addresses children as a target audience but also strives to entertain adults. Provide some additional examples for such dual target audiences and provide evidence in the examples for this dual addressivity.
2. In the case of theatre performances, the live audience can influence the dynamics of what happens on the stage. Have you experienced such instances yourself? Christmas pantomimes, a type of musical comedy with a long tradition especially in the United Kingdom, are well known for their interactions between the actors and the audience. The audience regularly joins in the fun, hisses at the villain, aws the poor victim or cheerfully disagrees with some of the characters with shouts of 'Oh yes, it is!' or 'Oh no, it isn't!' In opera productions, e.g. Mozart's *Don Giovanni* or Verdi's *Rigoletto*, the audience might interrupt the action by applauding and cheering after a beautifully performed aria. Describe some other ways in which the audience may interact with and influence, perhaps in much more subtle ways, what is happening on stage.
3. Is it the same when you read a poem silently to yourself or when you read it aloud to yourself or for an audience? You might want to try this out with Jennifer Wong's poem 'Itinerary' (2013) reproduced in Section 3.2 above. Describe the difference.
4. If you are a writer of poetry and fiction yourself, do you have a target audience in mind? If yes, how do you account for it? If no, what do you orient towards?
5. As pointed out in Section 3.6, popular television series are often discussed in online fan cafes and blogs, where viewers comment on and hypothesise about the artefact, compliment, complain and make suggestions addressed at the producers. For Korean television drama, Oh (2015) has shown that the producing team sometimes takes these comments for the continuation of the artefact into account. How would you try to incorporate this influence of the audience on the product in Figure 3.5?

Further reading

In this chapter, we have presented our own model of participation structure, which was, of course, inspired by others, most notably those by Bubel (2008) and Dynel (2011). For an overview and critique of these and other models, see Messerli (2017). Dynel (2011) applies her model of participation structure to *House MD*. This has also served as an inspiration for this chapter.

Part II

The pragmatics of story worlds

4 Genres of fiction

4.1 Introduction

Imagine you have some spare time and want to go to the movies with your friends. What to watch will be based on a decision process during which you negotiate things like time and place but of course also which movie to watch in the first place. If you do not have a particular movie in mind already, you might be guided by different criteria in your choice. Some of your friends are fans of actors, writers or directors and their choice will be guided by these considerations. Others base their decision on the genre of the artefact as advertised and browse the movie listing accordingly. Some love romance movies and comedies, others action movies, thrillers or horror movies, etc. Each of these labels produces certain expectations about what is to come and viewers and producers alike orient towards them. Therefore, a process of meaning making starts even before you actually engage with the artefact per se and continues during its consumption.

The same argument is valid for written fiction in the form of novels, play drama, poetry, etc. The title of a book, its cover and blurb or the title and visual appearance of a poem will all raise expectations in the reader as to what might be in store. In order to capture this phenomenon, in this chapter we will introduce the importance of the concepts of genre, text type, frame and activity type to continue the theme of fiction as communication. We will build our argument by first visiting structures of expectations in face-to-face communication as discussed in pragmatics and will then move to written texts more generally and then lead on to fictional artefacts.

4.2 Structures of expectation in face-to-face communication

The example of genres as advertised in movie ads and cinema listings is only one of many examples of labels that refer to structures of expectation and that order our world in the sense that they raise expectations of how an ensuing event can be classified and will unfold. It is a fundamental human trait to look for patterns and to draw on these when engaging in meaning making processes. In pragmatics, a number of terms are in use to refer to such recurring patterns in face-to-face communication. Drawing on the sociologist Erving Goffman's (1974) term 'frame', defined as structures of expectations, helps us to understand that people learn how to behave in recurring situations. Transactions of customers and clerks/shop assistants at the bank, post office, supermarket, etc. entail ritualistic elements of greetings, question and answer sequences, money transactions and farewells. Classroom interaction entails teachers, students, a particular infrastructure and ways of passing on knowledge. Human beings learn about how to appropriately navigate such daily situations by being socialised into a particular society from early childhood, by observing and by being prompted to produce adequate utterances (e.g. *thank you* and *please*, providing information, handing over money, etc.). This means that the term 'frame' entails both a historical dimension and a cognitive dimension. The historical dimension refers to the fact that it is the individual who has acquired the frame through socialisation in his or her own lifetime as well as the fact that the frame predated the individual (but see the possibility of change explained further below). The cognitive dimension refers to the fact that the person who has acquired knowledge about a frame will be able to draw on it as resource for meaning making in the future. People can even project how situations are likely to progress even if they have never experienced them themselves. There are many such instances of frames that are enacted usually in people's adult life for the first time. For example, (ideally) people will have heard or read about how job interviews work before they go to their first interview. Even first-time brides and grooms will have an idea of what to expect from the church ceremony or the civil act of registering the marriage. Other examples that come to mind are police interrogations, real estate negotiations for buying a house, or a speech at a funeral. The paths to making projections about these situations can be different. People might have attended a funeral where a speech was held, or accompanied friends in house-buying negotiations or weddings. In these cases, their roles were those of witnesses, audience or bystanders rather than the main interactants. However, knowledge, albeit of an incomplete and idealised type, can also be transported by means of fiction. We will return to this point in Section 4.5.

Thus, a frame is an umbrella term for a number of actions that belong together, and, importantly, it also includes knowledge of how they are ordered into sequences and who may or may not carry them out. The latter is referred to as the rights and obligations of the people enacting the frame. For example, during a trial in court, judges have the right to interrupt other members of the court and the accused, while the accused cannot self-select as a speaker and is restricted in his or her freedom of action to only answering questions. Teachers get to select students to speak and not vice versa. These examples clearly suggest that the concept of frame in its instantiation (i.e. the particular content of a frame) is culturally dependent while the fact that humans orient to frames in sense-making processes is in all probability universal. Levinson (1992) used the term 'activity type' to describe a very similar concept. His term highlights the importance of activities – or actions – in such prestructured events.

While frames guide actions and structure interpretation, this does not mean that they are static and unchangeable, nor that there is a limited set of frames. How classroom or court interaction ensues has changed over the centuries. Customer–clerk relations were probably different in subtle ways in the past. New (technological) innovations can change frames. Think, for example, about how to start a telephone conversation. In the past the ring tone was the only information available to the person receiving the call. Therefore the first exchanges were used to establish who was on the respective ends of the call. Now caller identification on your display will tell you who is calling, which makes spoken caller identification superfluous. Similarly, in a society where people are equipped with smartphones and access to online information, people in need of finding their way or finding information may turn to online solutions rather than asking passers-by.

As a final observation before moving on to expectations about written and fictional communication, we should stress that frames are often overlapping and often cannot be neatly organised in a linear fashion either. This is because they are tied to a particular society and to ideologies around understandings of roles. For example, we can subsume post office and bank interaction as customer–clerk frames, and we can make links between parent–child and teacher–student interaction when we draw on the concept of teaching and learning. However, usually there are other variables such as affection and closeness which will make the latter two scenarios slightly different. The term 'frame' should thus be interpreted not as a normative and prescriptive stance but as a cognitive guideline which activates expectations that are closely tied to a society's norms (see also Chapter 8).

4.3 Structures of expectation in written communication

The process of finding patterns and orienting to patterns in sense-making processes is not restricted to face-to-face interaction. When referring to written interaction, however, we usually speak of 'text types' or 'genres' rather than frames. Just like in face-to-face interaction, we take the context (or co-text) in which the text appears into account and interpret cues that evoke structures of expectations in us. An intuitive example is described by Bax (2011), who shows how the text type of a cooking recipe can be described along the parameters described in the left column of Table 4.1, ranging from location, topic focus, length, structure, discourse modes, style and register to grammar and lexis.

In line with the comments made about frames in face-to-face interaction, the boundaries between genres are fuzzy and characterised by intertextuality. This means that we can recognise a recipe quite easily in the cooking section of a magazine or a cook book, but sometimes recipes also appear in diaries, blogs or novels. Furthermore, there is variation in how instructions are rendered and whether there are pictures accompanying the recipe or not.

During our lifetime, we acquire a vast knowledge of different text types. This starts with children's stories where one of the earliest things children pick up is that English is read from left to right and top to bottom on the page and that the pages are turned from right to left. While this might seem self-evident, it is a convention and this practice differs, for example, in (historical) Chinese, Japanese or Hebrew. Over time, children also learn that stories have plots and high points and a moral message, which they will learn to *expect* from a children's book (see Chapter 5). Further examples of text types are letters, essays, school books, school report cards, newspaper and magazine articles, agony aunt columns, doctor's prescriptions, tax forms, bank statements, shopping lists, non-fiction books, user manuals, instruction books, or – to move to computer-mediated communication – text messages, blogs, tweets, status updates, encyclopaedia articles, etc. Being acculturated into recognising and using these text types means that people also actively draw on expectations when interpreting and classifying a text they encounter. The communicative purpose or function of a genre is thus its most distinctive feature (Swales 1990: 46). In Bax's (2011: 44–45) words, a genre schema is the 'mental construct which we draw on as we create and interpret actual text'.

Table 4.1 The relation between text functions and text features (abbreviated from Bax 2011: 50; see Locher 2017b: 76)

Features	Example: Recipe genre
Location	In a magazine or recipe book
Topic focus	How to prepare food
Visual aspects and layout Pictures, position of different parts, diagrams, colours	Frequently starts with a bold title and has pictures, perhaps with various colours to make it attractive
Length	Typically no longer than one or two pages
Structure	Title, picture, ingredients, instructions, etc.
Subjects/agents/focus Who is actually doing the actions? Subjects of the verbs?	Imperatives. The ingredients are in *describing* discourse mode and the instructions in the *interacting* discourse mode
Style and register Formal or informal? Related to any particular professional domain?	Typically relatively informal
Grammar Tense (past, present, future)	Imperatives, some conditionals (*if/when it is tender, then ...*)
Syntax (word order)	Standard, but simple
Length of sentences	Simple short sentences
Lexis Any jargon or technical language?	Cooking terms, names of foods, weights and measures

4.4 Structures of expectation in fiction

Turning our attention to fiction, we can state that just like frames and text types of the non-fictional type, genres of fictional texts provide a cognitive orientation structure. There is thus no need to assume that there are different cognitive processes per se at play when working with fictional texts (see also the discussion of the fuzziness of fictionality discussed in Chapter 2). Authors of fictional texts thus do not write in a cultural void but are influenced by fictional and non-fictional genres alike. They, as well as their readers, have been socialised into recognising these culturally dependent frames. This cultural knowledge will allow people to recognise patterns typical of, for example, the classic distinction between epic, tragedy, comedy and satire, as well as many other current and past genres from drama and melodrama, fairy tales, fan fiction, fantasy, horror, mystery, romance, thriller, to western, etc. As examples, see the text boxes, which contain brief definitions of lyric, epic, novel and gothic novel.[1] By recognising such genres, we form expectations about plot development, types of ending (happy, unhappy, open, etc.), focus on action/relationships/topic, set of characters, depth of character creation, attention paid to details (e.g. in detective stories), accuracy of background information, music, visuals, and much more.

'The Greeks defined a **lyric** as a song to be sung to the accompaniment of a lyre (*lyra*). A song is still called a lyric (the words in a song are known as lyrics) but we also use the term loosely to describe a particular kind of poem in order to distinguish it from narrative or dramatic verse of any kind.

A lyric is usually fairly short, not often longer than fifty or sixty lines, and often only between a dozen and thirty lines; and it usually expresses the feelings and thoughts of a single speaker (not necessarily the poet herself) in a personal and subjective fashion.' (Cuddon 2013: 411–412, italics in original, bold added)

'**epic** A long narrative poem, on a grand scale, about the deeds of warriors or heroes, incorporating myth, legend, folk tale [...] and history. Epics are often of national significance in the sense that they embody the history and aspirations of a nation in a lofty or grandiose manner.' (Cuddon 2013: 239, bold in original)

novel 'Derived from Italian *novella*, "tale, piece of news", and now applied to a wide variety of writings whose only common attribute is that they are extended pieces of prose fiction.' (Cuddon 2013: 477, italics in original)

'**Gothic novel/fiction** A type of romance [...] very popular from the 1760s until the 1820s. It had a considerable influence on fiction afterwards (still apparent in the 21st c.), and is of much importance in the evolution of the ghost story and the horror story [...].' (Cuddon 2013: 308, bold in original)

---

[1] Any introduction to literary terms will expand on these definitions and go into their historical development over several pages.

While readers/viewers use knowledge of genres as an orientation to make sense of what they read/see, at the same time there is no expectation of truth, accuracy or completeness of adherence to a genre or to frames depicted within an artefact. On the one hand, this can be explained with the fictional contract (i.e. readers'/viewers' acceptance of fictional texts as presenting fictitious characters and events; see Section 2.3). On the other hand, readers/viewers also expect that authors exploit genre expectations and play with them by breaking or/and adhering to them. This creativity is one of the things that makes reading and watching fiction pleasurable and novel. As Bax (2011: 27) puts it, '[t]exts draw on our mental ideas of genres, but may differ from those genres in various creative ways, or may mix genres creatively for particular and communicative purposes.'

To give some examples, Shakespeare's first folio categorised Shakespeare's plays into the three different genres that we are familiar with (comedies, histories, tragedies). Today's popular online streaming platform Netflix organises its content into over 200 main genre categories, which can have subcategories and are combinable with each other in searches. The online viewing platform Viki,[2] much smaller in scope and purpose, streams Korean, Japanese, Chinese and Taiwanese dramas and TV shows to an international audience, and classifies its content according to the following genres listed alphabetically:

> Action & adventure; Beauty; Biography; Challenges & competitions; Comedy; Costume & period; Created for Viki; Crime & mystery; Culture; Disaster; Documentary; Drama; Entertainment; Family & kids; Fashion; Film noir; Food; Horror & supernatural; Idol drama; Korean drama; K-pop; Lifestyle; Lifestyle & variety; Medical drama; Melodrama; Music; Sci-Fi & Fantasy; Short films; Sports; Telenovelas; Thriller & suspense; Travel; Variety; Web drama; Women

The individual artefacts are tagged and described with several of these labels and viewers can filter their searches of what to watch next with the help of the list.

The fact that viewers orient towards genre expectations can be nicely illustrated with another feature provided by Viki. When watching, the viewers can leave so-called timed comments directly linked to the video

---

[2] <https://www.viki.com> (last accessed 2 October 2020). Viki provides fans with software to add subtitles in their own language to the Korean/Japanese/Chinese originals. In this way, the platform draws on global lay translation and makes the artefacts accessible beyond English speakers. English still plays a major role on the platform since it is usually the first language into which the Asian artefacts are translated.

and they use these among other things to discuss plot development and genre conventions. Extract (4.1) displays a selection of such comments posted in the first episode of the Korean drama *Meloholic* (2017), which was labelled in the platform as belonging to the genres Korea, comedy, crime & mystery, Sci-Fi & Fantasy, Korean drama, idol drama and romance. The comments serve as evidence that the viewers indeed draw on their expectations about genre.

(4.1) Timed viewer comments on genre
 – Woaaaaaaw un drama qui commence par de la romance ?! Le ciel nous tombe sur la tête x) [woah a drama which starts with romance?! The sky is falling x)]
 – So Is this gonna be a mystery crime drama too?
 – well this is a new type of kdramas
 – Omg this kdrama is wild wtf 😂😂😂😂
 – Who produced this it's too much 😂
 – 😂😂😂😂 k dramas don't usually go this far but ok 😂😂😂
 – i cant believe this was included in a kdrama
 – this is so not the kind of Kdrama I'm used to 😂😂😂
 – WoW in 2017 we're definitely turning a page !
 – I am so not used to all this '\action\' in Kdramas but I'm okay with it! Carry-on!

The first comment in Extract (4.1) refers to the fact that there is a love declaration within the first couple of minutes in episode 1 of this drama. The writer displays knowledge of Korean romance drama conventions where such declarations are usually built up over several episodes and therefore come much later. To start with love declarations is perceived as unusual. The viewer thus points to an instance of genre expectations being broken. In the case of the second comment, the viewer wonders about the genre adherence of the drama and suggests that it could be a mystery crime drama in addition to whatever this particular viewer expected in the first place. The remaining comments refer to a scene in which sexual activity among characters is not only hinted at but shown fairly explicitly. The international viewers comment on this and thus display that they have gained knowledge about K-dramas usually not being explicit in this respect. The novelty of breaking the genre convention is thus commented on.

Another example of genre awareness – this time on the side of the producers – is taken from a humorous advertising campaign. As in the example given in the introduction with respect to choosing what to watch or read, the first expectations arise when looking at the title of a book/film or seeing the cover, blurb post or advertisement. The advertisers of the US film *He's Just Not That Into You* (2009) humorously exploit genre expectations in their potential viewers by producing a six-minute clip in which the three main male actors counter potential misgivings which might deter a male audience from watching the movie because of the genre label 'chick flick', which might evoke negative stereotypes from a masculine perspective. The label 'chick flick' with its potential negative connotation is thus brought up by the producers themselves and played with within the clip. The ad starts out as follows, directly addressing potential male viewers, with the three actors sitting on a sofa facing the camera:

(4.2) Introduction to '10 Chick Flick Cliches that are not in movie He's Just Not That Into You', 2009

1	Long:	^hi I'm Justin 'Long,
2	Cooper:	I'm ^Bradley Cooper,
3	Connolly:	and I'm ^Kevin ^Connolly.
4	Cooper:	and we're ^all in the movie *He's Just Not That Into You*.=
5	Long:	=^nah ^nah ^nah ^nah hold the phone. ((fending off gesture))
6		I ^know what you 'guys are there thinking=
7		=you are 'all thinking to yourselves=
8		=^oh fantastic great another ^chick flick this is just what I need I,
9		I ^just started dating this 'girl she's gonna drag me to see it=
10		=this [^sucks.]
11	Cooper:	[okay] 'first of all ^why are you so angry=
12		=it's 'just a movie= ((deep sigh by Long))
13		=and ^second of all you got 'nothing to worry about=
14		=you're ^safe seeing this film=
15		=we're going to tell you you 'might even ^enjoy it.
16		'cause *He's Just Not That Into You,*
17		it is ^not your typical chick flick.
18	Connolly:	and to ^illustrate that point we would like to 'present ^ten=
19		=^chick ^flick ^clichés that are ^not in this movie.
20		[continuation with title of the movie and ten enacted scenes for each cliché.]

You can find the ten clichés (or rather recurring elements which are part of potential expectations about the genre 'chick flicks') at the end of this chapter in Exercise 4. Before you read the list, ask yourself what your expectations are when somebody tells you that a movie is a chick flick. It is interesting that the list contains both plot-relevant clichés such as numbers 2, 4 and 7 but also many diegetic elements which have to do with music, camera angles and typical scenes that give the flavour of a light-hearted romance movie.

Delineating the many different fictional genres and their subgenres from each other is a largely futile endeavour due to the fuzziness of genres as such. However, as shown in Extract (4.1), it bears pointing out that there are different levels of genre expectations. The comments display cultural expectations about K-drama versus dramas in other parts of the world. For example, US and British telecinematic productions are nowadays more explicit in showing sexual activity and violence than in the past. Different cultures will develop different forms of narratives and performances (e.g. a limerick versus a haiku; a puppet theatre versus a shadow play). Genres can also be separated according to their medium. For example, Jahn (2003: F1.2) describes the genre of film in connection to (written and performed) dramatic play in general:

> a **film** is a multimedial narrative form based on a physical record of sounds and moving pictures. Film is also a performed genre in the sense that it is primarily designed to be shown in a public performance. Whereas a dramatic play is realized as a live performance by actors on a stage, a film is shown in a cinema (a 'film theater'), is not a live event, and can theoretically be repeated infinitely without any change. Like drama, film is a *narrative* genre because it presents a story (a sequence of action units [...]). Often, a film is an adaptation of an epic or a dramatic narrative (examples: Stanley Kubrick's adaptation of Anthony Burgess's novel *A Clockwork Orange*, Milos Forman's film of Peter Shaffer's play *Amadeus*). (Jahn 2003: F1.2, bold and italics in original)

Jahn highlights the narrative core of fictional texts in the comparison between film and dramatic play – a core which can also be argued to be key in most fictional genres (see Chapter 5). Genres can also be delineated with respect to prototypical content, as reflected in Table 4.1 and exemplified with the categories shown for the Viki streaming platform. We can further make a distinction with respect to what scenes are typically included, as shown in Extract (4.2), and continue this granularity up to the textual stylistic level. We can thus state that there are different levels on which expectations arise. As a result, genre expectations are scaffolded and interact in complex ways with each other. Evoking genres can thus work as creating common ground for meaning making processes.

Having highlighted different levels of fiction genres, we can continue with observations on the textual and diegetic level and thus return to a discussion of stylistic genre features, which we started when introducing Bax's taxonomy in Table 4.1 for non-fictional texts. For example, just as you can quickly distinguish a cooking recipe book from an instruction manual for operating your new coffee machine on a visual level, the text is usually differently presented in fictional text genres as well. Novels often have a table of contents and are organised in parts and chapters; plays are often organised in acts and scenes, include stage instructions and identify speakers; poetry collections often contain usually shorter texts that often are presented with a title, stanzas and verses, like the poem 'Itinerary' written by Jennifer Wong, presented in Chapter 3. The repeated use of 'often' in the previous sentence is crucial: we are only dealing with prototypical cues that point to a particular genre. However, the actual instantiation in a particular novel, play and poem is a creative act which can freely combine and mix elements.

This observation is also true for other stylistic elements of a fictional text such as typical sentence length, the use of imagery or rhyming. The author Anton Chekhov (1860–1904) has given a well-cited example for the textual level (Gurlyand 1904: 521). He argues that readers are aware that details given in a fictional text have been included for a purpose and that writers should only include relevant details in their texts. Therefore, if a gun is mentioned in a novel, this will raise expectations in the readers that this very gun will become important at a later stage in the plot. This technique has also been termed 'foreshadowing' when the gun indeed plays a part in the further development of the narrative and a 'red herring' when it does not. The point here is that readers are aware of this convention and that authors and producers can exploit this in either direction.

4.5 Frames within frames: intradiegetic and extradiegetic

As a final point, we return to the notion of frame introduced in Section 4.2 for face-to-face interaction. Throughout the creation of a story world, the notion of frames is exploited for effect by authors and producers within the storylines. For example, in a fictional rendition of a phone call, we rarely get to see the entire phone call from beginning to end. Instead, we are shown only what is relevant to the plot. The same goes for other activity frames. For example, it is enough for the readers to know that the characters are purchasing goods but we do not need to witness the entire interaction between the main character and the shop assistant to know that this frame has been activated. This means that authors can exploit the power of frame cues in order to create common ground with the readers for sequences of action as well as role understandings. The mere mention of 'going to the movies', 'having guests over', 'doing a job interview', etc. will activate these frames, including the perceived rights and obligations of the characters. To return to the example of *House MD*, the American medical drama series mentioned in

Chapter 3, the frame of doctor–patient interaction is evoked and then broken when the main character, Dr House, does not appear to care very much for his patients beyond seeing them as presenting interesting medical cases. The knowledge of individual frames can thus be activated within larger genre expectations in order to be maintained, broken or played with.

As just stated, using the power of frame cues to create common ground does not mean that the activated frame has to be enacted in its entirety. With respect to the fictional nature of texts, it is crucial to understand that the activated frame also does not have to be an exact match with the face-to-face counterpart. This point is important for two reasons. First, we should always be aware that we are working with fictional data which places cues strategically for effect (see also our discussion in Section 1.5). The artefact per se does not (and does not have to) make a claim for depicting 'reality'. For example, even though there are a number of popular and long-running hospital series which are famous for their meticulous checking of medical detail (e.g. *House MD, ER, Gray's Anatomy, Casualty*), this does not mean that linguists can study 'doctor–patient interaction', 'caretaker–patient interaction', or 'caretaker–caretaker interaction', etc. in the artefacts *as if* the interaction and language used in the artefact can replace actual recordings of non-fictional data and fieldwork in hospitals and wards. Sequences of action are usually clipped (i.e. the frame is not shown in its entirety), compromises are made (e.g. the sequence would entail multilingualism but is rendered in English only so that the audience can understand), and fictitious plot elements can create a deviation from more standard patterns. So, while we cannot draw any conclusions about the study of frames in their entirety, we have the option of exploring the cues and their underlying ideologies in their own right. For example, in the hospital series we can learn about how societal hierarchies are depicted in fiction (power, gender, age, education, etc.), what topics are considered worthy of being shown (e.g. patients and staff from different backgrounds; the effect of having access/no access to health care for different social classes), and how language is used to create similarity and difference in character creation (see Chapter 6).

Second, the connection between the intradiegetic and extradiegetic levels of communication is also important with respect to the direction of influence. In the examples above, it was always assumed that cues for frames derived from non-fictional interaction are strategically placed in the fictional text to create common ground. The direction of knowledge activation is from the non-fictional context to the fictional context. However, as discussed in Chapter 3 with respect to the participation structure of fiction as communication, there can be a back and forth between the intradiegetic and extradiegetic levels. People who are lucky enough never to have seen a hospital from the inside might gain (correct and incorrect) knowledge about hospitals and expected procedures, hierarchies and roles from the fictional artefacts. People who do have experience with hospitals will take the fictional pieces of information and map them against their own personal life experience. Similar observations can be made about police interviews, love declarations, court interaction, etc. For the latter, Machura et al. (2001) report to what extent people even outside of the United States are influenced by courtroom drama in their understanding of legal processes, even though their countries might have considerably different legal systems. This is not to imply that the audience is gullible or forgets the viewer contract, but that the meaning processes are interlinked, not separated cognitively and can influence each other.

The influence of fiction on the perception of reality and the interconnectedness between fiction and reality in general are in fact major research areas in many different fields within the humanities such as media studies, sociology, literary and culture studies, and history. The interconnectedness between fiction and reality also features prominently in scholarly fields that often are portrayed in fiction. For example, the medical humanities – among other things – explore how medicine is portrayed in fiction, or the field of law is well aware of the importance of law in film and offers courses in this area in order to discuss where the similarities and differences in the fictional renditions lie.

4.6 Conclusions

In this chapter we started out by making the case that structures of expectations play a crucial role for communication as discussed in pragmatics. We argued that these frames are equally important for face-to-face and written communication and then extended our discussion to fictional written and diegetic texts and the notion of genre.

Even before you read or watch a fictional artefact, genre expectations arise due to the context in which you consume the text. Genres thus present a cognitive orientation structure. Pointing out that genre is a fuzzy concept allows us to understand the process of creatively combining genre elements on different levels, such as cultural differences, content, modalities, forms, styles. The genre cues will contribute to the creation of meaning, and the scaffolding of different genre levels adds to the complexity of this process.

We wish to highlight that authors and producers have cues available with which they can create story worlds and exploit their indexicality for effect. We will return to the power of indexical linguistic cues once we talk about character creation especially in Chapter 6, where we discuss that how characters are made to speak through phonological, syntactic and lexical choices results in evoking strong associations about where characters are from (regionally, socially, ethnically, etc.). Next, however, we will turn to the discussion of the narrative core which links many fictional genres.

Key Concepts

Common ground, fictional contract, film, frame, genre schema, gothic novel/fiction, ideology, lyric, novel

Exercises

1. Drawing on Bax's (2011) list of text type features, pick a written non-fictional text type and try to complete the list in Table 4.1 (e.g. letters, essays, school books, school report cards, newspaper and magazine articles, agony aunt columns, doctor's prescriptions, tax forms, bank statements, shopping lists, non-fiction books, instruction books, text messages, blogs, tweets, status updates). How could you turn the description of this text type into a linguistics paper? What methodologies will you draw on?
2. How do you choose what to watch or read? What expectations do you have based on the cover of a book, the poster of a movie, or the trailer and blurb of an artefact? Think back to the last three movies/TV series you watched and the last three books you read. Discuss your selection practices with your colleagues.
3. Describe and define your favourite genre to your colleagues and explain what your expectations are based on. List at least ten features, including elements such as plot development, story world creation, and, in the case of performed genres, music and filmic character features. Do your expectations match your colleagues' or is there room for diversity?
4. The advertisers of the US film *He's Just Not That Into You* (2009) produced a promotional clip in which the three main male actors counter potential misgivings concerning the genre label 'chick flick' (see the discussion in Section 4.4). You can find the ten clichés they raise in the box below. Do these clichés match your own expectations

about romantic comedies or romances? Are there further clichés that have not been listed?

> **'10 Chick Flick Cliches that are not in the movie He's Just Not That Into You'**[1]
>
> 1. No falling-in-love montage
> 2. No speech where in order to win her over a guy tells a girl all the details he likes about her
> 3. No shots where heads fall into frame and land on pillows
> 4. Nobody chases anybody down to stop them from going somewhere to stop them from doing something
> 5. No elderly folks who say anything inappropriate
> 6a. No one is ever laughing and crying at the same time
> 6b. No one slides down a wall while crying
> 7. No scene where someone has a one night stand and shows up to work the next day and finds out that they actually slept with their new boss
> 8. No corky/sardonic/sassy best friend
> 9. No singing into random objects
> 10. No make-over montages

5. Fictional genre expectations are often broken for effect and often more than one genre label fits an artefact. Can you think of illustrations? For example, do you remember reading a book or poem, or watching a movie and you were surprised about a turn of events that you did not expect? For example, if you read the first novel *A Game of Thrones* (1996) in the book series *A Song of Ice and Fire* by George R. R. Martin (or watched the first season of *Game of Thrones*), were you taken aback by the fact that Ed Stark, one of the main characters, was killed quite unexpectedly, after the author had gone through hundreds of pages of building up the character? Can your surprise be explained with genre expectations that were broken?

Further reading

In this chapter we draw on Jahn (2003), Paltridge et al. (2011) and Giltrow (2017) for genre expectations in fiction, and on Bax (2011),

---

[3] Trailer at <http://www.imdb.com/video/screenplay/vi3392537369/> (6 minutes, last accessed 2 October 2020).

Clark (1996), Goffman (1974) and Levinson (1992) to link genre to discourse analytic concepts such as frame, activity type and common ground. Dynel's (e.g. 2012) work on *House MD* was also consulted. As Locher summarises in the context of describing the educational text genre of reflective writing:

> Linguistic approaches to genre developed out of literary and folklore studies (see Swales 1990: 33–44) and can be found within discourse analysis, corpus linguistics and text linguistics (see Schubert 2012: 14). Corbett (2006: 27) argues that a number of very productive research strands exist. In systemic-functionalist linguistics, researchers are concerned with collecting 'comparable texts and attempts to find in them predictable, goal-oriented elements that are characterized by similar realizational patterns' (Corbett 2006: 31). The new rhetoricians are more interested in a genre's historical context, while applied linguists focus on genres in order to be able to 'teach generic conventions to novices' (Corbett 2006: 31). We might add that corpus linguistics in general has furthered our understanding of genres with respect to corpus-derived grammars and to methodology (Biber 1988, 1989; Biber and Conrad 2009; Biber et al. 1999; Conrad and Biber 2001a, 2001b). (Locher 2017b: 75)

For medical humanities, consult Locher (2017b) and for law in film, Greenfield et al. (2010) and Machura and Robinson (2001).

5 The narrative core

5.1 Introduction

In literary studies the study of narrative, story and plot has a millennia-long tradition. Exploring how texts are composed is part of describing, analysing and understanding genres such as epic, tragedy, comedy and satire (see Chapter 4). What all of these genres will entail is a narrative core, which is transmitted in different ways. In this process we can distinguish the narrative as such ('anything that tells or presents a story'), the story ('a sequence of events involving characters') and the plot ('the logical and causal structure of a story') (Jahn 2017: N1.2, N1.2, N4.7). Often a story might contain a primary storyline and intertwined secondary storylines. However, the point is that readers expect and are looking for a narrative within the book, play or film (often also in poems and song lyrics) and will try to make sense of what they are presented with. This observation links back to the point made in the previous chapter that genre is a cognitive concept drawing on the prototypicality of story types. Taking a step back, we can thus say that fiction in general will give rise to expectations of being presented with a narrative, and genre cues specify the types of narratives further.

In this chapter we will discuss the cognitive and social function of narratives as discussed in pragmatics, both in fictional and non-fictional contexts. We will first explain the complex everyday storytelling conventions (Section 5.2) and will then make analogies to fictional texts with a narrative core (Section 5.3). In Section 5.4, we will turn to the concepts of story world creation and narratorial voice in particular as they represent a selection of important narrative techniques. In exploring the concept of narrative, we can both understand the concept of genre better and also prepare the ground for Chapters 6 and 7, where we will concentrate on the role of language in creating characters and the role of dialogues within storytelling in particular.

5.2 Stories as fundamental meaning making units in discourse

The study of oral narratives in linguistics started to gain momentum in the 1970s with seminal work by Labov (Labov and Waletzky 1967; Labov 1972, 1997, 2013) and has since then been a core interest in discourse analysis and pragmatics. The literary approach to narratives is much older. Nevertheless, it pays to first discuss oral non-fictional narratives in order to drive home the point that narratives are an all-pervasive discourse unit going beyond fictional genres. As Klapproth (2004) summarises, narratives are multifunctional in that they fulfil 'two fundamental human needs':

- a *cognitive* need: 'narratives are a means of structuring and processing personal human experience', and
- a *social* need: 'narratives are a means of communicating such experience to others and thus *sharing* it' (Klapproth 2004: 103, italics in original).

Stories are indeed all-pervasive in our lives. In fact, stories start even before our individual life times when future parents talk about living with the new family member or when they prepare siblings for the arrival of the new child by spinning stories of the type 'when you're a big sister, you'll . . .'. When growing up, we are immersed in storytelling in many different contexts. We hear adults tell each other what they experienced throughout the day or what they heard others saying and we develop the wish to share what we have experienced ourselves with others. Our parents may read a story to us and later we learn how to read ourselves. We may watch narratives on TV or nowadays on laptops, tablets and smartphones. We engage in play acting with our friends in which we create story worlds and characters and we learn how to navigate the fuzziness between fictionality and fact (see Chapter 2). After all, when we retell experiences about what happened to us in a past event, we cannot be entirely true to how a past experience exactly happened. Otherwise, this would mean that we would have to re-enact the event, which is impossible; instead, we summarise, set a scene succinctly and learn that some details can be left out in order to highlight others.

Learning how to tell a complete oral story of a past experience is something that needs to be practised and learned and is usually achieved by age nine to ten (Berman 2009: 355). Before this point, children's stories are often hard to follow because they cannot yet render the story worlds, characters, order of events and gist in a skilful way. Linguistic challenges such as reference (e.g. for place, person, time), narrative temporality (e.g. what action follows which, what happens at the same time) and connectivity (e.g. the use of 'and then', 'and meanwhile') develop over the course of several years (Berman 2009; Nelson and Khan 2019). As you can see from this list, telling a personal story is actually not all that different from telling a fictional story with respect to the complexity and skill needed.

When Labov and his team interviewed people in New York City for a linguistic analysis of variation in phonology and grammar, they asked them to share stories in order to produce non-scripted language.[1] These narratives were first used in order to analyse grammar and phonology. However, later Labov noted the similarity in how the stories were crafted and described the structure of such narratives of personal experience in his research. His definition is as follows:

> A narrative of personal experience is a report of a sequence of events that have entered into the biography of the speaker by a sequence of clauses that correspond to the order of the original events. (Labov 1997: 398)

He argues that a story needs to have a recognisable 'reportable event', i.e. one that 'justifies automatic reassignment of speaker role to the narrator' (Labov 1997: 406), and the most reportable event within a story is the 'point' of a story.

In order to play through Labov's narrative syntax, let us assume that you usually take the bike to work or university. While this is not reportable as such since it is a recurring event and everyone knows about you commuting by bike, this morning you actually had an accident since a careless driver who had parked his car opened the door without checking the rear mirror. As a consequence, you ran into the door, fell, and hurt yourself slightly. Thanks to traffic being light and no tram approaching (which it could have), no bigger disaster occurred. However, next to being upset at the incident taking place in the first place, you feel especially wronged because the driver never apologised and thought that it was your fault. You now want to share this upsetting and emotional experience with your friends. How do you go about it?

For example, you could start out by saying, 'You know what happened to me today?', which is called a story-opener move and is rhetorical in nature. You thus bid for speaker right in order to report on this event. Your friends will grant you this speaking right in order to understand

---

[1] The method used is the sociolinguistic interview during which interviewees are asked to produce language of the formal and informal type. In order to obtain non-monitored, free speech, sharing narratives turned out to be a suitable approach.

Table 5.1 Core elements of narratives of personal experience (Labov 1972: 370)

Name of narrative element	Leading questions
Abstract (optional)	What was this about?
Orientation	Who, when, what, where?
Complicating action	Then what happened?
Evaluation	So what?
Result or resolution	What finally happened?
Coda (optional)	The narrative is finished; bridges story world and world of the talk

the point of the story.[2] If you then do not deliver a clear narrative, your conversational partners (or audience) might ask, 'So what?' In order to fend off this question (which would imply that you are an unskilled storyteller and might be wasting your listeners' time), you will take care in constructing a linear narrative of causality, which also entails evaluation. This is what Labov means in his definition above when he talks about the sequence of clauses. The elements in Table 5.1 are part of a prototypical narrative of personal experience and some of them are shown in a schematised form of the flow of a narrative in Figure 5.1.

The abstract and coda are optional, i.e. they did not always occur in Labov's corpus. They function as dynamic boundary markers between the world of the talk and the world of the story, as Johnstone (1990) puts it and as shown in Figure 5.1. The arrows between the left and right parts of the figure indicate the transition between the two worlds and back. The world of the talk is the particular context during which a storytelling event takes place (e.g. during a coffee break between classes) and this context remains relevant even while the world of the story unfolds although it is not foregrounded. This is why the dark box for the world of the story is embedded in the world of the talk in Figure 5.1. The world of the story refers to the context in which the story unfolds.

The abstract succinctly summarises what the story is about ('You know, I was doored and my bike is a complete goner and on top of that this guy never apologised') and in the coda the audience members and storyteller might revisit aspects of the experience and ask follow-up questions ('Were you hurt badly?') until the topic is changed. The abstract and coda can also contain meta-comments as to how you

---

[2] This is what is meant by 'justifies automatic reassignment of speaker role to the narrator' (Labov 1997: 406), quoted above.

THE NARRATIVE CORE

```
World of the talk
       │
       ▼                World of the story
                        ┌──────────────────┐
  conversation ──────▶  │ abstract         │ ──────▶
                        │ (optional        │
                        │ announcement     │
                        │ of story starting)│        │
                        │                  │        ▼
                        │                  │      story
                        │                  │        │
                        │                  │        ▼
                        │ coda             │
                        │ (optional        │
  conversation ◀──────  │ announcement     │ ◀──────
       │                │ of story ending) │
       ▼                └──────────────────┘
```

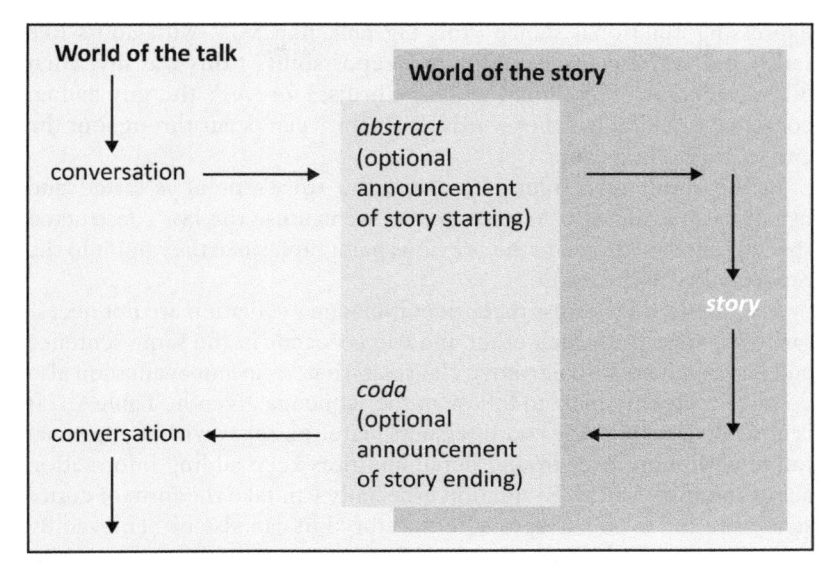

Figure 5.1 Structural conventions for personal experience storytelling (adapted from Johnstone 1990: 30)

classify the genre of your story (e.g. a traffic disaster story with you as victim, as opposed to a story of how you met your partner, etc.).

Within the story proper, orientation clauses tell the listeners who the 'characters' of the story are and when and where the event took place (e.g. you; a car driver who did not look in his side mirror when opening the car door; a potentially approaching tram in a busy and narrow street during early traffic hour). In the case where common ground is already shared, less detail can be given here (e.g. you and your audience are in the same city and your audience knows the city and your usual commuting path).

Narrative clauses explain the sequence of events and tell what happened by showing complicating actions. If you changed the sequence, a different story would emerge. In other words, the sequence implies a linear development of the story and causality. In our example, it matters that you mention the car door is opened first because that is what makes you fall.

The aspect of evaluation is a crucial element in narratives of personal experience. In order to make the audience understand that the story is worth listening to, the narrator might use adjectives and emotionally loaded nouns in the abstract to highlight relevance ('I had an accident and got such a scare') and use both modifiers such as adjectives expressing emotional stance ('this big tank-like SUV with doors like sails') and entire clauses to highlight reportability ('this was my worst bike accident ever'; 'I think I will have bruises forever'; 'this guy had no conscience at all'). In other words, evaluation can occur throughout the entire storytelling event.

In the result or resolution section, the story's point is stated and usually also evaluated. As an example, we can use the last constructed speech sentences given in the previous paragraph since they point to the reportability of the event.

It is important to stress that orientation and evaluation are not necessarily separate from each other and can co-occur in the same sentence and be combined with narrative clauses. Orientation and evaluation also do not necessarily have to follow in the sequence given in Table 5.1. It is entirely possible that you intersperse later passages within your narrative with more background detail and thus keep adding information about the story world. Evaluation especially can take the form of entire sentences and even passages within a story but can also be achieved by adjectives and verbs that express evaluative stance within other narrative elements.

What this research from sociolinguistics has demonstrated convincingly is to what extent everyday oral storytelling is both a skill and an interactional achievement. Storytellers need to gain the floor (i.e. speaking rights), then create a story world, present a sequence of events as belonging together, and make sure that the point of the story is understood and the purpose for the storytelling comes across.

Crucially, in interaction, the role of the audience should not be underestimated. People adapt their language according to who their addressees are, which is called audience design (see Bell's 1984 definition in Section 3.3). For example, a politician will use standard language in political, public speeches and avoid swearing and colloquialisms in professional contexts, but might use plenty of swearwords with family and peers. Or, a doctor is well-versed in medical jargon and uses it abundantly when talking to colleagues but avoids technical jargon when talking to patients in order not to jeopardise comprehension. A shop assistant might use a high number of grammatical and phonological features from a prestige variety when talking to customers, fewer when talking to fellow staff members, and the fewest when talking to friends or family. In the case of storytelling, the story is pitched to a particular audience: you tell stories differently when you address different target audiences such as children, peers, parents, etc. Furthermore, audience members can also influence the story and become co-constructors of the storytelling event. As Schegloff (1997: 97) stresses, '[o]rdinary storytelling is, ..., a coconstruction, an interactional achievement, a joint production, a collaboration, ...' For example, if your story abstract of being doored does not receive any uptake of sympathy and throughout the storytelling your audience does not make any appreciative or appalled noises, your story might become quite factual and short. In contrast, if your audience consists of fellow cyclists who maybe have had similar experiences and make the right noises of sympathy and might even add details to the orientation, then the story might get longer and include more details.[3]

So, what is at stake? In her work on narratives by Holocaust survivors as well as everyday storytelling, Schiffrin points out that what is at stake when we share stories is also identity construction, and we can add this function of stories to the fundamental cognitive and social human needs quoted at the beginning of this section. Schiffrin writes that we define 'ourselves through what we say, how we say it and to whom we say it' and continues to say that '[t]he way we tell our stories also reveals a self that exists within a cultural matrix of meanings, beliefs, and normative practices' (1996: 169, 170). Linde (1993: 123) adds to this point by stressing that narrative is 'an extremely powerful tool for creating, negotiating, and displaying the moral standing of self'. Therefore, a banal personal event such as having a bike accident can turn into a negotiation of identities where blame is assigned, where victims or heroic behaviour can be displayed and sanctioned or contested by the audience members.

The observations so far have been made about so-called high point stories, stories which have a clear point and climax (i.e. the story has a reportable event and thus a high degree of tellability; Labov 1972). In our daily experiences, however, there are many less fully-fledged narrative events. For example, when going to the doctors after an accident, patients need to recount a past experience. While in this case the retelling is less about triggering empathy and sharing emotions, patients still need to transform their past experience in such a way that a clear sequence of events emerges with enough orientation for the doctor to be able to follow (in fact, the concept of narrative is crucial for most medical professional and patient interaction; see Locher 2017b). Furthermore, Georgakopoulou (2007) has studied how teenagers who meet on a regular basis share stories. In addition to

---

[3] In the case where you have experienced an event which turns into a story together with others, these people can become co-storytellers as well by adding detail or taking over the storytelling. This phenomenon has been extensively studied among people who know each other well such as good friends or couples.

high point stories, the teenagers also engaged in sharing small scenarios of the type 'What if I met so and so tonight?'. Georgakopoulou has labelled these projections (in this case also jointly constructed) as 'small stories', and they typically do not contain any resolution. Dayter (2015) in her work on tweets posted by a group of ballet aficionados introduces the term 'tiny story' for the individual tweets. Looking at the individual tweets in isolation, they have a low degree of tellability and unclear narrative stance; however, looking at tweets over time, they can be read as belonging together and being turned into a biographical narrative. We might also engage in private fantasising and daydreaming (Klauk and Köppe 2014: 4), which we called 'spontaneous fiction' in Figure 1.1.

Our world is thus saturated with storytelling opportunities and these stories come in more and less elaborated forms. Once a storytelling context is established, a story schema is activated so that storytellers and listeners alike will orient towards it.

5.3 Stories in fiction: from starting point to intertextuality

After briefly outlining the importance of storytelling in our lives in general, we can turn to the fictional spectrum of storytelling and make links to the previous observations. We will first discuss the starting point of reading/watching/listening to a fictional narrative, then talk about story schemata within a genre, the fact that different genres can be activated within a story and different texts combined which results in intertextuality, and return to the concept of audience design. The choice of these issues is motivated by the link to oral storytelling where the same issues surface and are of pragmatic relevance. In the next section we will turn to the creation of story worlds and (briefly) character creation.

In oral high point stories people jointly construct a storytelling event through story openers which bid for the floor and audience members who sanction becoming listeners. So where is the starting point for engaging with fictional stories? This is not a banal question since our aim is to argue that engaging with a fictional artefact also activates an interpretation schema, which will make people look for narratives in general and for specific narratives in particular. For books, the selection is first made for children by their parents; later we might read on the recommendation of friends or librarians, because the school curriculum provides a list (canon), or because we follow recommendations published in journals and newspapers (e.g. the *New York Times* bestseller list or the Booker Prize nomination list in its long and short versions), personalised ads of online booksellers, or fan communities (sci-fi, mangas, graphic novels, particular authors, etc.). If you frequent libraries and bookshops, you may further be guided by the titles, the cover of a book or the blurb. Libraries and bookshops are often organised into thematic sections (e.g. mystery and crime, sci-fi and fantasy, novels), as well as the target audience (children, young adults, adults). If you browse online, shops such as Amazon will provide genre classification as well and will provide supplemental information on what other customers bought. No matter what you pick up and choose, you will expect to be confronted with a narrative that contains more or less fictitious elements (see Section 2.3 for the difference between fictitious and fictional) and roughly corresponds to the classification. So, if you pick up the latest book in the *Chief Inspector Gamache* series by Louise Penny or the *Inspector Lynley* series by Elizabeth George, two well-known contemporary crime novel authors, you will expect the two respective inspectors to appear in the novel and to solve murder cases. You will also expect to be presented with well-researched milieus since both writers are renowned for their meticulous background research.

These observations bring us back to genre as discussed in Chapter 4. There are many different fiction genres and they all come with expectations about narrative (containing love stories, disaster stories, action stories, etc.) and thus activate narrative schemata. In other words, they all have in common that there is some kind of communicative act which is transformed into the form of a narrative of a more or less elaborate type. There are narratives in the form of novels which span several volumes, create elaborate new worlds and are peopled by an abundance of different characters and creatures. There may be many different plot lines that together form the artefact. On the other end of this spectrum of narrative complexity, there might be brief poems or song lyrics about characters that still qualify as stories (i.e. 'a sequence of events involving characters'; Jahn 2017: N1.2; see also Chapter 10). What these texts thus all have in common is that they invite people to look for a narrative core.

This narrative core in its different instantiations is culture-dependent. For the classic Anglo-Western story tale, abundantly studied in folklore studies and literary and culture studies, Klapproth summarises the story schema as follows:

> Stories as protagonist-centred **PROBLEM-SOLVING** EPISODES
> This type of story focuses on a **main protagonist** involved in a problem-solving activity. Something (i.e. an **initiating event**) happens to the

protagonist, which creates a **problem** for him/her by either putting him/her in an undesired situation, or else by blocking his/her attainment of a desired situation. The protagonist responds to this initiating event by developing **the goal** (i.e. an internal motivating state) to solve this problem, and consequently engages in a (series of) **attempt**(s) to reach this goal. In his/her attempt(s) to solve the problem the protagonist may ultimately be either successful or unsuccessful, and the story will consequently result in either a happy or unhappy outcome. (Klapproth 2004: 160, bold added)

However, this is not to say that all narratives fit this schema, nor that narratives are predictable or need to progress in a preconceived manner. We have made the point before that there is fuzziness with respect to genre boundaries and that authors can play with the expectations of their readers. The previously mentioned crime novel series by Louise Penny and Elizabeth George are therefore not only about the ingenious work of the main protagonist inspectors but also about the development of relationships among colleagues, friends and family; expectations that might lean more towards the genre of a novel of developmental rather than crime fiction.

A well-known example of a humorous play on readers' expectations can be found in Laurence Sterne's *Tristram Shandy* (1762). For its time, this book is experimental in many ways by including figures, an entirely black page, empty chapters, censured text, etc. and its plot is anything but straightforward or progressing fast. The protagonist narrator includes a figure in which he visualises the digressions, flashbacks (or retrospection/analepsis) and flashforwards (or anticipation/prolepsis) within the narrative in the books up to the present point in the narrative (Figure 5.2). The fact that these non-linear storylines occur as such is not novel; the fact that they are talked about in a sequence of meta-discourse (i.e. the narrator reflects on his own storytelling technique), however, is surprising and was novel at the time since the story schema usually does not entail this element of meta-analysis.

Creative play with expectations about genres and plotlines therein is part and parcel of writing, and for readers/viewers, figuring out what is going on is part of the appeal of engaging with a fictional artefact in the first place. Drawing analogies between texts and real-life situations as well as drawing analogies between fictional texts further enriches this process and drives home once again the fuzziness of the concept of genre. This intertextuality (see text box) adds a level of meaning creation that draws on genre similarities but makes connections to particular texts. For example, Salman Rushdie's *Midnight's Children* (1981) draws

THE NARRATIVE CORE

> [152]
> CHAP. XL.
> I Am now beginning to get fairly into my work; and by the help of a vegetable diet, with a few of the cold seeds, I make no doubt but I shall be able to go on with my uncle *Toby*'s story, and my own, in a tolerable straight line. Now, 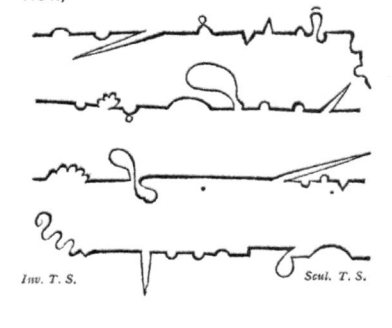
>
> *Inv. T. S.*   *Scul. T. S.*
>
> [153]
> These were the four lines I moved in through my first, second, third, and fourth volumes. —In the fifth volume I have been very good—the precise line I have described in it being this: 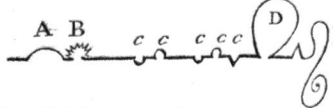
>
> A B   c c   c c c   D
>
> By which it appears, that except at the curve, marked A, where I took a trip to *Navarre*—and the indented curve B, which is the short airing when I was there with the Lady *Baussiere* and her page— I have not taken the least frisk of a digression, till *John de la Casse*'s devils led me the round you see marked D. — for as for c c c c c they are nothing but parentheses, and the common *ins* and *outs* incident to the lives of the greatest ministers of state ; and when compared

Figure 5.2 Extract of *Tristram Shandy* (Sterne 1762: Vol. VI, 152–153, italics in original)

on *Tristram Shandy* among other literature; Jean Rhys's *Wide Sargasso Sea* (1966), as a prequel to Charlotte Brontë's *Jane Eyre*, is full of intertextual links to the older text (see Chapter 2); Philip Pullman's *His Dark Materials* trilogy (1995–2000) can be read as an epic fantasy appealing to children but the author also weaves Milton's *Paradise Lost* (1667) and a critique and comment on Christianity into his texts. The more recent writing can be read in isolation and still works perfectly well; however, when a reader has knowledge of the older texts and access to the cultural background, the meaning making process becomes richer and multi-layered.

These observations on inclusion and exclusion of readers lead to the question of the target audience, i.e. the intended or ideal reader- or viewership, or the narratees. As mentioned above, in linguistics, we speak of audience design (see Section 3.3), a concept which highlights

> '**intertextuality** A term coined by Julia Kristeva in 1966 to denote the interdependence of literary texts, the interdependence of any one literary text with all those that have gone before it.' (Cuddon 2013: 367, bold in original)

that people will adapt their linguistic register to the context in which they wish to use language for effect. When writers and producers create a fictional artefact, they do not necessarily have to have a concrete readership in mind as many authors might claim that they are writing simply in their own voice. However, in many cases, stories are intended for a particular audience. This is especially true for telecinematic artefacts that are produced for profit. Just as the genre will influence the storyline expectations, the choice of language, level of intertextuality and complexity of plot and characters will favour some narratees over others. To give some examples, if a story plays in a multilingual context, the producers aiming at an English-speaking audience might still decide to stick with English only and sacrifice realism for comprehensibility. Other writers might intersperse their text with loanwords to give a passage a flavour of otherness (we will return to this point in Chapter 6). Children's stories cater to the level of language and psychological development of children of different age groups. They may contain artistic and/or humorous illustrations that appeal to all age groups. At the same time, they can also contain elements that are accessible to adults only and thus entertain more than one target group. The big blockbuster animated movies by Disney/Pixar and others generally are of this nature and thus appeal to the whole family. For example, in *Finding Nemo* (2003), the turtle surfing the ocean current might seem relaxed and fun to children but also represents a reference to youth culture through the use of 'be like' as a quotative ('and you were like woah'), 'Dude' and adjectives such as 'awesome', 'sweet' and 'totally'. The abundant use of 'Dude' is a reference to the Dude from *The Big Lebowski* (1998) and being high on drugs, a reference which will escape the children but will be known to most adults familiar with mainstream American movies from this decade. Keeping a particular audience in mind when writing and producing, however, does not mean that that there is an automatic or generic language use involved. Instead, we should stress the creative writing process again, which allows for free mixing of stylistic choices, while being aware that the narratees will draw on the meaning making processes outlined so far. After these more general observations, let us move to some language-specific comments and the creation of story worlds and narratorial voice.

5.4 Stories in fiction: story world and narratorial voice

Creating a story world is a fundamental task in all storytelling contexts. When and where does the story take place and who are the characters? Of course, novels do not usually start with a synopsis paragraph like in a face-to-face high point narrative, but any beginning of any novel will have to do the work of setting the stage and/or getting the reader interested in continuing to read. According to the American Book Review, famous first sentences include the following:

(5.1) A selection from the first ten entries taken from the American Book Review website[4]
1 Call me Ishmael. —Herman Melville, *Moby-Dick* (1851)
2 Lolita, light of my life, fire of my loins. —Vladimir Nabokov, *Lolita* (1955)
3 Many years later, as he faced the firing squad, Colonel Aureliano Buendía was to remember that distant afternoon when his father took him to discover ice. —Gabriel García Márquez, *One Hundred Years of Solitude* (1967; trans. Gregory Rabassa)
4 It was a bright cold day in April, and the clocks were striking thirteen. —George Orwell, *1984* (1949)
5 It is a truth universally acknowledged, that a single man in possession of a good fortune, must be in want of a wife. —Jane Austen, *Pride and Prejudice* (1813)

Sentences 1, 2, and 3 introduce characters within the story world: 'Ishmael' as a first person narrator, 'Lolita' addressed by another first person narrator, and 'Colonel Aureliano Buendía', one of the main protagonists of the novel, the protagonist's father and the fact that there is a firing squad. Sentences 3 and 4 set the scene with respect to time and place. In sentence 3, we are confronted with a prolepsis

> '**Deixis** is generally understood to be the encoding of the spatio-temporal context and subjective experience of the encoder in an utterance. Terms such as *I, here, now,* and *this [. . .]* are heavily context dependent and represent a kind of cognitive center of orientation for the speaker.' (Green 2006: 415, italics in original, bold added)

(flashforward) announced by means of 'many years later' and learn that there is a military or militia context ('the firing squad'). Sentence 4 gives a date and time of an unidentified year and alerts us to the fact that this world is different from ours since our clocks usually do not strike thirteen. In sentence 5, a topic statement is made most clearly among the five examples so that we expect the novel to be about match-making

---

[4] 100 best first lines from novels. American Book Review. <http://americanbookreview.org/100BestLines.asp> (last accessed 2 October 2020).

– in this case this first sentence functions very similarly to an abstract. If you were to continue reading after these first sentences, the story worlds would incrementally build up and create complex nets of personal, time and place deixis (see text box, p. 89). In the case of telecinematic artefacts, the visual possibilities take over or complement textual cues.

Consider now in more detail Extract (5.2), which shows the beginning of the prologue of N. K. Jemisin's *The Fifth Season. The Broken Earth: Book I* (2015):

(5.2) Jemisin (2015: x, italics in original, all other markings added)

```
 1                          Prologue
 2                       You are here
 3
 4   Let's start with the end of the world, why don't we? Get it over with and move
 5   on to more interesting things.
 6      First, a personal ending. There is a thing she will think over and over in
 7   the days to come, as she imagines how her son died and tries to make sense
 8   of something so innately senseless. She will cover Uche's broken little body
 9   with a blanket–except his face, because he is afraid of the dark–and she will
10   sit beside it numb, and she will pay no attention to the world that is ending
11   outside. The world has already ended within her, and neither ending is for the
12   first time. She's old hat at this by now.
13      What she thinks then, and thereafter, is: *But he was free.*
14      And it is her wary self that answers this almost-question every time her
15   bewildered, shocked self manages to produce it:
16      *He wasn't. Not really. But now he will be.*
17                             ***
18   But you need context. Let's try the ending again, writ continently.
19      Here is a land.
20      It is ordinary, as lands go. Mountains and plateaus and canyons and river
21   deltas, the usual. [...]
```

All personal pronoun references have been highlighted in bold. The first introduction to a voice is the 'you' in the title of the prologue and the 'us' in 'let's' (line 4), which indicates that a narrator is addressing either the readership or a character within the story directly and thus starts a dialogue. This addressee is returned to in line 18 again and this time it is clearer that the narrator is not talking to a character within the story because this character would not need this contextual information. The narrator introduces a female protagonist first not by name but by personal pronoun 'she' and reveals that this 'she' had a 'son', who died although the woman does not know how ('she imagines how her son died', line 7). The son's name is then shown to be 'Uche' (line 8), who was afraid of the dark when still alive. Any subsequent use of 'she'/'her' in this extract is then linked to the first introduction of the woman in a process of anaphorical linking. The pronouns 'he'/'his' refer to the introduced son Uche.

With respect to place (highlighted through underlining), we first learn that there is a 'here' (title of prologue) and that this here refers to a 'world', which appears to fall apart. We can work out that the female protagonist and her dead son are somewhere inside, since the world is falling apart 'outside' (line 11; this can be understood both physically and metaphorically). In line 18, however, the narrator acknowledges the lack of context given in the first sentences and places the story in 'a land' (line 19) and then starts to give more elaborate background information on the location. The geographical detail is no coincidence in this novel since grasping geographical processes will turn out to be a plot-driving element for the protagonist and her offspring who are magically endowed to manipulate and feel earth.

The first few lines also give us a sense of temporality. The title of the prologue creates a sense of co-presence through the use of 'here' (which is both spatial as well as temporal). We might then be surprised as readers that the story starts out with the end of the world (line 4), which in logical conclusion would also mean the end of the story. We learn then that there is a personal ending (line 6) and that the story continues after this endpoint after all ('in the days to come', line 7; the use of the future tenses; 'then, and thereafter', line 13).

Rather than starting with a neutral synopsis of the book, the lines quoted thus create a story world in crisis and engage the readers' interest in order to find out how this end of the world can be explained, how come Uche died, why there is an issue of suppression ('But he was free', line 13; 'He wasn't', line 16), and how come the female protagonist has already gone through the experience of the world falling apart (lines 11–12).

Picking up on textual cues is a fundamental process in reading. Authors are under no obligation to give the readers full access to story worlds and will indeed often withhold information, plant misleading information, or change narratorial perspectives for effect. How we are presented with cues will thus be co-determined by the (potentially changing) narratorial voice the authors choose to write in. In his overview chapter on 'narrative perspectives on voice in fiction', Hoffmann (2017) summarises the different possibilities and how they have been classified in the different traditions of literary and linguistic scholarship. Scholars have used the label 'perspective', and elaborated on 'mind style', 'multimodal and cognitive approaches to voice' as well as 'implicit characterization cues'. For a full rendition of this topic, we refer the reader to Hoffmann (2017) and Landert (2017). For the purposes of this chapter, we will first introduce some of the classic distinctions of types of narrators and types of focalisation for perspective before zooming in on some of the observations on mind style and cues.

A first important distinction is whether narrators appear as characters in the story and are thus part of the story or not. This distinction is meaningful since the different perspectives can be employed to give us different access to the story worlds. Jahn (2017, based on Genette 1980) refers to the result of these narratorial choices as homodiegetic or heterodiegetic narratives:

- In a **homodiegetic narrative**, the story is told by a (homodiegetic) narrator who is also one of story's acting characters. The prefix 'homo-' points to the fact that the individual who acts as a narrator is also a character on the level of action.
- In a **heterodiegetic narrative**, the story is told by a (heterodiegetic) narrator who is *not* present as a character in the story. The prefix 'hetero-' alludes to the 'different nature' of the narrator as compared to any and all of story's characters. (Jahn 2017: N1.10, bold and italics in original)

Furthermore, according to Hoffmann (2017, based on Genette 1972), the important definitions of focalisation (point of view in other frameworks) to describe perspective are 'zero focalisation', 'internal focalisation' and 'external focalisation':

> In zero focalisation, an omniscient narrator is capable of showing events from all possible spatio-temporal and cognitive vantage points. The narrator can slip into the minds and eyes of many different story characters and describe events at different times and in different places.
>
> Instead, in internal focalisation, the narrator adopts the restricted, subjective viewpoint of one of the story characters (the character-as-focaliser). In this configuration, the narrator's perspective is constrained by the character's personal, spatio-temporal and emotional point of view.
>
> The third category, external focalisation describes a (character-)external narrative viewpoint on the story world and its events. In contrast to internal focalisation, external narrators are unable to elicit the internal, mental state and thoughts of story characters. (Hoffmann 2017: 164)

Whichever strategy is used and whichever combination authors apply, the choice will give readers more or less access to story worlds and the thinking of characters within those story worlds. As texts develop, focalisations can also change. Table 5.2 summarises the rela-

THE NARRATIVE CORE 93

Table 5.2 Levels of focalisation (based on Martínez and Scheffel 2009: 67, reproduced with permission from Hoffmann 2017: 164)

Type of focalisation	Narrator-character relation
zero-focalisation	narrator **tells more** than character knows
internal focalisation	narrator **does not tell more** than character knows
external focalisation	narrator **tells less** than character knows

tions between the narrator and character in the type of focalisation involved.

Readers who are not literary scholars or pragmaticists will of course not label narrators with these concepts. However, they will start making assumptions about the knowledge state of the narrators, their mental state and their reliability with respect to giving access to the story world and the characters. While readers are aware that they are reading a fictional text (referred to as the willing suspension of disbelief or fictional contract; see Section 2.3), we assume that they will take information at face value until counter evidence is given.

Recall the example of *lonelygirl15* discussed in Chapter 2, where the video blogger's accounts were taken as real until revealed to be fictitious. In similar ways, narrators of whatever focalisation category are likely to be trusted first until cues are given that issues might be different. Consider the novel (and movie version of) *Atonement* by Ian McEwan (2001). The book is written in the voice of a third person narrator, who is not part of the story world. Only at the end of the book is it revealed that the previous parts are in fact a novel within a novel and that one of the characters of this very novel is the author of it who took the liberty of creating a happier ending than the 'real story' actually had. This 'move from anonymous implied author to embodied author-narrator' (Marsh 2018: 1331) in *Atonement* makes the readers revisit the entire reading experience and wonder how reliable the previous story is, not just with respect to the ending but also with respect to the other events that led up to it. This wondering brings to the foreground the powerful convention of the fictional contract since, of course, the readers know from the very beginning that the novel is fiction.

The notion of **mind style** is used to 'capture [...] a fictional individual's mental processes, including thoughts, memories, intentions, desires, evaluations, feelings, emotions, and so on' (Semino 2007: 169). This concept goes hand in hand with 'world view', which is argued to present the narrator's 'relatively permanent mental representations of the "reality" [she] inhabit[s]' (Semino 2007: 169). To distinguish the two in analysis, however, is often somewhat difficult. Studies of

> **Foregrounding** 'Giving unusual prominence to one element or property of a text, relative to other less noticeable aspects. According to the theories of Russian Formalism, literary works are special by virtue of the fact that they foreground their own linguistic status, thus drawing attention to how they say something rather than to what they say: poetry "deviates" from everyday speech and from prose by using metre, surprising metaphors, alliteration, and other devices by which its language draws attention to itself.' (Baldick 2015: 144)

mind style have often focused on those characters' minds which are somehow different or unique and, in connection with this, the characters' ways of thinking and reliability as potential narrators. As Hoffmann (2017: 174) points out, scholarly studies usually discuss characters that deviate from what readers might expect as the norm and whose style (linguistic and multimodal) is foregrounded (see text box). Studying what is unusual can help us understand texts in general. Foregrounding is also affected by contexts and can be a matter of degree. These concepts already set the stage for a discussion of characterisation more generally, which we will turn to in the next chapter.

To conclude this section, we can briefly point out another analogy between face-to-face storytelling practices and fiction. We have already made connections between the beginning of narratives, and have talked about orientation (time, place, characters, etc.) and the expectations which arise concerning complicating actions once the story schema is activated through genre cues. The concepts of characterisation cues and the study of mind style and world view give us access to the characters' being and understanding of their world. The remaining analogy has to do with 'evaluation'. Just as in the case of face-to-face oral high point narratives, evaluation is not reserved for the final paragraph or sequence of a novel or movie. On the contrary, evaluation is intricately woven into the textual fabric on all narratorial levels. A fruitful concept to capture the evaluative notion is stance, as defined by Landert:

> [S]tance [is regarded] as the expression of evaluative, epistemic and affective attitudes. [...] In fiction, stance can be realised both in character speech and in narratorial voice, and it can be expressed verbally as well as through non-verbal means, such as gestures and facial expressions. Studying stance can provide insights into characterisation, the dynamics between characters, plot development and narrative perspective. (Landert 2017: 489)

In linguistics, the term 'stance' describes those linguistic elements of an utterance that provide information on the speaker's attitude towards the content of the utterance, as in, '*Surprisingly*, he got a job.' The term 'epistemicity' is used for those elements that provide information on the inferential reliability of an utterance, as in 'He *may* have a job' or 'He *probably* has a job.' Some linguists treat these as distinct categories; others, like Landert (2017), take epistemicity to be a subcategory of stance. By looking at stance cues, we can thus learn something about evaluation on all levels of narrative. The concept is multifaceted and can be looked at in its grammatical instantiation as well as in its interactional form (i.e. through alignment of characters). If we revisit Extract (5.2) from the beginning of the *Broken Earth* trilogy, we see stance markers of several types. For example, evaluative stance markers can be found in lines 4 and 5 where the narrator judges the end of the world announced in the story as less interesting than what is to come ('Get it over with and move on to more interesting things') and assesses the land as 'ordinary' (line 20). There are epistemic stance markers, i.e. markers signalling knowledge states, in the use of future tense ('she will', e.g. line 8) and the foreshadowing per se ('in the days to come', lines 6–7; 'then, and thereafter', line 13), which tell the reader that the narrator has a privileged knowledge status about future and past events and has access to the protagonist's thoughts and feelings. Finally, there are also affective stance markers. The narrator characterises the female protagonist's state of loss and sorrow both by means of adjectives ('senseless', 'numb', 'wary', 'bewildered', 'shocked') and description of action (covering her son's body and keeping vigil, asking questions). These combined stance cues give readers access to the story world and in the continuation of the narrative will add up to an intricate interweaving of voices and positions. If the story was available in telecinematic form, further visual, auditorial and interactive stance markers would contribute to this picture too (see, e.g., Landert 2017, who discusses the visual and sound effects in a scene of *Mr. Robot* (2015) to illustrate this possibility).

5.5 Conclusions

Any scholar, reader or viewer of fictional texts will ask questions about the meaning of the text, just as any listener to an oral story will ask what this story that they are listening to is about. Looking for a narrative core is thus part and parcel of the narrative schema and the fictional contract. While this chapter does not support the idea that a text needs to have a single, identifiable reading/purpose, it is one of the givens that authors make textual choices of what to include and what to hide in texts and interweave intricate plot lines, digress, play to or play with readers' expectations. Depending on the authors' choices, the texts might receive different readings and be accessible to some target audiences and exclude other readers.

Together with the indispensable notion of genre and story schema, we therefore need to understand better how texts are read as forming parts of 'narratives'. The chapter argued that readers/audience members will both draw on their knowledge of everyday narratives and stories (from face-to-face highpoint stories to small stories and tiny stories in off- and online contexts) and their knowledge from having been socialised into recognising and making sense of fictional story types such as children's books, mangas, dramas, etc. From a pragmatic point of view, narrative is understood as a fundamental unit of human communication without which fictional narrative texts cannot be addressed. Narratives thus serve a social as well as cognitive function and are closely linked to character understanding and identity construction.

We have shown that the process of creating story worlds and moving the plot forward includes revealing aspects of time, place and character creation, the organisation of narrative actions into a particular temporal sequence, as well as the choosing of narratorial voice(s) for effect. In the next two chapters we will delve more deeply into the related phenomena of character creation as well as the role of dialogue in fiction.

Key Concepts

Audience design, deixis, external focalisation, focalisation, foregrounding, heterodiegetic narrative, highpoint story, homodiegetic narrative, internal focalisation, intertextuality, meta-comment, mind style, narrative, narrator, plot, small story, stance, story, story world, target audience, tiny story, voice, zero focalisation

Exercises

1. Have you ever been puzzled about a storyline after finishing a book or play or watching a movie? Choose one example of such a text and discuss the following questions: how did you deal with this situation? Does every piece of fiction need to have a clear narrative?
2. How does reading a physical book compare with reading an electronic version on your computer or e-reading device such as a Kindle? For example, bookshops appeal to many people when browsing for what

to read next because they can still physically touch the artefact and be attracted by its cover design. Books can also be put on special display tables, their covers can be put into scene, they can be thematically grouped and you can browse through them to discover whether the text appeals to you. Other people read entirely on electronic devices such as a Kindle and browse with the help of filters. When they read the book consecutively, they are not confronted with the author name or title (i.e. the app will simply open where they last stopped reading). Can you think of further differences? What do you think is the effect of these different reading habits?
3. Storytelling is all-pervasive in our lives and not just restricted to literary output. Discuss with your colleagues when you last told a story. What was it about? How did you get the attention of your listeners? How did you make sure that you could finish telling the story? Did your audience participate in your storytelling? Were you satisfied with the uptake? Why did you decide to share the story in the first place?
4. Usually a person acquires a set of stories that they tell throughout their lives (e.g. how they survived an accident, how they met their partner, how they . . .). Do you have a repertoire of such stories? How do you adjust the story according to whom you tell it? What remains the same, and what might change?

Further reading

In this chapter we draw on Jahn (2003), Landert (2017) and Rimmon-Kenan (2002) for input on narrative, voice and stance in fiction. For those readers interested in the competing narrative theories and the concepts they use for voice, Hoffmann (2017) presents an accessible introduction from which we have also quoted here. Dayter (2015, 2016), Georgakopoulou (2007, 2016), Johnstone (1990), Klapproth (2004), Labov and Waletzky (1967) and Labov (1997, 2013) gave us the background on oral narratives, small stories and tiny stories. For further discussion of how story worlds are created, also consult insights from text world theory in stylistics (e.g. Gavins 2007, 2016).

6 Character creation

6.1 Introduction

In the previous chapters we have highlighted the narrative core and genres of fictional texts and have talked about how story worlds are created. In this chapter we will discuss the linguistic cues through which the characters of these story worlds are shaped. Consider the following transcript of a Berlitz language school commercial (Berlitz 2006), which can be considered a humorous mini-narrative. It shows two actors in German coastguard uniforms in front of radar monitors in an office with dimmed lights. A senior coastguard explains technical gadgets to a new coastguard in fast and clipped German (see translation in italics) and then leaves the newbie alone in the room. The comments in brackets in (6.1) show the actions that are visible in the clip.

(6.1) Berlitz language commercial, 2006, 37 seconds

1	Senior:	das hier ist mein Sektor.	((points to his sector))
		'this is my sector'	
2		^das hier =	((gives the gadget a pat))
		'this here'	
3		=ist das ^wichtigste Gerät des ^Küstenwächters.	((Newbie takes seat))
		'is the most important gadget for coastguards.'	
4		^das Gerät und das Gerät	((points to both gadgets))
		'this gadget and this gadget'	
5		^Überlebensradar. ((puts hand on gadget, gives N. a pat on shoulder,	
		'survival radar'	takes coffee and leaves the room))
6	Speakers:	((beeping sound, static noise))	
7		... mayday mayday.	((noise, N. rocks his chair))
8		... hello can you hear us=	((N. looks around))
9		=^can you hear us can you XX= ((noise, N. orients towards speakers))	
10		=over.	
11		we are sinking,	((N. spins a button, is at a loss))

12		^we are sinking.
13	Newbie:	((pushes the button from the microphone))
14		^hello. ((moves closer to the microphone))
15		^this is the ^German ^coast ^guards. ((speaks slowly and hesitatingly))
16	Speakers:	((a static noise comes from the speakers))
17		… we are **sinking** we're ^**sinking**. ((N. looks around))
18	Newbie:	what are you ^**thinking** about? ((N. looks around, speaks hesitatingly))
19		Improve your English ((slogan appears, accompanied by Beethoven's
20		Berlitz Language for life *Ode to Joy*))

This clip stresses humorously that lacking in foreign language skills can jeopardise lives and that Berlitz as a language school can help improve linguistic skills. Turning to character creation, this mini-narrative uses visual cues to create a professional coastguard setting and sets up a contrast between the senior officer who introduces the equipment in clipped language and the newbie who acts insecurely by looking around hesitatingly and who is not in command of the situation. The humour is derived from a linguistic pun since the German newbie confuses the initial unvoiced sibilant s-sound in 'sinking' with the unvoiced fricative th-sound in 'thinking'. This accent feature adds to the non-professional character creation and makes fun of an accent feature commonly associated with German speakers of English.

Exploiting accent features, visual comportment and clothing are some of many possibilities for character creation (speech, appearance, action). Since fictional characters have to be created by means of language alone or in combination with visual and action cues, the chapter deals with the indexical role of language and comportment for identity construction. We will explore how regional, social and ethnic linguistic variation is employed in character creation. In addition, multilingualism in fiction is introduced as another important linguistic indexical resource for characterisation. The final two sections are on alienation effects in the case of story worlds that play in the past or in the future and on the challenges of translating characterisation cues. The chapter draws on linguistic theories of dynamic identity construction and discourse analysis, which are key issues in pragmatics.

6.2 Multimodal cues in character creation

In linguistics, the indexicality of linguistic cues has been discussed in the field of the study of identity construction, anthropology, discursive psychology and variationist linguistics. As quoted in Chapter 5, we define 'ourselves through what we say, how we say it and to whom we say it' (Schiffrin 1996: 169). Importantly, how we say things can change depending on whom we address (see our discussion of audience design in Sections 3.3 and 5.2) and what we wish to achieve. Manipulation of style can be conscious, but often we also use linguistic features subconsciously. In either case, we reveal aspects of our identity to others and through this engage in identity construction. Such cues can be of a lexical, morphological, syntactic or phonological nature and index different social realities such as regional, social or ethnic belonging, as well as past, present or future temporality. These cues can change over time and are bound to societal ideologies.

> In the postmodernist sense **identity construction** is understood as 'the social positioning of self and other' (Bucholtz and Hall 2005: 586).
>
> Identity 'is intersubjectively rather than individually produced and interactionally emergent rather than assigned in an a priori fashion' (Bucholtz and Hall 2005: 587).

While variationist linguistics explores how groups of speakers who differ in gender, social class, age and ethnicity express themselves differently, recent scholars of identity look at identity as a dynamic concept which draws on the indexical nature of cues in a constructivist manner (see text box). This means that the composition of cues can be quite unique, exploiting their indexicality in specific ways; for example, speaking like an older (age) upper class (social cue) woman (gender) with white background (ethnicity cue). There are no hard boundaries between features, and their indexicality is bound to place and time and societal ideologies.

Turning to fictional data, we can follow this constructivist tradition and postulate that authors and producers can exploit the indexicality of linguistic features as shorthands to draw characters. So, for example, in the Berlitz clip above (Extract (6.1)), characters are positioned vis-à-vis each other and the contrast makes their individual characteristics come to the fore. In addition, Androutsopoulos (2012: 141) reminds us of the importance of audience design and argues that 'characters and their speech are designed so as to enable (imagined target) audiences to identify with or sometimes distance themselves from them'. The contrast or alignment is thus not only created between the characters within the fictional world but also between the target audience members and the characters. In this process of pragmatic meaning making, language ideologies are activated (what it means to speak with a social/regional/ethnic accent, etc.).

CHARACTER CREATION

To illustrate aspects of this, let us look at how the protagonist the Dude in the American movie *The Big Lebowski* (1998) describes himself in Extract (6.2), which occurs a good 13 minutes into the movie. In this scene, the Dude meets the second character in the movie whose last name is also Lebowski. Because of sharing the same name, the Dude has been harassed instead of Mr Lebowski. The Dude meets Mr Lebowski in the latter's office in his mansion to clarify the issue and to be recompensed. Mr Lebowski (JL) sits imposingly behind his desk and is in business attire, while the Dude wears a washed-out cardigan, T-shirt, shorts and sneakers, is laid back and slouches in a kind of armchair facing Mr Lebowski's desk.

(6.2)   *The Big Lebowski*, 1998, at 12.59
1   JL: are you 'employed Mr ^Lebowski?
2   D: what wait ^wait,
3   let me let me 'explain ^explain 'something to you.   ((rubs his eyes))
4   ^uhm..
5   ^I am ^not Mr 'Lebowski.   ((points at himself))
6   ^you're Mr 'Lebowski.   ((points at JL))
7   ^I'm the ^Dude.   ((gesticulates))
8   so that's what you ^call me.
9   you ^know?
10   ^uh..   ((slaps his leg))
11   ^that or uh=..   ((gesticulates))
12   his ^Dudeness or uh=..   ((JL nods and looks around))
13   ^Duder or uh=..
14   you ^know,
15   el 'Duderino,   ((gesticulates))
16   if you're ^not into the whole ^brevity thing.
17   ^uh--

What comes to the fore in this small scene is the contrast that the Dude wishes to draw between himself and his namesake. They differ not only in their attire and economic affluence but also in their world views and even in the way they behave and comport themselves. These differences are summarised in the contrast between the proper names 'Mr Lebowski' versus 'the Dude'. This act of naming thus continues to add to the characterisation of the protagonist already established previously to this scene. The audience can then place itself on this wide cline from the Dude to the businessman.

Following the fictional contract, the target audience is of course well aware that the characters are not real. The cues that are presented, however, will draw on analogies to real life, i.e. exploiting the indexicality

Table 6.1 Explicit, implicit and authorial cues (Culpeper 2001, as summarised in and adapted from Bednarek 2010: 101–102)

Explicit cues	Self-presentation (character gives explicit information about self)
	Other-presentation (character gives explicit information about other character(s))
Implicit cues	Conversational structure (e.g. turn length, turn-taking, turn allocation, topic shift, topic control, incomplete turns/hesitations, interruptions)
	(Non-)adherence to conversational maxims;* conversational implicature*
	Lexis (Germanic vs Latinate, lexical richness/ diversity, surge features/affective language, terms of address, key words)
	Syntactic structure
	Accent and dialect
	Verse and prose
	Paralinguistic features (e.g. tempo, pitch range/variation, loudness, voice quality)
	Visual features: kinesic features and appearance (e.g. stature, clothing, facial expression, posture)
	Context: a character's company and setting
	(Im)politeness strategies or features
Authorial cues	Proper names
	Stage directions

* See Section 10.3 for an explanation of maxims and implicature.

of linguistic features in a particular context, as well as on knowledge gained through previous exposure to narrative genres and their character repertoire (villains, lovers, heroes, anti-heroes, etc.). Audience members will build an idea of a persona based on such cues and will revise and adjust their impressions incrementally. As Culpeper (2001: 10) puts it, 'the cognitive structures and inferential mechanisms that readers have already developed for real-life people might be used in their comprehension of characters', and these readers will pay particular attention to cues because they assume that they were inserted into the text consciously and for effect.

The examples of cues discussed so far can be predominantly found in the ways characters are made to speak, i.e. in dialogue (see

Chapter 7). However, character creation also occurs in how characters are described (by a narrator, the characters themselves or other characters), through their (described and/or enacted) appearance (clothing, hair, make-up, demeanour, etc.) and action (Bednarek 2010). In his 2001 book entitled *Language and Characterisation*, Culpeper gives us a set of concepts with which to systematically describe characters. They are listed in Table 6.1. From the list presented there we can glean the richness of possibilities for combining character-building cues of linguistic and multimodal nature. In the next sections we will illustrate the use of some such cues by focusing on regional, social and ethnic variation, followed by observations on multilingualism, alienation effects and translation challenges.

6.3 Contrasts: regional, social and ethnic variation in past and present

What linguistic indexical cues are available to be chosen for effect by authors and producers? Here is some more linguistic background. The ways in which individuals speak are shaped by their upbringing. It matters where and when they were born, who raises them and with whom they interact. We speak of dialects when a variety of a language shares lexical, phonological and grammatical features according to geographical distribution. And we speak of an ethnolect when a group of speakers shares the same ethnicity and because of historical and cultural processes has developed shared ways of speaking (again with respect to lexical, phonological and grammatical features). In the case of a sociolect, the reason for the groupings is due to class distinctions. We speak of an idiolect when an individual uses a combination of linguistic features unique to him or her. Table 6.2 (p. 104) gives examples of these four concepts. Finally, these 'lects' are often put in contrast with a standard variety (a 'lect' in its own right) that for historical and social reasons might enjoy a higher prestige than other varieties.

While these concepts seem to be neatly distinguishable at first sight, they can of course overlap to a certain extent and features can be mixed (e.g. a working-class person from Manchester with a Pakistani background). To make matters even more complex, individuals often master both standard and non-standard varieties and can adapt according to whom they are speaking to (this is referred to as intra-speaker variation, as opposed to inter-speaker variation). Usually it is assumed that the more standard varieties carry more prestige, which is called overt prestige. However, in the sense of in-group creation, non-standard forms are also valued and carry covert prestige.

Table 6.2 Reasons for variation

Reason for variation	Linguistic term	Examples
Regional	Dialect	Scouse (Merseyside), Brummie (Birmingham), Appalachian, New York City
Ethnic	Ethnolect	African American Vernacular English, Chicano English
Social	Sociolect	Working-class English, upper-class English
Combinations	Social dialects	Cockney (working-class London and surrounding areas), Estuary (middle-class London and Home Counties)
Combinations	Ethnic dialects	New York Latino English, Multicultural London
Individual	Idiolect	An individual's personal ways of speaking

When turning to fictional artefacts, the authors and producers can use the features that identify the lects as shorthand to draw a character. Importantly, this sketching does not have to pass the fidelity test through linguists or the group of people who are represented. In other words, the linguistic features need be neither complete nor entirely accurate or consistent in order to create an artistic effect. Sometimes a small deviation from an expected standard norm, such as an accent, lexical choice or grammatical pattern, is enough for the positioning of the characters as belonging to a particular group of people.

Consider the series *The Tudors*, which aired between 2007 and 2010, and follows the life of King Henry VIII of England. This means that we are dealing with events which took place in the sixteenth century when people spoke Early Modern English. However, although Early Modern English is much more accessible to Present-day English speakers than Old English or Middle English, the majority of the audience members could still be expected to struggle if the text were entirely in Early Modern English. And, as a matter of fact, the vast majority of the series is filmed in standard British English. However, there are a number of features which are interspersed throughout which give the characters a feeling of being genuinely from the past. To illustrate this, look at Extract (6.3). The scene shows how Anne of Cleves (who speaks German and whose text is subtitled for viewer access) is introduced for the first time to her future husband.

(6.3) *The Tudors*, 2009, Season 3, Episode 7, at 25.30–28.05
((Henry enters the room in haste in order to meet Anne of Cleves, who is in the presence of her entourage. Anne is taken aback and insecure. She bows. Henry is clearly displeased and frowns. He asks her to rise.))

1   Henry: ^Madam?   ((Henry gestures to make her rise))
             ... ((He approaches her and kisses her mouth; Anne is at a loss; Henry is irritated.))
2   'I am here to ^welcome you to my 'realm.   ((Henry bows))
3   I trust you are ^comfortable 'here?
4   ... before your ^journey to 'London?   ((spoken hesitatingly))
5   Anne: ^Thank you your 'Majesty.   (((spoken timidly))
             ((silence))   ((She looks at him, is taken aback but does not speak))
6   Henry: I will ^see you **anon.**

((Henry turns around and leaves the room hastily with his entourage. Anne looks astonished and discouraged. Anne sits and talks to her ladies in waiting.))

7   Anne: Ich hätte mehr 'Unterricht beim ^Herzog nehmen sollen.
                                                         ((desperate voice))
             Subtitle: 'I should have taken more lessons from the Duke'
8   ^Englische Manieren sind ganz ^anders als unsere.   (((she holds her forehead))
             Subtitle: 'English manners are very different from ours!'

((Cut to another room which is filled with music and people who walk around engaging in small talk and feasting. A guard is positioned in the background. Henry storms in angrily and people take a bow.))

9   Henry: **I like her ^not.**   ((shouting, Henry addresses two advisors))
10   do you ^understand me.
11   **I ^like her ^not.**   ((in pronounced manner))
12   ^call a meeting with the ^council.

((Cut to a different location, the council has assembled before Henry (sitting on the throne). He gets up, angry.))

13 Henry: It 'seems,
             ((addresses the assembled council, approaching them individually))
14   that 'princes in marriage suffer ^more than poor men.
15   since ^they have to take what is ^brought to them.
16   while ^poor men,
17   are at liberty to 'choose.
18   I have been ^deceived about Anne of 'Cleves.

In line 6, Henry uses the word 'anon', which means 'in a little while' and is no longer in much active use but still largely understood. It has an archaic ring to it. Henry's assessment of his new wife 'I like her not' (lines 9 and 11) is rendered in accurate Early Modern English negation since, at the time, the do-auxiliary was only in the process of gaining ground ('I don't like her') but not yet established entirely. While perfectly understandable, this small grammatical variation has the effect of contrasting present-day expected usage (as illustrated in the lines around the quoted examples) with past usage and thus creates a flavour of Early Modern English by means of contrast. Interspersing such features is enough to transport us back in time in combination with the setting and comportment of the characters. The language chosen is therefore indexing England through accent and a different time period through grammar and lexis.

In other instances, linguistic cues are used to create a social class distinction. The best-known written examples are the play *Pygmalion* by George Bernard Shaw (1914), and its musical and movie adaptation *My Fair Lady*. The text is particularly well-suited for illustration because the plot itself is also about linguistic identity construction. The play is about linguistics professor Henry Higgins who bets with his friend Colonel Pickering that he can linguistically educate the working-class girl Eliza Doolittle in such a way that she can pass as a duchess. Compare Extract (6.4), where the readers meet Eliza for the first time. The scene takes place in London in front of Covent Garden where a family is trying to hail a cab in pouring rain. The mother and daughter are berating the son Freddy for not being more efficient in finding a cab. They are conversing in a standard variety of the time. The stage instructions are in italics; the Flower Girl Eliza Doolittle's text has been rendered in bold for ease of reference.

(6.4)   *Pygmalion*, Act I (Shaw [1914] 1983: 15–17, italics in original, bold added)

1   FREDDY. Oh, very well: I'll go, I'll go. [*He opens his umbrella and dashes off*
2   *Strandwards, but comes into collision with a flower girl, who is hurrying in for shelter,*
3   *knocking her basket out of her hands. A blinding flash of lightning, followed instantly*
4   *by a rattling peal of thunder, orchestrates the incident*].

5   THE FLOWER GIRL. **Nah then, Freddy: look wh' y' gowin, deah.**

6   FREDDY. Sorry [*he rushes off*].

7   THE FLOWER GIRL [*picking up her scattered flowers and replacing them in the*
8   *basket*] **Theres menners f' yer! Te-oo banches o voylets trod into the mad.** [*She sits*
9   *down on the plinth of the column, sorting her flowers, on the lady's right. She is not at*
10 *all an attractive person. She is perhaps eighteen, perhaps twenty, hardly older. She*
11 *wears a little sailor hat of black straw that has long been exposed to the dust and soot*
12 *of London and has seldom if ever been brushed. Her hair needs washing rather badly:*
13 *its mousy color can hardly be natural. She wears a shoddy black coat that reaches*
14 *nearly to her knees and is shaped to her waist. She has a brown skirt with a coarse*
15 *apron. Her boots are much the worse for wear. She is no doubt as clean as she can*
16 *afford to be; but compared to the ladies she is very dirty. Her features are no worse*

17　*than theirs; but their condition leaves something to be desired; and she needs the*
18　*services of a dentist].*
19　THE MOTHER. How do you know that my son's name is Freddy, pray?
20　THE FLOWER GIRL. Ow, eez ye-ooa san, is e? Wal, fewd dan y' de-ooty bawmz a
21　mather should, eed now bettern to spawl a pore gel's flahrzn than ran awy athaht
22　pyin. Will ye-oo py me f'them?[1] [*Here, with apologies, this desperate attempt to*
23　*represent her dialect without a phonetic alphabet must be abandoned as unintelligible*
24　*outside London.*]
25　THE DAUGHTER. Do nothing of the sort, mother. The idea!

What we see in the stage instructions in lines 8–18 is a description of Eliza as being not particularly attractive, but, more importantly, clearly from a different social class than the previously introduced characters. Her hat is not well-kempt, her hair unwashed, her clothes are shoddy and shapeless and working clothes rather than stylish. She does not seem to be able to afford a dentist and is only 'as clean as she can afford to be; but compared to the ladies she is very dirty' (lines 15–16). This contrast is exacerbated once Eliza starts speaking in Cockney English, which is rendered in eye-dialect, i.e. non-standard spelling to indicate different sounds. The stage instructions point out that not everyone will in fact be able to know how this sounds (lines 22–24) due to the general rarity of writing in dialect.

Before we comment on this further, consider Extract (6.5) from the final act after Eliza's training and her transformation. She had left without farewell and is now returning to a distraught Higgins. Eliza enters a room in which Higgins's mother, Higgins and his friend Colonel Pickering are already convened.

(6.5)　*Pygmalion*, Act V (Shaw [1914] 1983: 120, italics in original)

1　*Eliza enters, sunny, self-possessed, and giving a staggeringly convincing*
2　*exhibition of ease of manner. She carries a little work-basket, and is very much*
3　*at home. Pickering is too much taken aback to rise.*
4　LIZA. How do you do, Professor Higgins? Are you quite well?
5　HIGGINS [*choking*] Am I— [*He can say no more*].
6　LIZA. But of course you are: you are never ill. So glad to see you again, Colonel
7　Pickering. [*He rises hastily; and they shake hands*]. Quite chilly this morning,
8　isn't it? [*She sits down on his left. He sits beside her*].
9　HIGGINS. Don't you dare try this game on me. I taught it to you; and it doesn't
10　take me in. Get up and come home; and don't be a fool.

---

[1] A possible translation into standard English is: 'Oh, he is your son, is he? Well, if you'd done your duty by him as a mother should, he'd know better than to spoil a poor girl's flowers and then run away without paying. Will you pay me for them?'

In Extract (6.5), Eliza speaks in Standard English, engages in small talk and thus conveys that she has mastered the values of Higgins's class. In contrast, Higgins is not in control and is upset about her behaviour. This play is of course not only using linguistic cues for character creation but is in itself a comment on language use and the power of language ideologies and the effects of exclusion and social injustice.

Now, when we read a Shakespeare play or Milton text today, we might obtain a similar sense of archaic language as described for Extract (6.3) above, an effect which the authors clearly did not have in mind as they were writing for their contemporaries. In a similar sense, even the standard English and the comportment of the upper class as well as the working class displayed in the *Pygmalion* examples might strike today's audience as outdated. The indexical field that a cue taps into is therefore culture and time dependent and might not be accessible to all audiences in the same way. Hodson makes this point for dialect representation in fiction:

> Thinking of dialect representation in terms of 'the indexical field' thus allows for the fact that different people will respond to any given dialect representation in different ways, and also that those meanings will shift over time; as Agha has noted, 'cultural value is not a static property' (Agha 2003: 232). (Hodson 2016: 426)

> 'Film uses language variation and accent to **draw character** quickly, building on **established preconceived notions** associated with specific regional loyalties, ethnic, racial or economic alliances.' (Lippi-Green 1997: 81, bold added)

Dialect and sociolect representation in written fiction (i.e. eye-dialect) and performed artefacts are often used in dialogue to indicate how a character is to be seen in contrast to other characters or the audience (see text box). Eye-dialect in particular has often run the risk of ridiculing the character or of implying illiteracy and stigma. This interpretation itself, however, reveals how (little) the non-standard forms are valued at any given time (at least in the English context[2]). So, Shaw is quite right that the rendition of Cockney is challenging in its written

---

[2] Both authors of this book are Swiss and their dominant languages are two different varieties of Swiss German as well as Standard German in diglossic distribution. In general, people identify with their dialects in Switzerland more than with the standard. The dialect therefore carries no stigma of being uneducated or from a lower social class.

form in Extract (6.4) above, because the unconventional letter combinations are hard to follow. He also exploits them to evoke the stigmatisation of illiteracy which is part of the plot of this play. Taavitsainen and Melchers (1999: 13) report that '[i]t is mostly the low and the rural that are presented as speakers of non-standard; humorous parts are attributed to minor characters and non-standard language to side episodes.'

While this observation might be accurate for many texts, this point is of course not valid for those poets and authors who write in non-standard language exactly in order to express belonging and realism and not as a shorthand for characterisation in order to boost the standard speakers in a process of contrast creation. Consider, for example, the work of the Scottish novelist Irvine Welsh, the many African American writers who employ African American Vernacular English in their writing for empowerment, or authors from former British colonies who write in their own English varieties and thus appropriate English as their own. What remains generally valid though is the activation of the indexical field to which not everyone has equal access. We will return to this point when we talk about the depiction of multilingualism in Section 6.4.

To illustrate the complexity of how characterisation cues interact, let us look at one more example which creates a contrast between regional and ethnic linguistic cues, drawing on lexis, accent and syntactic differences. It is taken from the American movie *My Cousin Vinny* (1992). The contrasts that are being established are between Southern US English and New York Italian-American English and, by extension, the Southern US way of life and the New York Italian-American way of life. The scene shows Vincent Gambini (VG) examining a witness in court in Alabama. He is defending his cousin, a young college freshman who was mistakenly apprehended as a murder suspect on his way to college from New York City to UCLA. The cousins are New York Italian-Americans. The witness is Sam Tipton, the shop owner of the gas station and small Sac-O-Suds convenience store where the murder took place. He identified the suspect.

(6.6) *My Cousin Vinny*, 1992, at 1.20.15–1.24.02

((Context: In court, the lawyer Vincent Gambini questions the witness Sam Tipton in the presence of Judge Chamberlain Haller, the jury and the public.))

1 Judge: Mr 'Gambini,
2   ^your witness.

((3 lines of interaction between a different lawyer and the second accused person omitted.))

6 Gambini: Mr ^Tipton.
7   when you ^**viewed** the..   ((gesticulates))

8		'defendants ^walking from their ^car into the ^Sac-O-Suds,	
9		what ^angle was your 'point of view?	
10	Witness:	**they was** ^kind of walking ^**towards** me when they entered the 'store.	
11	Gambini:	and when they ^left,	((gesticulates))
12		what ^angle was your point of view?	
13	Witness:	**they was** 'kind of walking ^away from me.	((VG reflects))
14	Gambini:	^so would you ^say that you got a better ^shot of them going ^in,	
		((points with his index finger in one direction))	
15		and ^not so much coming ^out? ((points in the other direction))	
16	Witness:	you could ^say that.	((looks down))
17	Gambini:	I ^did say that.	((gesticulates))
18		would ^you say that?	
19	Witness:	^yeah. ((VG's girlfriend in the audience vehemently nods her head))	
20	Gambini:	is it ^possible..	((gesticulates))
21		the ^two **'youds--** ((judge moves his head closer to VG))	
22	Judge:	uh the two ^**h-what**?	((VG looks at judge))
23		. . . ^h-what was that ^word?	((VG approaches the judge))
24	Gambini:	uh,	
25		^what word?	
26	Judge:	two ^**h-what**?	
27	Gambini:	^what?	
28	Judge:	did you say ^**youds**?	
29	Gambini:	^yeah,	((nods))
30		two ^**youds**.	
31	Judge:	^what is a ^**youd**?	
32	Gambini:	^oh,	((gesticulates apologetically))
33		^excuse me your 'Honour.	((gesticulates))
34		two <PLC ^**youths**. PLC>	((walks towards witness))
35		. . . is it ^possible,	((gesticulates))

((Interaction omitted, Gambini attempts to find out whether a different murder suspect could have entered the shop, the question prior to line 75 is about what the witness had for breakfast.))

75	Witness:	^**eggs and ^grits**.	
76	Gambini:	^eggs and ^grits.	((looks around))
77		^I like grits 'too.	((witness nods his head))
78		^how do you 'cook your ^grits?	((gesticulates))
79		you like 'em ^regular ^creamy or **al ^dente**? ((witness looks puzzled))	
80	Witness:	. . . just ^regular I ^guess.	
81	Gambini:	^regular.	((moves his head))
82		^instant grits?	((frowns))
83	Witness:	**no 'self-respecting ^Southerner uses ^instant ^grits**. ((looks at a lady from the jury; the lady smiles))	

84		I take ^pride in my ^grits.	((VG nods his head))
85	Gambini:	^so,	
86		Mr ^Tipton,	((starts walking around))
87		^how could it take you ^fi=ve minutes=	((gesticulates))
88		=to ^cook your ^grits,	((addresses the jury))
89		when it ^takes **the 'entire grit-eating world**..	((walks around in front of jury))
90		<PLC ^twenty ^minutes? PLC>	

In Extract (6.6) we see linguistic cues, action cues and appearance cues being used to draw contrasts between the witness, the judge and Gambini. Let us first consider the witness. The transcription does not show this but the vowel pronunciation reveals a Southern lengthening of vowels and diphthongs throughout and the witness speaks in a slower pace. This phonological feature is combined with syntactic non-standard marking ('they was' instead of 'they were', lines 10 and 13). The witness also proudly identifies as a 'self-respecting Southerner' (line 83), who eats 'grits' (a corn porridge famous in the South), and shows confusion over the adjective 'al dente' in his facial expression (line 79). In contrast, Gambini outs himself as an Italian-American by using the loanword 'al dente' first (line 79). He speaks at a fast pace and uses the dental d [d] sound instead of the fricative th [ð] ('youds' instead of 'youths', e.g. line 21). This feature is typical of Italian-Americans in New York. Gambini also speaks considerably faster than the Southern witness and judge and uses a noticeable amount of gesticulation, which is in contrast to the other two characters, who hardly move at all. He is dressed in a three-piece suit whose flamboyant trim and burgundy colour manage to give the air of a circus master rather than a serious professional lawyer. The judge, dressed in black robes, reveals that he is from a different group than Gambini because he does not understand the latter's pronunciation of 'youths' and requests a clarification of the word (lines 22–23). The question particle 'what' is pronounced with a distinctive 'h' [hwɒt] sound in initial positions, which in turn confuses Gambini. It takes the two a number of turns (lines 21–34) until they understand each other. Considering conversational structure, the judge uses his right to interrupt Gambini and ask for clarification. This power to self-select and interrupt is the prerogative of a judge during trials and can thus also be considered a characterisation cue in addition to his clothing and speech features.

In this scene, the action, speech and appearance cues are of explicit and implicit nature. They are creatively combined and exploited for character creation and for highlighting difference between the involved characters in a humorous way. The combination of cues and concepts ultimately results in a contrast between different ways of life within the United States and thus reflects ideologies and values as well (see Chapter 8).

The variation illustrated in this section drew on variation within English. In the next section, we will turn to cues that draw from the multilingual indexical field for character creation.

6.4 Multilingualism in fictional character creation

When we pick up a book with an English title written by an author who is a native speaker of English, we probably expect it to be written in English, no matter where and when the book's story world is set. However, our world is in fact fundamentally multilingual. This is even true for societies which pursue an ideology as a monolingual people. For example, consider the importance of English in the United States despite the fact that the nation is made up of people from many different linguistic backgrounds and that English is not mentioned in the constitution.[3] Fictional texts are under no obligation to depict the complex linguistic situation of a particular milieu or context, but authors and producers can choose to give their artefact the flavour of multilingualism and achieve various pragmatic effects by doing so, 'such as scene creation/enrichment, character creation, the creation of humor, the display of social criticism, realism and ideological debates of difference and belonging' (Locher 2017a: 297). So, in addition to language variation within the same language family (dialects, sociolects, ethnolects, idiolects), there is widespread multilingualism in societies which can find its way into fictional artefacts.

Bleichenbacher summarises the ways in which multilingualism cues in fictional texts appear by means of four concepts:

- Elimination: '[A]ny speech that would have been in another language is completely replaced with an unmarked standard variety of the base language' (Bleichenbacher 2008: 24)
- Signalisation: '[T]he replaced language is explicitly named in a metalinguistic comment' (Bleichenbacher 2008: 24)
- Evocation: '[C]haracters speak a variety of the base language that is characterized by interference (transfer) from the language they would

---

[3] The constitution of the United States does not mention English or any other language as a national or as the only language. There are, however, a number of states which postulate English to be the dominant language. This discussion is subsumed under the slogans English-only and English-plus. For reviews, consult Wiley (2004, 2014).

Table 6.3 A taxonomy of multilingualism in fictional texts (based on Mareš 2000a, 2000b, 2003, reproduced with permission from Bleichenbacher 2008: 24)

	Most distant from depicted reality			Closest to depicted reality
Strategy	Elimination	Signalization	Evocation	Presence
Treatment of other languages	Neither used nor mentioned	Named by the narrator or by characters	Evoked by means of L2 interference phenomena	Used
Audience awareness of other language(s)	Depends on ability to process extralinguistic hints	Through metalinguistic comments	Depends on correct interpretation of interference phenomena	Full
Audience comprehension of content	Full	Full	Full, unless the audience is unwilling to listen to nonstandard speech	None, unless the other language is somehow translated

really be speaking', e.g. accent, short code-switches (Bleichenbacher 2008: 24)
- Presence: '[T]he other language is no longer replaced at all' (Bleichenbacher 2008: 25)

Elimination means that there is erasure of multilingualism where the plot and characters suggest its presence. The text is therefore maximally accessible for the target audience, but furthest removed from realism (see Table 6.3). In the case of signalisation, the text is still entirely in one language, but the presence of other languages is explicitly mentioned. The process of evocation is an extension of signalisation. However, in this case, characters display certain linguistic cues associated with the additional language, such as an accent or accessible vocabulary from the additional language. In Extract (6.7), the latter two functions are combined. It is taken from *The American* by Henry James (1877), and shows a brief extract of a dialogue between the male American protagonist and his French addressee in the Louvre. The main protagonist wants to buy a painting from the young lady.

(6.7) *The American* (James 1877: n.p., italics in original, bold added)
1   'How much?' said our friend, **in English**. *'Combien?'*
2   *'Monsieur* wishes to buy it?' asked the young lady **in French**.

Signalisation appears in bold, i.e. the narrator informs the reader in a meta-comment that the direct quotation in the same sentence was uttered in English or in French. However, evocation is also present in the italicised words 'Combien' and 'Monsieur'. Finally, in the case of presence, more than one language is used in line with what the plot calls for.

The effects of including or excluding aspects of multilingualism on comprehension are listed in the last row of Table 6.3. Full presence means that there are also risks in going for a realistic representation because the audience might not have access to the linguistic codes. However, this effect may be desired. Consider Extract (6.8) from the movie *Lost in Translation* (2003). The main protagonist is in Japan but does not understand Japanese. He has been hired for a commercial by the Japanese whisky company Suntory. The scene takes place during the shooting of this commercial. The Japanese director gives an out-pouring of instructions about how to act to the protagonist in Japanese. The text in italics is performed in Japanese and not made accessible by means of subtitling to the audience; it was later translated in the *New York Times* (Rich 2003).

(6.8) *Lost in Translation*, 2003, at 8.41 (Rich 2003, italics indicate Japanese)
1   Director (in Japanese to the interpreter): *The translation is very important, O.K.? The*
2   *translation.*
3   Interpreter: Yes, of course. I understand.
4   Director [in Japanese]: *Mr. Bob-san. You are sitting quietly in your study. And then there is*
5   *a bottle of Suntory whiskey on top of the table. You understand, right? With*
6   *wholehearted feeling, slowly, look at the camera, tenderly, and as if you are*
7   *meeting old friends, say the words. As if you are Bogie in 'Casablanca,'*
8   *saying, 'Cheers to you guys,' Suntory time!*
9   Interpreter: He wants you to turn, look in camera. O.K.?
10 Bob: That's all he said?
11 Interpreter: Yes, turn to camera.
12 Bob: Does he want me to, to turn from the right or turn from the left?
13 Interpreter (in very formal Japanese to the Director): *He has prepared and is ready*
14 *And he wants to know, when the camera rolls, would you prefer that he turn to the*
15 *left, or would you prefer that he turn to the right? And that is the kind of thing he*
16 *would like to know, if you don't mind.*
17 Director (very brusquely, and in much more colloquial Japanese): *Either way is fine.*
18 *That kind of thing doesn't matter. We don't have time, Bob-san, O.K.? You need*

19		*to hurry. Raise the tension. Look at the camera. Slowly, with passion. It's passion*
20		*that we want. Do you understand?*
21	Interpreter (in English, to Bob): Right side. And, uh, with intensity.	
22	Bob:	Is that everything? It seemed like he said quite a bit more than that.
23	Director [in Japanese]:	*What you are talking about is not just whiskey, you know. Do you*
24		*understand? It's like you are meeting old friends. Softly, tenderly. Gently. Let*
25		*your feelings boil up. Tension is important! Don't forget.*
26	Interpreter (in English, to Bob): Like an old friend, and into the camera.	
27	Bob:	O.K.
28	Director:	*You understand? You love whiskey. It's Suntory time! O.K.?*
29	Bob:	O.K.
30	Director [in Japanese]:	*O.K.? O.K., let's roll. Start.*
31	Bob:	For relaxing times, make it Suntory time.
32	Director:	Cut, cut, cut, cut, cut! (Then in a very male form of Japanese, like a
33		father speaking to a wayward child) *Don't try to fool me. Don't pretend you*
34		*don't understand. Do you even understand what we are trying to do? Suntory is*
35		*very exclusive. The sound of the words is important. It's an expensive drink.*
36		*This is No. 1. Now do it again, and you have to feel that this is exclusive. O.K.?*
37		*This is not an everyday whiskey you know.*
38	Interpreter:	Could you do it slower and?
39	Director:	*With more ecstatic emotion.*
40	Interpreter:	More intensity.
41	Director (in English): Suntory time! Roll.	
42	Bob:	For relaxing times, make it Suntory time.
43	Director:	*Cut, cut, cut, cut, cut! God, I'm begging you.*

The translator present in the scene does not translate the director's verbose instructions nor Bob's contributions verbatim but summarises in brief statements only (lines 9, 21 and 26). This causes the protagonist to become insecure (lines 10 and 22) and leaves the non-Japanese speaking target audience equally in the dark with respect to what exactly was said. The protagonist's feeling of being lost in translation thus becomes the audience's feeling too and both protagonist and viewers are aligned in their experience.

Including multilingual cues in fictional texts can have diverse effects. An important one is of course character creation. However, multilingual cues can also be used for patina in order to create a sense of realism, such as street signs or background dialogue in the language of the place where the scenes take place. In general, some of the important functions are the creation of realism, social criticism and humour (see Bleichenbacher 2008; Locher 2017a). In Extract (6.8), we have already seen how a realistic setting can get the protagonist and the audience closer or aligned. Social criticism can play a role in numerous ways. Consider the *Pride and Prejudice* (Jane Austen, 1813) movie adaption *Bride and Prejudice* directed by Gurinder Chadha in 2004. The Victorian setting is transported to India and present-day times. As a consequence, the middle-class girls to be married off speak English with an Indian accent, lexis and syntax and are cast in contrast to the two affluent male characters, who speak English English and American English. Throughout the movie, social contrasts are made salient and negotiated not just by plot but also by linguistic cues.

> **Linguicism** refers to 'ideologies, structures, and practices which are used to legitimate, effectuate and reproduce an unequal division of power and resources (both material and immaterial) between groups which are defined on the basis of language' (Phillipson 1992: 47).

There is nothing inherently humorous in multilingualism per se. In fiction, however, one of the major effects is to draw on multilingual linguistic cues for humorous and stereotyping effects. In her work on accent in movies, Planchenault (2015, 2017) shows how a French accent characterisation cue is used to convey a simplified and reductionist, hence stereotypical view of what it means to be French (e.g. 'romance' or 'bon vivant'). In cases where cues are systematically used in a reductionist and negative manner (i.e. not empowering), we speak of cases of 'linguicism' (see text box). We encountered an instance of linguicism in Extract (6.1), where the German coastguard's lack of foreign language skills and his German accent are correlated with his being insecure and incompetent. In a seminal study, Lippi-Green (1997) found that positive Disney movie characters up to that time were associated with mainstream varieties of English, while negative characters were associated with stigmatised varieties. In the same vein, using mock Russian, German or Spanish cues for humorous effects in English movies ultimately can result in linguistic racism, especially when these strategies are combined with associating the characters with negativity. Following up on Lippi-Green's findings, Bleichenbacher (2008) confirmed this general trend for Hollywood movies but also stated that the genre per se can override the stereotyping.

6.5 Alienation effects: past and future

In the previous sections we have seen how multilingualism and linguistic variation of a geographical, social and ethnic kind can find its way into fiction by means of linguistic cues for characterisation and/or story world creation. Contemporary fictional texts draw on the current indexical fields to create effects. But what to do when the texts play in the past or in the future?

In Extract (6.3) from *The Tudors* quoted above, we have seen that small archaisms can suffice to create a linguistic impression of the past. In other contexts, writers and producers have to put even more thought into their product. For example, if you want to produce the passion of Jesus Christ, your story plays during the Roman period in a multilingual context (Roman, Aramaic, Hebrew, Greek). Most productions targeted at an English audience simply go for making the characters speak English (although often with a British accent, since American accents are associated with modernity). A notable exception is Mel Gibson's (2004) rendition, *The Passion of the Christ*, which, in an attempt at maximum realism, makes the characters speak in Latin, reconstructed Aramaic and Hebrew, as well as in Greek as a lingua franca. The text is then made accessible to the audience by means of subtitling.

In cases of past and future imagined story worlds, such as fantasy and science fiction, authors and producers also need to 'dress up their characters' in meaningful linguistic attire. Just as a spattering of Early Modern English features make the text appear archaic to present-day readers, the inclusion of alienation techniques allows for unique characterisation. A well-cited example is the Jedi Master *Yoda* in the *Star Wars* series, who, while using English vocabulary, systematically speaks in different syntax patterns. Rather than using subject-verb-object, he uses object-subject-verb ('Patience you must have, my young padawan'; 'Truly wonderful, the mind of a child is'). The text is still comprehensible but creates an othering effect. In extreme cases, entirely new languages are created such as Elvish in Tolkien's *Lord of the Rings* epic, Klingon in the *Star Trek* TV and movie series, or Dothraki in the *Game of Thrones* TV series adaptation. Just as present-day linguistic cues need be neither complete nor entirely accurate to create a characterisation effect, the same can be said for the inclusion of multilingualism in general and the use of invented languages in particular. In other words, 'the quantity of these foreignisms is not game-changing since even small inclusions of elements other than the base-language can already create a defamiliarisation or alienation effect that suffices to signal to readers that they are dealing with a different world' (Locher 2017a: 311).

6.6 Translation challenges for character positioning

Linguistic characterisation cues are particularly challenging in translation processes. If you think of the power but also of the subtlety of the indexical cues, this will not come as a surprise. The regional, social, ethnic and time cues are tied to indexical fields and as such to a particular society in a particular time and place. As a consequence, the indexical power of the cues does not travel well into other languages because there is no one-to-one correspondence in societies along which lines (region, social class, age, ethnicity, etc.) people distinguish themselves when speaking. For example, Queen (2004) studied how African American Vernacular English in American movies has been dubbed into German. Since there is no comparable ethnic group in Germany, there was no easy way to face this challenge. There is regional variation but it would have created a very different effect if the African American Vernacular speakers were made to speak in a Southern dialect (e.g. Bavarian) in contrast to standard speakers. Since ethnic markers were not available, Queen found that the solution was to adopt a language which was associated with urbanity and young people rather than regionality and ethnicity. This results in a contrast but not the one of the original.

If you revisit all of the examples in this chapter, it becomes clear that none of their linguistic characterisation cues is easy to translate. Quite often, there is thus a process of reduction and simplification of the contrasts established in the original. However, if the characterisation contrast through linguistic means is plot relevant, it cannot easily be left out. This is especially the case in translations of *Pygmalion*, quoted in Extracts (6.4) and (6.5), where finding solutions for translations is imperative since part of the appeal and the point of the plot would be lost otherwise.

6.7 Conclusions

The creation of characters who people the story worlds is a fundamental aspect of narration. In this chapter, we have shown that action, appearance and speech jointly contribute to characterisation. Readers and viewers will pick up the indexical force of cues in a process of analogy to real-life situations but will interpret these cues within the play frame, i.e. in light of the fictional contract. Characters build up incrementally in the process of reading and viewing.

We also addressed how complex these indexical processes can become. There are processes of reduction at play in the sense that reality would generally be more complex and display more cues than fiction. At the same time, creative combinations are possible. We have stressed that it is not necessary to be accurate and complete and thus to depict a faithful rendition of the linguistic combination of cues of a real-life person. Drawing on the fictional contract, the readers and viewers know that the cues are meant as pointers to add information for characterisation. Their quantity and accuracy are thus less important than the fact that they are used to create a contrast either between characters in the story world or between the characters and the target audience. However, the cues can only reach their full potential if the audience has access to the linguistic indexical field.

Characterisation cues can be used for empowerment as well as negative stereotyping (the latter resulting in linguicism). Studying them from the point of view of meaning making and pragmatics is thus a rewarding area of research since we can study the creativity in which cues are combined and explore what effects their use achieves in light of linguistic ideologies. We will continue this topic in Chapter 8 where we will add the study of comportment and impressions of politeness and impoliteness to characterisation.

Key Concepts

Alienation effect, characterisation cues, dialect, ethnolect, functions of multilingualism (elimination, signalisation, evocation, presence), identity construction, ideology, idiolect, index and indexicality, linguicism, meta-comment, regional variation, sociolect

Exercises

1. In movies and TV series, characters are made to speak in standard and non-standard ways. Discuss how the choice of which linguistic variants to use adds to characterisation. Can you think of artefacts where such features are used to set characters off from each other? (See also Exercise 2.)
2. The African American author Toni Morrison contrasts the voice of the narrator with the dialogue between Sethe and her mother-in-law Baby Suggs in the following extract from the beginning of *Beloved* (1987: 5–6), a novel which plays at the end of the nineteenth century in the United States. Which linguistic features can you detect in the different parts of the extract? What is the effect of the created contrasts in light of character creation?

1   Counting on the stillness of her own soul, she had forgotten the other one:
2   the soul of her baby girl. Who would have thought that a little old baby could
3   harbor so much rage? Rutting among the stones under the eyes of the engraver's
4   son was not enough. Not only did she have to live out her years in a house palsied
5   by the baby's fury at having its throat cut, but those ten minutes she spent pressed
6   up against dawn-colored stone studded with star chips, her knees wide open as the
7   grave, were longer than life, more alive, more pulsating than the baby blood that
8   soaked her fingers like oil.
9   'We could move,' she suggested once to her mother-in-law.
10 'What'd be the point?' asked Baby Suggs. 'Not a house in the country ain't
11 packed to its rafters with some dead Negro's grief. We lucky this ghost is a baby.
12 My husband's spirit was to come back in here? or yours? Don't talk to me. You
13 lucky. You got three left. Three pulling at your skirts and just one raising hell
14 from the other side. Be thankful, why don't you? I had eight. Every one of them
15 gone away from me. Four taken, four chased, and all, I expect, worrying
16 somebody's house into evil.' Baby Suggs rubbed her eyebrows. 'My firstborn. All
17 I can remember of her is how she loved the burned bottom of bread. Can you beat
18 that? Eight children and that's all I remember.'

In this fictitious interaction from the nineteenth century, Toni Morrison uses the word 'Negro', which, like the N-word, is considered highly offensive today. What is the effect of the use of 'Negro' in this passage?

3. Some fictional characters in movies and TV series are famous for their regional or social linguistic features. For example, Hagrid displays dialectal features in the *Harry Potter* book and movie series, while other characters do not. This characterisation feature might be challenging in translation, dubbing and subtitling. Why? Can you think of further examples?

4. How much multilingualism is too much for a fictional artefact? Have you ever read a book or watched a movie when you felt left behind as a reader/viewer due to not being able to understand the language(s) used in the artefact? What was the effect of this situation on you with respect to comprehension and enjoyment of the artefact? (See also Exercise 5.)

5. Consider the following extract from Chimamanda Ngozi Adichie's (2013: 74) novel *Americanah*, which tells the story of a young Nigerian woman, Ifemelu, who emigrates to the United States in order to study there. In the extract, she is still in high school in Nigeria and talks to Obinze, a classmate she falls in love with. They talk about their hometowns. What is the role of Igbo in this extract?

1   'Ahn-ahn! One of my uncles goes to your village all the time!' he told her.

2   'I've been a few times with him. You people have terrible roads.'
3   'I know Abba. The roads are worse.'
4   'How often do you go to your village?'
5   'Every Christmas.'
6   'Just once a year! I go very often with my mother, at least five times a year.'
7   'But I bet I speak Igbo better than you.'
8   'Impossible,' he said, and switched to Igbo. '*Ama m atu inu*. I even know
9   proverbs.'
10 'Yes. The basic one everybody knows. A frog does not run in the afternoon for
11 nothing.'
12 'No. I know serious proverbs. *Akota ife ka ubi, e lee oba*. If something bigger
13 than the farm is dug up, the barn is sold.'
14 'Ah, you want to try me?' she asked, laughing. '*Acho afu adi ako n'akpa dibia*.
15 The medicine man's bag has all kinds of things.'
16 'Not bad,' he said. '*E gbuo dike n'ogu uno, e luo na ogu agu, e lote ya*. If you
17 kill a warrior in a local fight, you'll remember him when fighting enemies.'
18 They traded proverbs. She could say only two more before she gave up, with
19 him still raring to go.

6. The process of using language and action to create your own identity is connected to and similar to shaping fictional protagonists. Discuss where you monitor your language use (e.g. in class, at home, at your job, in your peer group, . . .) and how you do this (i.e. what features change). Have you observed other people speaking and behaving differently in various contexts?

Further reading

In this chapter we draw on Bednarek (2010, 2017), Culpeper (2001), Culpeper and Fernandez-Quintanilla (2017), Hodson (2014, 2016), Planchenault (2015, 2017) and Locher (2017a) for fictional character creation, and on Bucholtz and Hall (2005, 2008) and Locher (2008a) for discursive identity construction in linguistics.

Part III

Themes in the pragmatics of fiction

7 The performance of fiction

7.1 Introduction

Novels regularly depict characters who talk to each other. Plays, movies and television series consist to a large extent of characters who talk to each other. Verbal interactions are an essential part of fiction, and they have received increasing scholarly attention, especially in film dialogues (e.g. Kozloff 2000) and in dialogues in television series (e.g. Bednarek 2018). In this chapter, we want to explore the different pragmatic aspects of dialogue in all forms of fiction. As Kozloff (2000: 121) has pointed out, dialogue in fiction is never realistic, it is always designed for us. In a play by Shakespeare, this is particularly obvious. The characters often talk in what is known as iambic pentameters, i.e. each line consists of five pairs of syllables in which the first syllable is unstressed and the second is stressed. It is clear that nobody, not even at the time of Shakespeare at the end of the sixteenth and the beginning of the seventeenth centuries talked like this in their daily lives, even if the lines sound quite natural and speech-like to us. Characters in our daily soap operas do not speak in iambic pentameters but their lines have also been carefully crafted. If they sound like everyday spontaneous interactions, it is to a large extent because they have been designed to sound like that by the author or script writer and the actors. Narrative texts have additional options. They can represent the interactions between characters in an indirect way by summarising the content of what they say to each other through a narratorial voice (see Section 5.4), or they can present the actual but, of course, fictitious words of the interaction. The written language represents the words of the fictitious spoken interactions in a stylised way.

Spoken language differs from written language in several important respects. One of the most obvious differences is the amount of planning and editing that speakers or writers can use. Speakers must generally plan their utterances on the spot, and they cannot edit what

> Bednarek (2017: 130) defines **dialogue** in fiction as 'shorthand for all character speech, whether or not this speech is by one character (monologues, asides, voice-over narration, etc.), between two characters (dyadic interactions) or between several characters (multi-party interactions)'.

they have already said. They can repeat something that they have already said or say it again in a different way. They can point out explicitly that what they have just said was not what they meant and so on, but they cannot erase what they have already said. As a result, transcriptions of spoken language often display the evidence of this planning process, such as truncated turns, repetitions, hesitation phenomena, self-corrections or pauses. Writers, on the other hand, can edit their texts, take time to think about the next thing they want to write and remove parts of their text with which they are not sufficiently happy. In some registers of written language, for instance informal emails or in exchanges of instant messages, writers take very little time for planning and editing. These forms may therefore bear some resemblance to spoken language.

In fictional language, the situation is more complex. Actors who perform a play have learned their lines by heart. They do not have to plan their utterances in the same way as speakers in everyday conversations. Furthermore, they know in advance who speaks next and how the plot unfolds. However, actors may perform characters – on the basis of the author's or scriptwriter's text – who often hesitate, or characters who interrupt other characters and so on. Even in written dialogues in novels, an author may want to imitate some of the features that are typical of natural conversations. In these situations, features such as pauses, hesitations, repetitions or truncations are not the result of the actual planning and editing process but devices to imitate this process. We call features which have their origin in the planning and editing process of spontaneous conversations 'features of orality', and in this chapter, we explore how they are used in fictional texts.

But first we turn to the function of dialogues in fiction in general in Section 7.2. In an obvious way, they are representations of fictitious speech exchanges that take place between the depicted characters, and in that sense, they may be taken as imitations of interactions as they could have happened in real life. But in addition, they serve several functions that they do not normally perform in everyday interactions. In Sections 7.3 and 7.4, we turn to the features of orality and assess to what extent they are – or may be – caused by the constraints of spontaneously producing spoken language and to what extent they are being used in a stylised way to flag a sentence or utterance as spoken and spontaneously produced.

7.2 The role of dialogue in fiction

Since a narrative can be told entirely without dialogue, i.e. entirely through narrators who summarise and report (telling rather than showing), the inclusion of dialogue is a conscious stylistic means (showing rather than telling), which can have a diverse range of effects (see text box). As pointed out above, it is far more than an imitation of dialogue in real life, and for this reason it has attracted the interest of scholars who have tried to disentangle the different functions. Our own presentation of functions in Table 7.1 is based on these earlier models (in particular on the work by Kozloff 2000 and on Bednarek's 2017 and 2018 adaptation of this work) as well as insights gained on the use of constructed dialogue in oral narratives in face-to-face interaction (Tannen 1989). But we have rearranged the functions into different categories, and we have tried to make the model applicable to all forms of fiction in spite of the fact that different forms of fiction make different uses of these functions.

> 'In a **showing mode** of presentation, there is little or no narratorial mediation, overtness, or presence. The reader is basically cast in the role of a witness to the events.'
>
> 'In a **telling mode** of presentation, the narrator is in overt control [...] of action presentation, characterization and point-of-view arrangement.'
>
> (Jahn 2017: N5.3.1, bold added)

Table 7.1 gives an overview of four groups of functions that can co-occur. The first group describes the inclusion of dialogue that is plot-relevant in that the action enacted in the dialogue drives the plot forward and can create a number of effects on the reader (immediacy, involvement, etc.). The second function links the indexicality of oral and stylistic features of dialogue to character creation. The third group highlights that characters can be made to impart contextual knowledge to the readers and viewers, while the last group of functions points to the effects of stylistic choices and audience appeal. We will illustrate these categories in turn but wish to stress that they can co-occur within the same stretch of dialogue.

Table 7.1 The roles of dialogue in fiction (overlap possible)

Representation of speech exchanges with plot consequences
Enactment of verbal exchanges between characters for plot advancement
Using dialogue to control evaluation and interpretation
Creating immediacy, engagement, emotional involvement

Characterisation
Characterisation of characters through ways of speaking, appearance and action

Presentation of narrative context
Addition of narrative details such as locations, names of characters, background information (off-stage action)
Presentation of realistic verbal context for main action

Stylistic function and audience appeal
Poetic uses of language, such as figures of speech, rhyme, metre
Humour, irony
Language style to appeal to specific audiences

7.2.1 Representation of speech exchanges with plot consequences

The most obvious function of dialogue in fiction is, of course, the representation of a speech exchange which 'enacts/shows' a plot moment rather than 'describes' a plot moment and thus constructs narrative causality. Fictitious characters are shown to interact with each other in a wide range of situations. Characters argue with each other, they insult each other, compliment each other, apologise, declare their love, bribe others, talk of their despair and so on. For example, in a crime novel, rather than describing the plot-relevant moment when a perpetrator killed someone in a cruel way, we might read the words that the killer uttered when killing and we read the last words of the victim. The choice of dialogue for this plot-relevant moment transports the reader into the here-and-now of the story world and thus creates suspense, immediacy and involvement. This function of dialogue has also been highlighted for the use of 'constructed dialogue' in personal oral narratives in face-to-face contexts (Tannen 1989). 'Constructed dialogue' is used as a term because the storytellers have the choice to summarise the past action but choose to reconstruct an action through dialogue. In doing so, they rarely – if ever – recall the exact phrasing but adapt the phrasing to their needs and the needs of the target audience. For example, in work on how people tell stories about interactions with doctors, Hamilton (1998) found that the storytellers preferred withholding their own negative assessments of the doctors' communication skills and, instead, used dialogue to show how the doctors behaved in a way that was deemed unhelpful. In this way, the storytellers left the judging of the doctors to the listeners. This created involvement in the listeners, and, at the same time, the storytellers were able to present themselves as victims rather than as people who simply judge doctors in a negative way without evidence. In fiction too, just as in personal oral narratives, the choice to use dialogue rather than description allows the readers and viewers to make their own evaluation of the characters' behaviour and to become involved in the story world. This function of dialogues can thus be used to control audience evaluation. The representation of speech exchanges with plot consequences is thus a powerful tool for advancing plot, controlling audience evaluation, and creating immediacy, engagement and emotional involvement.

Consider Extract (7.1) from George Orwell's novella *Animal Farm*, published in 1945, in which anthropomorphic characters, i.e. animals with the power of speech, interact with each other. (It is of course the fictional contract that lets us accept talking animals.) The extract is from the first chapter in the novella and appears after four paragraphs of descriptive contextualisation.

(7.1) *Animal Farm* (Orwell 1945: 7–8)
1   All the animals were now present except Moses, the tame raven, who slept on
2   a perch behind the back door. When Major saw that they had all made themselves
3   comfortable and were waiting attentively, he cleared his throat and began:
4   'Comrades, you have heard already about the strange dream that I had last
5   night. But I will come to the dream later. I have something else to say first. I do not
6   think, comrades, that I shall be with you for many months longer, and before I die,
7   I feel it my duty to pass on to you such wisdom as I have acquired. I have had a long
8   life, I have had much time for thought as I lay alone in my stall, and I think I may
9   say that I understand the nature of life on this earth as well as any animal now living.
10 It is about this that I wish to speak to you.'

On the first page of Orwell's novel Major had already been introduced as a prize Middle White boar on Mr Jones's Manor Farm. After the drunken farmer had gone to bed, all animals, except for the tame raven, had congregated in the big barn in order to listen to Major, who was going to tell them about his dream. Here, Major launches into a long speech in which he rouses the farm animals to stand up against the injustice of their oppressed lives, and he teaches them the revolutionary song 'Beasts of England'. Thus this speech clearly has a very important function in the development of the narrative, in the course of which the animals start a revolution against their oppressor, Mr Jones. Rather than just telling the readers that Major wants to incite the other animals to such a revolution, the readers witness its beginning by means of dialogue and are invited to make analogies with political events in real life. Kozloff (2000) also refers to this function of dialogue as rendering thematic messages and as controlling viewer evaluation and emotions.

7.2.2 Characterisation

However, Major's speech has additional functions. It immediately characterises both the speaker, Major, and his relationship with the other animals. The second function listed in Table 7.1 on characterisation, therefore, focuses on 'how' something is being enacted and thus adds to character creation (see Chapter 6). Major starts his speech with the address term 'comrades' (line 4), which is used for fellow socialists or fellow communists. He repeats it within the first two lines and thirteen more times over the next five pages of his speech. The speech is also characterised by a very formal style of carefully selected formulations. Major says, 'I do not think, comrades, that I shall be with you for many months longer' (lines 5–6); he does not say, 'I am going to die soon.' And he says, 'I feel it my duty to pass on to you such wisdom as I have acquired' (line 7); he does not say, 'I am going to tell you what I think.' Thus, he is shown as a character who formulates his thoughts carefully, and who balances his socialist communion with his audience with a rather reserved and elevated style. Some readers might perhaps have thought that if animals could talk, they would talk in very simple language, but in this opening paragraph of Major's speech, he is portrayed as thoughtful, eloquent and rather formal.

In Chapter 6, we showed in more detail how characters are created in fiction. In that context, conversational behaviour in terms of conversational structure, word choice, syntactic structures and so on was mentioned among several other ways in which authors create characters (see Table 6.1). The contrast between a narratorial voice and character voices can create interesting effects. For example, a narrator voice might be rendered in standard English (e.g. the *Harry Potter* narrator), while characters speak in dialects, sociolects or ethnolects, and/or different registers (e.g. Hagrid in *Harry Potter*). This contrast then sharpens the difference between the voices and adds to character creation. A novelist such as Orwell in *Animal Farm* can use a narratorial voice to describe characters in more detail, and indeed the narrator briefly describes the impressive and prize-winning figure of Major in this first chapter: 'He was twelve years old and had lately grown rather stout, but he was still a majestic-looking pig, with a wise and benevolent appearance in spite of the fact that his tushes had never been cut' (Orwell 1945: 5–6, not shown in the extract). But apart from that, Major is described and characterised almost entirely through the way he speaks, and the readers are thus invited to form their own impression, which is, however, steered by the chosen features. The other animals do not speak in this first chapter.

In the case of TV series, Bednarek (2017: 142) adds that 'how' characters speak can create continuity of characters which allows viewers to recognise and easily identify them. This argument could be further explored with book series as well, unless the plot entails that characters change significantly, and this change is expressed by means of language.

7.2.3 Presentation of narrative context

Some functions of dialogue in fiction are particularly important for specific forms of fiction. In plays, for instance, there rarely is a narrator on the stage, and some narrative details have to be integrated into the dialogue. This is particularly true for plays which are enacted on a stage with only minimal scenery and stage props. Shakespeare's plays, for instance, were originally performed on a more or less empty stage in broad daylight, and much of the scenery had to be created in the audience's mind through the dialogue of the characters on stage. In Extract (7.2), Shakespeare's *Hamlet* (1600) opens with a scene of two night guards.

(7.2) William Shakespeare, *Hamlet*, 1.1.1–11
  1 *Enter* BARNARDO *and* FRANCISCO, *two sentinels.*
  2 BARNARDO
  3   Who's there?
  4 FRANCISCO
  5   Nay, answer me. Stand and unfold yourself.
  6 BARNARDO
  7   Long live the King.
  8 FRANCISCO   Barnardo?
  9 BARNARDO   He.
10 FRANCISCO
11   You come most carefully upon your hour.
12 BARNARDO
13   'Tis now struck twelve. Get thee to bed, Francisco.
14 FRANCISCO
15   For this relief much thanks. 'Tis bitter cold
16   And I am sick at heart.
17 BARNARDO

18		Have you had quiet guard?
19	FRANCISCO	Not a mouse stirring.
20	BARNARDO	
21		Well, good night.
22		If you do meet Horatio and Marcellus,
23		The rivals of my watch, bid them make haste.

These opening lines are not part of the main plot of the play, but they set the scene for what is to follow. The two night guards, or sentinels, address each other with their names and thus the audience learns who they are. Barnardo further reveals that it is the middle of the night, and it is bitter cold. If we imagine a similar situation in real life, the guards might well make a reference to the time of the day, especially if Barnardo has arrived a little late for the appointment, and they might comment on the coldness of the night. But in the context of a real conversation, they would be stating the obvious by providing information that is available to both of them anyway. For example, the fact that Horatio and Marcellus are 'the rivals of my watch' (line 23) is probably mutually known. In the fictional context of a theatre stage, their words have an additional significance because they transport the audience from a hot afternoon in London in The Globe theatre to a bitterly cold night in which one night guard arrives to relieve another of his duties. The night guards may have carried torches or lanterns as an additional element to conjure up a scene in the darkness of the night. In the further course of this and the next scene, the audience learns that the scene is set in Elsinore (1.2.173) and on the battlements of a royal castle (1.2.212). Thus, the dialogue is not only part of the narrative action, but it also fills in narrative details that are important for the audience in order to be able to make sense of the action. (Compare Extract (7.1) from *Animal Farm*, where much of the necessary contextualising information is given in the descriptive paragraphs before the dialogue.)

The dialogue can also be used to relate events that take place off-stage, and in fact the first act of *Hamlet* is full of narrations of events that have taken place earlier. In the first scene (1.1.78–94), Horatio, Hamlet's friend and fellow student, tells Marcellus how thirty years ago their old king had won a battle against the King of Norway, which accounts for the war preparations that are going on in Denmark at this point in time. The new King of Norway, young Fortinbras, appears to be gathering together an army and may be on his way to revenge his father. In the second scene (1.2.195–211), Horatio tells Hamlet how Marcellus and Barnardo had been approached by a ghost in the shape of the old king, Hamlet's father. In the third scene, Laertes, who wants to return to France after having come home to Denmark for the coronation of the new king, admonishes his sister Ophelia for her relationship with Hamlet. When their father, Polonius, joins them, he questions her about the relationship and she concedes (1.3.98–99), 'He hath, my lord, of late made many tenders / Of his affection to me.' Thus, we learn about the relationship between Ophelia and Hamlet through these dialogues. And finally, in the fifth scene (1.5.59–73), it is the Ghost, in the shape of Hamlet's father, the late King Hamlet of Denmark, who tells young Hamlet that he had not died through the poison of a serpent but through poison that his brother Claudius poured into his ear while he was sleeping in the garden.

From a pragmatic perspective, it is important to realise that dialogue in fiction overlaps to some extent with dialogue in non-fictional texts but that there are also functions that are different from our everyday interactions. In normal conversations, we adjust our conversational contributions to our addressees. We generally do not tell them what we assume that they already know. In a play, the author has to consider both what each character knows about the other characters and what the audience already knows or is still in need of knowing. The audience learns about the important narrative details through the communicative needs of the depicted characters, and sometimes the characters communicate to each other in order to satisfy the information needs of the audience. Marcellus asks Horatio about the reasons for the war preparations and as a result Horatio tells him – and the audience – the story about the battle with the old King of Norway. Laertes and Polonius admonish Ophelia to be very careful in her dealings with Hamlet and as a result the audience learns something about Hamlet's recent advances towards Ophelia. And the Ghost urges Hamlet to revenge his murder and as a result the audience learns early in the play that Hamlet's father had been murdered, even though there is, of course, the problem, at least for Hamlet, that the credibility of this information depends on the dubious source of a ghost.

Sometimes, authors also create dialogue that merely fills in a realistic verbal background to the main action. The night guards in the opening scene of Hamlet quoted above take several turns to identify each other. This does not belong to the main action of the play, but it provides a realistic background to this particular scene. In the darkness of the night, they have to identify each other verbally and with a password. It is the newcomer to the scene, Barnardo, who asks the first question, 'Who's there?' (line 3), which is immediately challenged by the night guard on duty, Francisco, 'Nay, answer me. Stand and unfold yourself' (line 5). The answer, 'Long live the King' (line 7), appears to function as a password. Kozloff (2000: 47; see also Bednarek 2017: 137) calls this 'adherence to expectations concerning realism', that is to say some fictional dialogue merely serves as a background of ordinary conversational activities, or 'verbal wallpaper' as Kozloff (2000: 47) calls it. What she has in mind with this term are scenes in which characters order food in a restaurant, or exchange brief greetings or small talk with extras playing waiters, traffic wardens, hospital staff and so on. These interchanges do not advance the plot but provide a plausible context that appears to be authentic. In a movie, such interchanges generally occur against the appropriate visuals. They reinforce the scenery of a restaurant, a roadside accident or a hospital with some verbal embellishment. In contrast, the interchange between Barnardo and Francisco is both verbal embellishment of a visual scene (the greeting exchange) as well as contextualising the play and the scene as such (setting place and time). In a crucial sense, it actually creates the scene.

7.2.4 Stylistic function and audience appeal

The fourth category of functions of dialogue is called 'stylistic function and audience appeal'. This includes what Kozloff (2000: 34) and Bednarek (2017: 132) call the 'exploitation of the resources of language', which means, for instance, poetic use of language, humour and irony, linguistic innovation, intertextuality, but also the use of dialogue in creative ways that are not usually associated with non-fictional dialogue. Sitcoms, for example, usually have a fast-paced dialogue track with one humorous punchline following another, which might also be imbued with irony.

> **Voice-over** in film: 'There are two major meanings: (1) Representation of a non-visible narrator's voice (voice-over narrator); (2) representation of a character's interior monologue (the character may be visible but her/his lips do not move).' (Jahn 2003: F3.2, emphasis removed)

Fictional dialogue can go beyond the normal forms of dialogue that we are familiar with from our everyday real-life experience. We have already seen an animal talk in Extract (7.1). In fiction, we also often find depictions of inner monologues when characters talk to themselves. Take, for instance, the famous soliloquy of Shakespeare's *Hamlet*, 'To be, or not to be – that is the question' (3.1.55), in which Hamlet agonises over his own inability to take revenge for the murder of his father. Here we are privy to Hamlet's innermost feelings and emotional turmoil in a way that would be very unusual in real life. In telecinematic fictional texts inner monologue/thought might also be rendered as direct speech uttered by the characters or even subtitling (e.g. in Woody Allen's *Annie Hall* the thoughts of the characters are sometimes rendered in subtitles as an additional layer to the spoken dialogue). Furthermore, extradiegetic narrators and characters can use voice-over to tell a story or to address the audience directly (see text box). In the context of fiction, we accept this possibility of using dialogue as part of the fictional contract (see Chapter 2).

In this section, we have looked at the different functions that dialogue in fiction can serve. In the following sections, we zoom in on the ways in which dialogue is created in order to give it the air of spontaneous face-to-face interaction. For this purpose, it is necessary to first have a closer look at the planning process that goes into the production of spoken language that is produced on the spot. This planning process accounts for some of the typical features of everyday spoken language.

7.3 Planning, production and interaction

Spoken language is highly complex. When we talk to each other in everyday interaction we have to plan what we are going to say next on several different levels simultaneously. In Section 3.2, we introduced the term 'synchronous communication' for this type of interaction. Utterances are produced at the same time that they are received. We have to think about what we are going to say next, the anecdote, for instance, that we want to use to entertain our interlocutors, the arguments that will make our point in a debate, or the answer that will respond adequately to a question that has just been addressed to us. At the same time, we have to think of the words that we can use for what we want to say and the order in which we want to use them. We have to plan the syntax of the sentences that we produce. There is pronunciation to attend to and the way in which we stress certain words to emphasise them and so on. We also have to pay attention to the reactions of our interlocutors with whom we take turns at talking. We have to react immediately when they have stopped talking. If we realise from their facial expression that they are baffled, annoyed, pleased or pleasantly surprised by what we say, we can – in real time as it were – adjust what we are saying, retract what we have just said, correct something, add another argument, give additional reasons or reinforce a compliment that we have just made. Much of this planning happens below our level of consciousness and it goes on while we are talking ourselves or listening to what our interlocutors say. We use the term 'online planning' for this.

Offline planning, on the other hand, refers to situations of asynchronous communication (see Section 3.2), in which the content and the actual wording are planned in advance and the sentences are produced some time before their transmission to the addressee. The typical situation here might be an email message, a short text message or indeed an entire book. We may jot down our sentences at high speed without giving them much thought or we may ponder for a long time over every single word and spend a long time rewriting entire passages, but in each case we plan and compose a message before it is transmitted to the addressee. In quasi-synchronous situations, the time lag between composition and transmission is very short, as in the case of a short text message, while in asynchronous situations it may be very long, perhaps even centuries long as in the case of books that were written a long time ago.

The distinction between online planning and offline planning neatly distinguishes between spontaneous interaction and books, such as novels, but the distinction gets more complex if we also consider play texts or movie scripts and performed fiction. Figure 7.1 gives an outline of some of the complexity of the interaction between planning and production in the context of the language of fiction. It shows that the categories 'planning', 'production', 'type of orality' and the 'reasons for orality features' cross the boundaries of spontaneous interaction,

Type of text	Spontaneous interaction	Performed fiction			Written fiction	
Subtype		Improv theatre	Plays	Movies, TV series	Play texts, movie scripts	Dialogues in narrative texts
Planning	Online				Offline	
Production	Online			Frozen	None	
Type of orality	Genuine			Staged	Represented	
Reasons for orality features	Orality features largely consequence of online planning and production			Orality features partly consequence of online production, partly used for narrative purposes	Orality features used for narrative purposes	

Figure 7.1 Orality in spontaneous interaction, performed fiction and written fiction

performed fiction and written fiction. We will unpack this claim in what follows.

In the first column on the left, we have spontaneous interaction as a benchmark for all the different forms of fictional language in this figure. Spontaneous interaction is planned and produced in the very situation in which the utterances are transmitted from the speaker to the addressee. The speakers may need time to think about what to say next, they react spontaneously to their interlocutors, they may say things which they want to repair as soon as they have said them and so on. This is a situation of true orality. Obviously, some of these features of orality may be produced for special effects. A speaker may pretend to be planning an utterance very carefully or may say something as if it had slipped out accidentally. It is also important to realise that different situations of spontaneous interaction may differ very considerably in the frequency of such features. In some situations, perhaps an interaction between a supervisor and a student, there may be a relatively high number of hesitations because the topics under discussion are complex and require careful thought and precise formulations. In other situations, perhaps a spontaneous chat between two students on the way to the next lecture, there may be very few hesitations. On a different dimension of orality, some interactions may show only a few interactional features, such as interruptions or fighting for the floor, while in others, especially if there are more than two speakers eager to contribute to the conversation, there may be many such features.

> **'Improvisation**, in theatre, the playing of dramatic scenes without written dialogue and with minimal or no predetermined dramatic activity. The method has been used for different purposes in theatrical history.' (The Editors of Encyclopaedia Britannica 2017, bold in original)

The second column lists improvised theatre, or improv theatre for short. This is already a form of performed fiction. Actors improvise various fictional scenes and interactions, perhaps on the basis of suggested keywords from the audience. In this situation, the actors have to plan and produce their utterances on the spot with very little time for preparation in advance. Of course, they may have rehearsed similar situations beforehand and they may even include elements that they have used on previous occasions, but most of the production appears to be entirely spontaneous in a way that mirrors spontaneous interaction, and features of orality may occur as a result of the online planning and production. However, in this situation, such features may also be produced to characterise the character that the actor is performing.

Self-repairs and hesitations, for instance, may be the result of the actor's need to plan what to say next or may be the result of the actor impersonating a hesitant and insecure character. For very skilled and professional actors, it is probably more of the latter, while for less experienced actors it may be a bit of both.

In theatre plays, actors generally perform interactions that have been scripted as part of the roles that they are performing. The details of what the character has to say have been specified in advance, and the actors have learned them by heart, and, in addition, they also know the lines of their co-actors. They know how they are going to react, and at what precise point they will claim or cede the floor. Thus, the planning is offline, but the production still occurs in the actual situation, which may occasionally lead to slips of the tongue, mispronunciations and other mishaps, especially for less experienced or non-professional actors, as well as creative ad libs. The offline planning is combined with an online production. Features of orality, as a consequence, may be partly due to the online production but generally they are performed for narrative purposes. The actors perform repairs, hesitations, interruptions and so on because they have been scripted by the author of the play. Here, the orality is – to a large extent – staged.

Movies and other telecinematic artefacts are similar to plays. The actors also perform roles that have been carefully scripted in advance. However, in this case, we talk of frozen production. The end product that is shown to the audience is the result of many takes and of the director's selection of the version that finally goes into the movie. Once the product is finished, the orality features remain frozen, whether they were originally produced more or less accidentally, as in spontaneous interaction, or for specific narrative purposes. But here, too, we should expect quite a lot of internal variation. Some films appear to be more scripted than others, some films favour a 'natural language' effect, others prefer poetic, non-everyday language.

In the case of written fiction (see the header 'written fiction' in Figure 7.1), i.e. play texts, movie scripts or dialogues in narrative texts, one might suspect a complete absence of features of orality, but this is not the case. They do occur, even though they are clearly not the result of an online planning process. They are carefully scripted for narrative purposes and in order to represent orality. Features of orality perform important functions in the planning and production process, and they are accordingly frequent in spontaneous interactions, where they are expected and, therefore, largely inconspicuous. When they are used in situations where they are not caused by the planning and production process, they become more conspicuous and their significance increases.

THE PERFORMANCE OF FICTION   139

They are not a result of the online planning and production process. They are performed in this way to draw attention to the online planning and production process. In the words of Gregory (1967: 188, as quoted in Rossi 2011: 25), they are 'written to be spoken as if not written'.

Thus, as we will show in the rest of this chapter, a general decrease in the frequency of features of orality from left to right in Figure 7.1 is paralleled by a corresponding increase in the significance of these elements. But, as pointed out above, the situation is somewhat more complex because of considerable variation within the individual boxes of Figure 7.1.

7.4 Features of orality

So far, we have talked of features of orality as if they were a more or less coherent group of elements. We now need to have a closer look at these elements, and for this purpose we put them into two different groups even if there is some overlap between them. Group 1 comprises elements that are part of the planning process, including fast speech processes, self-repairs, hesitations and so on. Group 2 includes elements that have to do with the interaction between the conversation partners and the way in which they organise speaking rights. Who is allowed to speak when? And at what point can another speaker take over? Table 7.2 gives an overview of relevant examples for each group. As far as possible the illustrations are taken from Extracts (7.3), (7.4) and (7.5), which we will discuss in some more detail below.

Let us illustrate some of these features with two short extracts taken from the crime comedy *The Big Lebowski* (1998), one of which you have already encountered in Chapter 6 when discussing character creation. As a result of mistaken identity, the notorious slacker Jeffrey 'the Dude' Lebowski is assaulted by two criminals who want to extort money from him. When he later confronts his namesake, the eponymous Big Lebowski, in order to get compensation, the following exchange ensues between the wealthy philanthropist Jeffrey Lebowski (JL) and the Dude (D), also called Jeffrey Lebowski.

(7.3)   *The Big Lebowski*, 1998, at 12.59 (previously shown as Extract (6.2))
  1   JL: are you 'employed Mr ^Lebowski?
  2   D: what wait ^wait,
  3   let me let me 'explain ^explain 'something to you.   ((rubs his eyes))
  4   ^uhm..
  5   ^I am ^not Mr 'Lebowski.   ((points at himself))
  6   ^you're Mr 'Lebowski.   ((points at JL))

140   THE PRAGMATICS OF FICTION

Table 7.2 Examples of features of orality

Planning and repairing	
Contractions	'you're', 'I'm', 'what's'
Fast speech	'lemme', 'gonna'
Planners, hesitators	'uh', 'um'
Self-repairs	'a wider fe-, sorry a wiser fellow'
Pauses	...
Repetitions	'wait, wait'
	'let me let me', 'explain explain'

Interaction	
Adjacency pairs	question – answer
	greeting – greeting
	offer – acceptance/rejection
Address terms	'dude', 'man', 'Mr Lebowski', 'Eve', 'Kate', 'my Lord'
Turn-taking signals	Response elicitors, question intonation, falling intonation, eye gaze
Attention signal	'hello'
Response elicitor	'eh?'
Discourse marker	'well', 'oh', 'right', 'now', 'you know', 'I mean', 'I see'
Response form	'yeah', 'ya', 'uh-huh', 'okay', 'no', 'really!'
Corrections	Correcting other speaker
Interruption, overlap	Two speakers speak at the same time

```
7      ^I'm the ^Dude.                              ((gesticulates))
8      so that's what you ^call me.
9      you ^know?
10     ^uh..                                        ((slaps his leg))
11     ^that or uh=..                               ((gesticulates))
12     his ^Dudeness or uh=..         ((JL nods and looks around))
13     ^Duder or uh=..
14     you ^know,
15     el 'Duderino,                                ((gesticulates))
16     if you're ^not into the whole ^brevity thing.
17     ^uh--
```

On the word level, there are such everyday phenomena as the contraction of 'you are' to 'you're' (line 6), 'I am' to 'I'm' (line 7) or 'that is' to 'that's' (line 8). At the phrase level we have repetitions in lines 2 and 3, and we have a whole range of planners and hesitation phenomena. There are a number of short pauses indicated by double full stops, and there are six planners (five 'uh's and one 'uhm'; see text box), some of them slightly lengthened as indicated in the transcription by an equals sign. In line 4, the Dude uses 'uhm' before he launches into the explanation that he wants to give to his namesake, and when he wants to give him further alternatives of what he himself should be called, every new name is preceded by 'uh', which gives the impression that he briefly reflects on what else might be an appropriate name for him. We do not know to what extent these features were part of the script and thus authorial or whether the actor Jeff Bridges,

> Elements such as *uh* and *um* are variably called hesitators, filled pauses or **planners** in the relevant literature. In British English they are usually spelled *er* and *erm*. The speaker uses them to fill in time while thinking of what to say next. They fill in what otherwise might have been silence. It makes clear that the speaker still wants to continue his or her turn. There is more to come. He or she is planning what to say next (see Tottie 2016).

who plays the Dude, created them as part of his characterisation of the Dude.

In Extract (7.4) from the middle of the movie, the Dude (D) is sitting at a bar in a bowling alley and is visibly down. He is joined by the character 'the Stranger' (S), who only appears in three scenes of the movie (prologue, middle, epilogue), and wears a cowboy hat and cowboy attire. Both are facing the barkeeper (B), who puts in a quick utterance and serves S's drink, but otherwise remains invisible.

(7.4) *The Big Lebowski*, 1998, at 59.50

```
1   S:  d'ya have a ^good ^Sarsaparilla?          ((S addresses B; D looks at S))
2   B:  Sioux ^city ^Sarsaparilla.                ((D puts his glass down; S nods))
3   S:  ^yeah,
4       it's a ^good ^one?                        ((to B))
5       <P how are ya ^doin' there ^dude? P>      ((D quickly looks at S))
6   D:  ^not too ^good ^man.                      ((fiddles around with his drink))
7   S:  one of ^those ^days,                      ((looks knowingly and kindly at D))
8       ^eh?                                      ((nods))
9   D:  ^ya.
10  S:  ^well,
11      a ^wiser fella than ^myself once ^said..
12      'sometimes you eat the ^bar,     ((bangs on the table; B puts drink on counter))
13      much 'obliged,                            ((to barkeeper))
14      and 'sometimes the ^bar..                 ((looks at D))
15      ^well..
16      ^ea=ts ^you.
```

17	D:	uh-huh.	((takes some nibbles))
18		that's some kind of ^Eastern ^thing?	((eats them))
19	S:	^far from it. ((turns his head; D looks at S; S raises his drink to D))	
20		. . . I like your 'style ^dude.	((takes a sip))
21	D:	uhm ^well,	((smacks his lips))
22		I ^dig your 'style ^too ^man.	((gesticulates))
23		got a whole ^cowboy thing ^goin'. ((S takes a sip of his drink; puts it down))	
24	S:	. . . ^thankie.	((looks at D who grabs his drink))
25		it's this ^one ^thing,	
26		^dude.	
27	D:	and what's ^that?	((takes a sip and slurps))
28	S:	d'ya ^have to use so many ^cuss words?	((D puts his glass down noisily))
29	D:	what the ^fuck are you ^talking 'about.((S chuckles and turns around his seat))	
30	S:	<P okay ^dude,	
31		have it ^your ^way.	((gets up and leaves))
32		take it ^easy ^dude. P>	
33	D:	yeah, thanks man.	((D looks after S))

The two characters in this movie extract take turns in a way that seems very much like an everyday interaction of two almost strangers at a bar. The first question is uttered by the Stranger and is addressed to the barkeeper (line 1). It concerns the soft drink that the Stranger wants to drink. After that the Dude and the Stranger launch into a brief conversation that starts with a very conventional conversation opener 'How are ya doin' (line 5), but the Stranger also uses the address term 'dude', which is both a turn-taking device handing over the speaking turn to the person so addressed but also an involvement feature creating rapport between the speaker and the addressee (and, of course, it happens to also be the name of the character). The Dude responds in a slightly less conventional way by admitting that he is not very well, and they continue by taking turns in quick succession. Many of the linguistic elements that they use are directly used to negotiate their interaction. In line 8, the Stranger uses the response elicitor 'eh?' They ask each other direct questions (lines 18 and 28), and they use a variety of short response forms, such as 'yeah' (line 3), 'ya' (line 9), 'uh-huh' (line 17) and 'okay' (line 30).

There are also several instances of the discourse marker 'well' (see text box). In line 10, the Stranger uses it to introduce his wisecrack about eating the bar or being eaten by the bar as an analogy of good and bad days. The discourse marker here serves as a framing device on the structural level. In line 15, the Stranger uses the same discourse marker to briefly hesitate before the punchline and thus to give it more prominence. In line 21, the Dude uses 'well' in conjunction with the planner 'uhm' to respond to the compliment that he has just received from the Stranger. Here it functions as a qualifier on the interactional level.

The two extracts from *The Big Lebowski* illustrate a broad range of the features of orality listed in Table 7.2. The movie is what we called a case of performed fiction and frozen production (Figure 7.1). As such, the extracts represent what is supposed to look like spontaneous interaction, and therefore evidence quite a number of such features.

> **Discourse markers** are stand-alone words or short phrases, such as *well, right, now, you know, I mean* or *I see*. They often occur at the beginning of an utterance and generally they can function as structural devices that help to segment discourse units or as interactional devices that signal something about the relationship between the speaker, the addressee and the message (see Biber et al. 1999: 1086).

However, some of these features also occur in written fiction as extracts (7.5) and (7.6) illustrate. The first extract is taken from the novel *Rules of Civility*, by the American novelist Amor Towles, published in 2011. It is mainly set in the late 1930s in New York. Eve and Kate are sitting in a posh restaurant where they have just been disturbed by the noise of two boisterous guests at a nearby table. Kate is the I-narrator of the novel.

(7.5) *Rules of Civility* (Towles 2011: 115–116, italics added)
1 The two drunkards suddenly stood. They reeled past us with bursts of laughter.
2 —*Well, well,* Eve said dryly. *Terry Trumbull. Was that you making all that*
3 *racket?*
4 Terry came about like one of those little boats that children learn to sail in.
5 —*Eve. What a great surprise . . . .*
6 If it weren't for twenty years of private schooling he would have stammered it.
7 He gave Eve an awkward kiss and then looked inquiringly at me.
8 —*This is my old friend, Kate,* Eve said.
9 —*Pleasure to meet you, Kate. Are you from Indianapolis?*
10 —*No,* I said. *I'm from New York.*
11 —*Really! Which part of town?*
12 —*She's not your type either, Terry.*
13 He turned to Eve looking like he was about to parry, but then thought better of
14 it. He was sobering up.
15 —*Give my best to Tinker,* he said.
16 As he retreated, Eve watched him go.
17 —*What's his story,* I asked.

The short conversation that develops between Kate, Eve and Terry (one of the two noisy guests) shows some of the same features of orality that we have seen in the previous extracts. But apart from two contractions ('She's' in line 12 and 'What's' in line 17), the pause/silence in line 5, indicated with '...', and the repetition of the discourse marker 'well' (line 2), there are no features that are directly linked to the planning or repairing of the utterances. There is no indication that there were any hesitations or self-corrections, for instance. On the contrary, there is a meta-comment from Kate, the I-narrator, that somebody with less rigorous schooling than Terry would most likely have stammered if he had been in his place (line 6).

On the interactional level, there are no interruptions or overlaps, but there are very clear turn-taking signals, such as questions directed at the interlocutor. Direct forms of address, e.g. in line 9, pick out one specific addressee in the group of four. In the imagination of the reader, it is clear that Terry not only verbally addresses the I-narrator at this point but that he also turns his attention to her and looks at her. Eve uses the discourse marker 'well' in reduplicated form to greet one of the two noise-makers (line 2), and Kate and Terry both use response forms ('No' in line 10, 'Really!' in line 11) to respond to each other's utterances. The narratorial voice is interwoven in the dialogue and also indicates turn-taking in that Terry's gaze is interpreted as a question by Eve ('and then looked inquiringly at me', line 7). The textual presentation on the page also helps the readers to identify speaker shift (imagine reading the text without the line breaks and hyphens) and thus detecting dialogue.

Extract (7.6) is again taken from Shakespeare's *Hamlet*. It is a scene towards the end of Act 1, immediately after Hamlet's encounter with the Ghost in which he has learned that his father had not been killed by a poisonous snake as everybody had been made to believe but by his uncle Claudius, who is now the new king. Hamlet promised the Ghost to take revenge, and he is clearly disturbed by what has just happened. Horatio and Marcellus now seek him out and call for him in the darkness of the night. They are deeply worried for their friend who has just gone off to meet a ghost.

(7.6)   William Shakespeare, *Hamlet*, 1.5.113–125
    1   *Enter* HORATIO *and* MARCELLUS.
    2   HORATIO
    3   My lord, my lord!
    4   MARCELLUS
    5   Lord Hamlet!
    6   HORATIO   Heavens secure him!

```
 7  HAMLET
 8      So be it.
 9  MARCELLUS    Illo, ho, ho, my lord!
10  HAMLET
11      Hillo, ho, ho, boy, come and come!
12  MARCELLUS
13      How is't, my noble lord?
14  HORATIO              What news, my lord?
15  HAMLET
16      O, wonderful.
17  HORATIO      Good my lord, tell it.
18  HAMLET
19      No, you will reveal it.
20  HORATIO
21      Not I, my lord, by heaven.
22  MARCELLUS            Nor I, my lord.
23  HAMLET
24      How say you then – would heart of man once think it? –
25      But you'll be secret?
26  HORATIO, MARCELLUS   Ay, by heaven.
27  HAMLET
28      There's never a villain dwelling in all Denmark
29      But he's an arrant knave.
30  HORATIO
31      There needs no ghost, my lord, come from the grave
32      To tell us this.
```

In Extract (7.6) there are no indications of any hesitations, planners, repetitions or corrections. But there are many features of interaction. In fact, the utterances are tightly interlinked by specific turn-taking devices. At the beginning of this scene, Horatio and Marcellus take turns to shout for Hamlet and to pray for him ('Heavens secure him!', line 6). Hamlet's turn, 'So be it' (line 8) might be the end of the soliloquy of the previous scene in which he promised to take revenge, or it may in fact be a response to Horatio's 'Heavens secure him!' 'Illo' and 'Hillo' are variations of 'holla' or 'hallo' (lines 9 and 11). They are used here as what is technically known as attention signals. Horatio and Marcellus use address terms in most of their utterances ('my lord', 'Lord Hamlet'). Horatio and Marcellus urge Hamlet to speak with questions (lines 13 and 14) and a request (line 17). Such utterances are normally analysed as the first part of an adjacency pair (see text box). They require a response by the addressee. But here it takes several such openings for Hamlet to respond. Hamlet responds with an answer that is not sufficiently informative, so that Horatio has to insist on getting the full story. When Hamlet in turn questions his friends' confidentiality (lines 19 and 25), both Horatio and Marcellus immediately respond, in one case even in unison (line 26).

> **Adjacency pairs** are sequences of utterances that are produced by two different speakers, usually in adjacent position. The nature of the first utterance specifies the expectation of what type of utterance is required in response. A question, for instance, requires an answer, a greeting requires another greeting, an invitation requires an acceptance or rejection and so on.

It is also noteworthy that most of the utterances of this extract are very short. They are shorter than a line, which leads to shared lines, in which one of the character's lines finishes before the end of the metrical line, which is then picked up by another character. This is clearly indicated by the layout of Extract (7.6), for instance in lines 3, 5 and 6, which form one metrical line that consists of three brief utterances. In addition, many utterances are not syntactically complete sentences. Lines 3, 5 and 9, for instance, consist entirely of address terms and attention signals. Lines 16 and 26 consist of response forms. Lines 21 and 22 are elliptical answers which also lack a verb. The overall impression is one of great urgency and insistence, which is heightened by the fact that Hamlet's responses fail to be informative.

This is, of course, not a normal everyday interaction, but a carefully crafted dialogue that characterises the tension of the situation, the anxiety of Horatio and Marcellus and the troubled state of mind of Hamlet. The features of orality are carefully selected for this purpose. They stress the quick-fire interaction between the characters, even though they do not appear to interrupt each other. In one case two characters speak at the same time (line 26) but they speak in unison. In a similarly intense and animated conversation in real life, we might expect speakers to speak at the same time, to interrupt each other or to repeat themselves, which might make it difficult for bystanders to understand what is going on. But this interaction is deliberately designed for the audience to convey the urgency and the apprehension of the entire scene.

7.5 Conclusions

In this chapter, we have focused on one of the core topics of pragmatics: the structure and use of conversation. In particular we have looked at the use and representation of dialogue in fictional texts of various types. Drawing on the crucial distinction between showing and telling, we first elaborated on the functions that the inclusion of dialogic passages can fulfil in fiction. This allowed us to point out the multi-functionality of dialogue in fiction and the creativity for which dialogue can be employed. Ranging from showing plot-driving moments, characterisation of protagonists, giving background information or contextualisation to using dialogue for stylistic effects, the use of dialogue is truly multiplex. Next we explored how planning, production and interaction are presented in fiction of different types. By juxtaposing spontaneous interaction with performed and written fiction, we explored how features of online planning can appear in fiction as forms of staged and represented orality for different effects. Finally, we demonstrated the occurrence of oral interactional features as well as features due to planning and repairing that are rendered in fictional texts. Once again, we pointed to the multi-functionality of the inclusion of these features in fiction.

This chapter connected in a number of ways to issues raised in previous chapters. First, we highlighted that the fictional contract introduced in Chapter 2 allows us to buy into the idea that thought can be represented in dialogue form or that animals talk, etc. and that features of orality do not have to be shown in their entire complexity in order to evoke orality and realism of dialogue. Second, comparing spontaneous interaction, performed fiction and written fiction with respect to their inclusion and rendition of orality and enactment allowed us to tap into the viewer's genre expectations, linking to Chapter 4. Third, since the inclusion of dialogue can push the plot of the narrative on (Chapter 5), among other functions, we demonstrated one means of how narrative causality can be enacted. Finally, we pointed out that dialogue adds to the characterisation of protagonists as introduced in Chapter 6. Dialogue can thus carry indexical meaning for region, social class, education, age, etc. In the next chapter, we will turn to another core topic in pragmatics and discourse analysis – the rendering of politeness and impoliteness in language – in order to continue our discussion of how language in use and fiction relate.

Key Concepts

Adjacency pair, dialogue, discourse marker, features of orality, improvisation, offline and online planning, planners, showing mode, telling mode, voice-over narrator

Exercises

1. If you revisit the examples which include dialogue presented in the previous chapters, can you assign one or more functions of dialogue listed in Table 7.1? Look in particular at Extracts (3.2) and (3.3) (*House MD*) in Chapter 3 and Extracts (6.2) (*The Big Lebowski*) and (6.4) (*Pygmalion*) in Chapter 6.
2. In Extract (6.8) (*Lost in Translation*) in Chapter 6, a fictitious film crew is in the process of recording a whisky commercial. The commercial consists of one line of dialogue, 'For relaxing times, make it Suntory time.' Who is the addressee of this line? And to what extent can we assign any of the functions of dialogue presented in Table 7.1 to this one-liner?
3. What is the difference between *being told* what happened by a narrator and *being shown* what happened through the dialogue of the involved characters? How do the two ways of giving us access to the story world differ in their emotional effect?
4. The following extract is taken from the novel *The Hitchhiker's Guide to the Galaxy* by the British author Douglas Adams ([1979] 2005: 137). The novel started out as a radio play, which may account to some extent for the oral quality of the depicted conversation. The novel is an example of mock science fiction full of outrageous improbabilities, in which the planet Earth is casually destroyed to make room for a galactic bypass. The only survivor is Arthur Dent, who is here stranded on the planet Margrathea, where he happens to bump into an old man. The following extract is part of their conversation. Identify as many features of orality as possible (see also Jucker 2015).

```
1    He looked gravely at Arthur and said, 'I'm a great fan of science, you know.'
2    'Oh ... er, really?' said Arthur, who was beginning to find the man's curious,
3    kindly manner disconcerting.
4    'Oh yes,' said the old man, and simply stopped talking again.
5    'Ah,' said Arthur, 'er ...' He had an odd feeling of being like a man in the act
6    of adultery who is surprised when the woman's husband wanders into the room,
7    changes his trousers, passes a few idle remarks about the weather and leaves
8    again.
9    'You seem ill at ease,' said the old man with polite concern.
10   'Er, no ... well, yes. Actually you see, we weren't really expecting to find
11   anybody about in fact. I sort of gathered that you were all dead or something ...'
12   'Dead?' said the old man. 'Good gracious me no, we have but slept.'
13   'Slept?' said Arthur incredulously.
14   'Yes, through the economic recession, you see,' said the old man, apparently
15   unconcerned about whether Arthur understood a word he was talking about or
16   not.
```

Further reading

The model of the role of dialogue in fiction that we presented in Section 7.2 is inspired by Kozloff's (2000) work in film studies and also draws on studies in conversation and discourse analysis dedicated to the role of constructed dialogue in oral narratives (e.g. Bednarek 2017; Tannen 1989). Further inspiration was gained from Bednarek (2010, 2018), Bublitz (2017), Jucker (2015), Norrthon (2019), Piazza et al. (2011), Quaglio (2009), Richardson (2010), Rossi (2011) and Toolan (2011).

8 Relational work and (im/politeness) ideologies

8.1 Introduction

In this chapter we are concerned with ideologies of comportment in linguistic and multimodal form. We will demonstrate how assessments of such comportment result in character creation in fictional artefacts and add to plot development. This topic combines concerns within the pragmatics of fiction with interpersonal pragmatics, a perspective in pragmatics which gives the interpersonal and relational element of communication centre stage. It builds on insights about frames of expectation (introduced in Chapter 4 on genre and expanded on in connection with narratives in Chapter 5) and on the indexicality cues introduced in Chapter 6 on character creation.

To illustrate what is at stake here, consider unemployed and single mother Erin Brockovich, the main character of the US movie of the same title (2000), who is desperately looking for a job in order to put food on the table for her three children and get out of debt. In scenes shown before Extract (8.1), Erin is seen going to court because of a car accident and it is implied that she had lost her case because she was the socially weaker person (Jaguar-driving male, medical doctor versus single, unemployed, twice divorced mother) and because she swore in court. The swearing portrays her as someone who is socially inept. After many futile attempts at getting job interviews, she simply shows up for work at the law firm where she was a client earlier. The boss of the law firm, Ed Masry, confronts her in an open plan office and their confrontation is witnessed by many staff members.

(8.1) *Erin Brockovich*, 2000, at 13.10–14.32
    1   Ed: ^Erin?
    2   how's it ^going?
    3   Erin: 'you never called me ^back.   ((confrontational stance))
    4   I left ^messages.

5	Ed:	you 'did well ^I I I didn't know that 'uh,
6		^Donald seems to think that ['you said that --]
7	Erin:	[there's] ^two things that aggravate me Mr 'Masry?
8		being ^ignored,
9		and being ^lied to. ((assertive and accusatory glance))
10	Ed:	I never ^lied. ((objecting incredulously))
11	Erin:	you 'told me things would be ^fine.
12		and they're ^not.
13		I ^trusted you.
14	Ed:	I'm 'sorry about that [I really ^am--] ((staff members observe, worried faces))
15	Erin:	[^I don't need] 'pity,
16		I need a ^paycheck.
17		and 'I've ^looked.
18		but when you've spent the ^past six years raising babies= ((fast and upset))
19		=it's ^real hard to convince someone to give you a 'job that pays worth a damn=
20		=are you ^getting ^every ^word of this down honey= ((at staring office worker))
21		=or am I talking too 'fast for you. ((office worker turns away, taken aback))
22	Ed:	I am ^sorry about that I 'really am but we have a full 'staff right [now so --]
23	Erin:	[^bullshit] if =
24		=you ^had a full staff this ^office would return a client's damn=
25		=^phone call. ((secretary stares shocked))
26	Ed:	((staring at her with an expression of incredulity))
27	Erin:	I'm ^smart I'm 'hard-working and I'll do 'anything and I'm ^not leaving=
28		=here without a 'job.
29	Ed:	((exhaling)) ((incredulous, then compassionate look))
30		((13 sec. silence)) ((everyone is staring; Erin becomes aware of her situation))
31	Erin:	don't make me 'beg. ((whispering, desperate face, not looking at Ed))
32		if it doesn't work 'out,
33		'fire me.
34		don't make me 'beg. ((brief eye contact))
35		((5 sec. silence)) ((Ed looks at her))
36	Ed:	^no benefits. ((Ed nods at her))

What we see in this scene is the staging of multiple breaks of frame expectations. With respect to dress code, Erin is singled out as the 'other' and is contrasted to the other office workers. While all employees in the somewhat cramped office space wear office attire, Erin wears high heels, a short skirt, and a revealing leopard-print T-shirt. (She has, however, donned a cardigan over the T-shirt.) Her way of dressing thus breaks the expectations about how to dress in a respectable law firm as an employee. With respect to how to start a new job, Erin has broken several conventions as well. She basically hired herself, jumping the job interview or employment negotiations. With respect to language, her level of adversarialness in a situation where she is in a weaker hierarchical position is noticed not only by her future boss but also by everyone in the office witnessing the interaction. In particular, her use of swearwords ('damn', lines 19 and 24; 'bullshit', line 23) raises eyebrows. During the scene, Erin plays out several roles: the former client whose expectations were violated because her case was lost and her calls were not returned (lines 3–13), and that of someone in desperate search for a job (line 14 onwards). Combining multimodal elements of character creation, the scene, which is still part of the introductory phase of the movie, manages to position Erin as an assertive and active, yet unconventional person, who does not mince her words and will go to great lengths to secure herself a job to support her children.

The formation and development of relationships is often at the heart of fictional plots or at least often an important part of the plot. To study the interpersonal function of language in fiction is thus a fruitful research path. There is the tradition of studying forms of im/politeness surface structures in fiction in light of character portrayal and development; the characters' use of polite or impolite language will then lead to characterisation of them as polite or impolite human beings, who know/do not know/do not care about social conventions. These judgements can be made on the intradiegetic and extradiegetic level (characters judge each other; narrator comments) and/or can be made by the viewers and readers. These readings do not necessarily have to be aligned. For example, characters might be portrayed as finding each other's ways of speaking and behaving perfectly acceptable, while their norms might clash with the viewers' mainstream understandings of comportment. These effects can be created by the characters employing certain language indexicals (e.g. the use of swearwords in Extract (8.1)), by other characters commenting on linguistic behaviour (e.g. the office workers staring and raising their eyebrows) and by authorial cues assigning relational traits to characters (e.g. by narrators describing characters in written fiction as considerate, warm-hearted, rude, ruthless, etc.). Exploring how interpersonal issues are foregrounded in fictional texts allows us to uncover ideological understandings about interpersonal relations in particular cultural contexts (e.g. gender roles, power roles) and how they are transformed into fiction.

To address the issues raised, Section 8.2 will give a brief introduction to im/politeness studies and its connection to identity construction. In Section 8.3, the emergence of ideologies in fiction in general and im/politeness ideologies in particular will be discussed. Section 8.4 turns to swearing as one pivot where im/politeness ideologies emerge and will show how its inclusion or exclusion is also influenced by societal constraints imposed on the creation of fictional artefacts.

8.2 Relational work and (character) identity construction

Im/politeness studies have a long tradition in pragmatics. This is because scholars wanted to find out how language in use is structured beyond grammatical rules and thus focused on pragmatic rules. A sentence might be formulated in perfectly grammatical English, but its level of politeness might not be pitched right in the context in question. If a person wants a window closed by someone else, she can catch someone's eye and merely grunt in the direction of the window. An imperative 'close the window', a conventionalised question 'can you close the window?', or statements such as 'it would be good if the window were closed' or 'it is cold in here' can all realise the speech act of request, i.e. getting the window closed by someone else. Adding mitigators/hedges such as 'please' or 'maybe' can tone down the request somewhat. The level of indirectness (grunting or an indirect statement) can give the addressees the possibility of ignoring the request. There is thus vast variation in how speech acts are formulated and the difference is not on the propositional level (i.e. the message that the window should get opened is clear in context) but on the interpersonal level. So why is there so much variation?

Im/politeness research argues that the variation is due to face-negotiations of the interactants. Face is a metaphor to describe how people take each other's projected identities into account (see text box, p. 154). All people have face to gain, lose, or defend and they can maintain, challenge or boost someone else's face. The technical terms proposed here are face-maintaining, face-enhancing and face-aggravating behaviour. Crucially, this face-negotiation is always at play and not only in marked cases where im/politeness as etiquette is foregrounded. We use the term 'relational work' rather than 'im/politeness' (see Locher and Watts 2005, 2008; see also text box, p. 154), because relational work is a technical concept that allows us to study the entire spectrum of relational negotiations. In the remainder of the chapter, we will use the term 'relational work' to describe the interpersonal cues and negotiations we observe and the term 'im/politeness' in cases where we can detect clearly surfacing ideologies about comportment.

The concept of frames of expectations was introduced in detail in Section 4.2 and is also key to the understanding of relational work. Frames of expectations about a particular activity type are acquired in processes of socialisation. Frames evoke knowledge about action

> According to Goffman (1967: 5) **face** is seen as 'the positive social value a person effectively claims for [her/himself] by the line others assume [s/he] has taken during a particular contact.'

> **Relational work** 'refers to all aspects of the work invested by individuals in the construction, maintenance, reproduction and transformation of interpersonal relationships among those engaged in social practice' (Locher and Watts 2008: 96) and it includes linguistic and other modes of interaction.

sequences and the rights and obligations belonging to the interactional roles of the interactants. This entails expectations about how to be properly addressed and talked to in the particular context of the frame.

Furthermore, judgements about the level of relational work involve emotions that are tied to one's understanding of self. This link to identity construction in connection with relationship negotiation is key (for an overview, see Locher 2008a). People can feel wronged and upset if their rights evoked by a role are disregarded (see Chapter 9). For example, in the case of using swearwords during a court trial (briefly mentioned above in connection with Erin Brockovich's backstory), use of inappropriate language might result in a severe reprimand by the judge and might cause the judge to have a negative opinion of the defendant or witness. Positive and negative emotions in connection with relational work thus have to do with judging the level of relational work with respect to the norms that belong to the particular frame in its socio-cultural context.

> Eckert and McConnell-Ginet (1992: 464) define a **community of practice** as 'an aggregate of people who come together around mutual engagement in an endeavour. Ways of doing things, ways of talking, beliefs, values, power relations – in short, practices – emerge in the course of this mutual endeavour.'

The norms that belong to particular frames are heavily imbued with societal ideologies. To disentangle these is no easy feat and often impossible in fictional and non-fictional data alike because ideologies might be intertwined. For example, ideologies on gender, power, age and what it means to comport yourself according to a society's norms in order to be judged a polite member of society might be intricately interlaced. Swearing by women is generally less tolerated than by men; women who act assertively in offices of power might be perceived as not feminine; older people who dress according to the latest trend in teenage fashion and use the latest linguistic innovations from youth culture might not be taken seriously, neither by teenagers nor their peers. Additionally, societal norms are not static and can change over time. They might also be challenged and changed in more local communities of practice that develop their own ways of doing things (see text box). Fictional texts can aim explicitly or implicitly at making such norm negotiations and their underlying ideologies visible.

Returning to the question of why there is so much variation in the realisation of speech acts, we claim that face-negotiations are influenced by all of the concepts raised in the previous paragraphs and find their expression in linguistic choices (among other indexicalities such as appropriate clothing, comportment, etc.). Which linguistic strategies or combination of strategies are appropriate in a particular context depends thus on many factors that have been discussed in many approaches to im/politeness (e.g. Brown and Levinson 1978, 1987; Lakoff 1973; Leech 1983, 2014; Watts 2003). In Table 8.1 we summarise the issues presented so far and present an overview of these factors in groups. Despite their presentation in clusters, they are not hierarchically listed and are all assumed to interact with each other simultaneously. They are personal factors, relationship factors, frame factors and participation structure factors. The questions in the second column of Table 8.1 describe what interactants might ask themselves. However, while the questions imply a rational approach to linguistic choices, we do not claim that speakers and addressees work through the list and tick off boxes one by one. What counts as a pragmatically adequate linguistic choice is a matter of learning through life-long socialisation processes. Assessing the impact of a strategy or choosing one might often be instantaneous. In other

Table 8.1 An open list of potential factors influencing the choice of relational work strategies with respect to the imposition of a particular speech act in its socio-cultural context

Personal factors	Pertinent questions
Face of the speaker	How is the speaker's own face endangered through the interaction? Can the speaker enhance or maintain his/her face through the interaction? What costs or benefits to face are involved when engaging in interaction?
Face of the addressee	How is the addressee's face endangered through the interaction? Can the interaction enhance, maintain or challenge the addressee's face? What costs or benefits to face are involved?

Table 8.1 (*continued*)

Personal factors	Pertinent questions
Identity construction	What consequences does the speaker's and addressee's choice of relational work strategies to challenge/maintain/enhance face in interaction have with respect to their identity construction?

Relationship factors	Pertinent questions
Distance	Are the interactants close or distant?
Power	Is there a power difference between the interactants or are they hierarchically equal? Is one participant allowed to exercise power over the other within the context of the frame?
Status	Do the interactants differ in status (even in hierarchically equal contexts, interactants might differ with respect to the status they have gained in the group)?
Affect	Do the interactants like or dislike each other?
Density of network	Do the interactants know each other just from one type of interaction or do they have multiple ties?
Relationship history	Have the interactants a history of previous encounters or are they meeting for the first time?

Frame factors	Pertinent questions
Roles of interactants	What roles do the interactants embody in the context of the encounter?
Rights and obligations	What rights come with each role? What obligations come with each role? What effects would maintaining or challenging these rights and obligations have?
Sequences of actions	Are there expected actions that belong to the frame? Are they obligatory or can they be left out?
Norms and ideologies (local and cultural level)	Does the frame evoke particular norms of conduct with respect to societal norms such as the role of gender, power distribution, freedom of speech, etc? What effects would adherence or non-adherence to these norms and ideologies have?

Participation structure factors	Pertinent questions
Private communication	Is the interaction accessible only to the interlocutors?
Overhearer and witnesses	Can others witness the interaction?
Persistence	Is the interaction in a form that can be recalled later (taped or written communication) or is it ephemeral?

cases, much agonising over how to phrase a concern appropriately can go into choosing (see the cartoon in the Exercises section).

The first group of factors pertains to face-negotiations and the resulting identity construction. An important issue to assess is thus whether what you are about to do presents an imposition on the addressee (e.g. a request for a job), restricts the addressee's action environment (e.g. being forced to answer) or in any way challenges the identity of the addressee (e.g. disagreeing) or yourself (e.g. denying/being denied a request). Both the speaker's and the hearer's perspectives and the cost and benefit for both sides enter into consideration. Importantly, these considerations are context- and culture-dependent. There are both societal ideologies on appropriate comportment that influence these assessments and local norms that might also challenge the societal views to a certain extent. Revisiting Extract (8.1) above, Erin commits an enormous imposition on her former lawyer by putting him in the uncomfortable position of having to call her out for having employed herself. Both Erin's face and Ed's face are in a vulnerable position and both their identities as boss and potential future employee are at stake.

With respect to relationship factors, distance, power, status, affect, density of network and the relationship history have an impact on the selection of relational work strategies. It thus matters whether interactants have a close or distant relationship and whether their roles position the interactants as equals or with a power difference (i.e. whether one person has power over the other). What status the interactants have in a group can influence the choice of linguistic strategies. It is important whether interlocutors know each other from different contexts or just one (e.g. your co-worker might be in the same sports club). It also matters whether people meet for the first time or have had a long history together, and whether they like or dislike each other. In the case of Erin and Ed, there is no closeness yet between the characters. Her position in relation to him is also powerless since he has the power to hire her or let her go during the extract, which is dramatised through the long pauses in lines 30 and 35. The lawyer's status is higher from a societal perspective, and Erin's low social status is driven home by the story so far and her way of dressing and using language. Interestingly, Ed and Erin now know each other in two different capacities as we see a transition from lawyer–client to boss–employee during this short extract and they can already look back to a joint history.

All of these considerations are tightly linked to the group of factors that centres on the frame evoked in interaction. It matters in what roles people meet (as client–lawyer, boss–employee, teacher–student, family members, etc.) and how these roles are defined in their societal context, including rights and obligations of the interactional partners. The fact that Erin offers her work power in this unconventional manner is perceived as breaking frame conventions by Ed as her future boss and all the other characters in the scene. Ed's rights to see her résumé and offer her the job are violated. In contrast, Erin claims that her rights as a client have been violated as her phone calls were not returned, and she also implies that she was not given a chance to follow the expected action sequence of a job interview. This in turn evokes societal ideas on gender and injustice.

The last group of factors pertains to the participation structure of the encounter and the persistence of the communication that is produced. It matters that Ed and Erin are enacting their dispute in front of intradiegetic witnesses, as is made clear by Erin's aside to the office worker ('are you getting every word of this down honey or am I talking too fast for you', lines 20–21) and her starting to whisper in an attempt to keep the dialogue for Ed's ears only (lines 31–34). This implies that being rejected or having to beg is bad enough on its own but having to do it in public exacerbates the potential face loss. The viewers in turn are made privy to the negative evaluations of Erin's unconventional process of getting herself a job by the bystanders but they also witness that her pluck is successful. The factor persistence refers to the mode of communication. While face-to-face interaction is generally ephemeral (i.e. once spoken, the utterances cannot be reproduced for evidence), recorded interaction and written interaction are persistent and can be revisited and reperused. For example, quite some effort and thought is put into personal and business letter writing since how the addressee is addressed and in what register the text is composed will influence how the writer will be judged. In the case of our example, the scene is staged as ephemeral on an intradiegetic level, but it is persistent data on the level of viewer–artefact.

When looking at the key issues involved in relational work (face, identity construction, relationship negotiation, frames, norms, ideologies, emotions, participation structure), it becomes apparent to what extent the concepts are interconnected and interwoven. There is no simple hierarchy of these concepts as they are evoked and oriented to at the same time. In the next sections, we will explore further how relational work surfaces in fictional context.

8.3 Relational work in fiction

Studies on relational work using fictional data have been conducted on plays and novels (e.g. Jucker 2016, 2020; Jucker and Kopaczyk 2017;

Kizelbach 2017), and more recently telecinematic data (e.g. Dynel 2015, 2017; McIntyre and Bousfield 2017). What this research shows is that relational work is all-pervasive in fiction as well as in real life due to the relational element never being absent in language use. However, moments of relational work can be staged for effect in fiction. Extract (8.1) is part of the character positioning of the two main characters Erin and her boss Ed, who will become work partners who respect and like each other in the continuation of the movie. The scene can be argued to complete the introductory phase of the movie and works as a transition to the remaining plot of the movie.

As a further case in point, consider Extract (8.2) from the US TV series *The West Wing* (1999), where we see awareness of imposition as well as role understanding staged over several turns in the fictional context of two White House employees. C.J. Cregg (White House Press Secretary) walks into Sam Seaborn's (Deputy White House Communications Director) office in order to obtain information on how the US census works. This information is important to her since she needs to do a press briefing later.

(8.2) *The West Wing*, 1999, Season 1, Episode 6, at 6.20–8.02
```
1   Sam:  ^hey.
2   C.J.: ^hey.
3         that was all..
4         ^great,
5         what you just ^said there.
6   Sam:  ^what did I just ^say?        ((walks towards his suit jacket and puts it on))
7   C.J.: ^not so much what you ^said,
8         but the ^way you ^said it.
9   Sam:  the ^census ^has to be taken ^seriously.
10  C.J.: ^tell me about it.
11  Sam:  you ^know..
12        it's not ^glamorous but..
13        you ^know?
14  C.J.: ^sure.
15  Sam:  you ^need something?          ((fumbling around with papers on the desk))
16  C.J.: did ^you get a ^haircut?
17  Sam:  ^no.
18  C.J.: you look ^good today.         ((Sam looks at C.J.))
19  Sam:  thank ^you.
20        you ^too.
21  C.J.: new ^suit?
22  Sam:  ^no.
```

23	C.J.:	you look ^good.	((Sam walks away from his desk))
24	Sam:	what do you ^need ^C.J.?	
25	C.J.:	a ^tutor.	((C.J. follows, they leave the office))
26	Sam:	a ^tutor?	
27	C.J.	^yes.	
28	Sam:	a ^tutor?	
29	C.J.	^yes.	
30	Sam:	what ^for?	
31	C.J.:	^Sam,	
32		I read my ^briefing book last night on the ^commerce bill regarding the ^census =	
33		=and there are ^certain ^parts of it that I don't ^quite 'understa=nd. ((gesticulates))	
34	Sam:	^I can help you out.	
35		which ^parts?	
36	C.J.:	^well..	
37		^all of it.	
38	Sam:	^all of it?	((looks at C.J.))
39	C.J.:	^yes.	
40	Sam:	you don't understand the ^census.	
41	C.J.:	I don't 'understand certain ^nuances.	((gesticulates))

A viewer might wonder why 41 lines are needed to get the two characters to agree about exchanging information on the census. A more efficient version would could have been staged like this:

(8.2 abbreviated)

1	Sam:	^hey.	
2	C.J.:	^hey.	
3	Sam:	you ^need something?	
4	C.J.:	a ^tutor.	((C.J. follows, they leave the office))
5	Sam:	what ^for?	
6	C.J.:	^Sam,	
7		I read my ^briefing book last night on the ^commerce bill regarding the ^census=	
8		=and there are ^certain ^parts of it that I don't ^quite 'understa=nd. ((gesticulates))	
9	Sam:	^I can help you out.	
10		which ^parts?	
11	C.J.:	^well..	
12		^all of it.	

So, why is there so much more text? There are two reasons for this. The first has to do with the census being the topic of this particular episode, and the script writers use these two characters in a fictionalised teaching exchange in several scenes throughout the episode to inform the viewers about the technical details of this topic (Extract (8.2) is the first scene in this sequence). If we think back to the role of dialogue in fiction (Table 7.1), the exchange is used for plot advancement and to control viewer interpretation. The length of the sequence stresses the importance of the census for this episode and that it is not a trivial matter nor easy to understand since C.J., who is well educated, has trouble understanding its process.

The second reason has to do with character creation and relationship formation. While the two characters have been working with each other for a while, what is staged here is C.J.'s awareness of imposing on Sam's time and her reluctance to admit lacking in knowledge (lines 33 and 41). This reflects their hierarchies and identities. Both hold important key positions in the White House, but C.J. clearly does not want to ask directly for a favour. By using several compliment insertion sequences on Sam's input on the census in a prior meeting, his haircut, and his clothes (lines 3–23), she gets Sam to pick up on the fact that she wants something from him ('you need something?', line 15; 'what do you need C.J.?' line 24) and to offer help himself rather than her having to ask for it ('I can help you out', line 34). Sam might have felt upset if C.J. had simply imposed on his time directly and expected him to tutor her, which is not in his job description. Since she goes to considerable lengths in cushioning her request, she aligns him with her and also allows him to embrace a task that is not usually what he does in his job. In doing so, she demonstrates awareness of the imposition and concern for Sam. As a result, he might judge her attempt at face-boosting as positive (albeit transparent). What is staged here is linguistic gift giving in the form of compliments to prepare and mitigate an imposition. What is at stake are primarily power hierarchies and status concerns which are negotiated through quick and witty dialogue sequences. The fact that Sam cannot withhold a certain element of sarcasm when he states in a deadpan voice 'you don't understand the census' (line 40) reveals that C.J. had a hunch her request might be ridiculed and she might appear incompetent, an impression she goes to great lengths to avoid. The extent to which relational work is foregrounded in this example is quite remarkable and might be taken by some viewers as being over the top, while others might enjoy the back and forth between the characters as part of their relationship negotiation.

One of the tenets of relational work is that all interaction contains a relational aspect even if the interaction at stake is content and information oriented. For example, even in scientific journals that report on medical research, there are conventions that the authors abide by in order to adhere to the expectations of their learned colleagues (e.g. the use of medical jargon, an agreed-upon and established way of presenting theory, method, data and results, etc.; see Table 4.1 for parameters in genre description). Not adhering to these factors will result in a negative impression of the scholar's capability to understand conventions. Adhering to the conventions will result in identity construction of a scholar who knows the ropes. In fiction, too, we can discuss all the examples presented so far in this textbook in light of relational work. The easiest entry point is character creation and identity construction. For example, recall Extract (6.2), where the Dude explains to the Big Lebowski how to address him in an adequate manner, thus creating a difference between the two people who share the same name. Extract (6.6) from *My Cousin Vinny* showed a courtroom scene where the judge interrupts the lawyer Gambini, which is his right as judge, and Gambini accommodates to the judge by pronouncing the word 'youths' especially carefully since it caused misunderstanding the first time he used it. Both characters orient towards their interactional roles and in doing so uphold the courtroom frame. However, there are also fictional texts where im/politeness ideologies and how they reflect a society's beliefs are part of the plot itself. The examples from Shaw's play *Pygmalion* in Chapter 6 present a case in point since the plot discusses how language can be used to create personas and how ideologies of comportment can be learned and acquired and then used for effect. The play thus deals with language and comportment on a meta-level, i.e. politeness ideologies are explicitly talked about and reflected on. We will explore the idea of meta-discussions as well as the emergence of im/politeness ideologies further in the next section.

8.4 Fiction as locus for discursive im/politeness ideologies

Fiction can give us access to ideologies that shape comportment in the present and the past. The previous two examples were taken from US telecinematic artefacts. We can, however, also turn to fictional texts written in more distant times and witness relational work negotiations in historical contexts, from the twentieth century right back to medieval times (for an overview, see Jucker 2020). What we need to keep in mind is that relational work is shaped by the ideologies and norms of its time. In other words, what might have been intended to signal a particular type of relational work to the audience of the time (e.g. the display of considerateness or insult through the choice of address terms or swearing) might escape the present audience or might evoke different effects. This has to do with the fact that both linguistic expressions and their semantic and pragmatic connotations as well as the norms and ideologies that they evoke can change over time. In addition, both present and past writers may play with the rendition of the ideologies of their time for effect since they are not bound to presenting them accurately. This means that scholars need to carefully interpret the fictional data in its context (as far as this is possible) and cannot easily jump to conclusions about the relational indexicalities of past linguistic choices.

Taking Jane Austen's (1775–1817) work as a case in point, present-day readers might find the roles that the female main characters are assigned in the texts excruciatingly restricted. In a somewhat simplified summary, these female main characters, who belong to the English gentry, are confined to particular tasks such as supervising the household, reading, flower arranging, singing and playing the piano, going to dances, and waiting for a suitable marriage proposal, etc. They do not have the possibility of choosing their occupation, going to university or finding a suitable marriage partner on an online dating app, which might be taken for granted by present-day readers. For readers at the time, however, this restriction of the female protagonists' action possibilities will not have been all that surprising since the role women were assigned at the beginning of the nineteenth century did not foresee such independence. From a gender perspective, these depictions give us insights into the gentry women's position at the time and they also demonstrate how Austen subtly criticises this system by showing how her protagonists cope with it. Fictional texts can thus reveal gender ideologies and also question such ideologies at the same time. We also find evidence of how gender ideologies are intertwined with ideologies on how to properly comport oneself. To know one's place, to be a gracious host, to do one's duty in charity work, etc. are all factors that contribute to how a character is judged.

To demonstrate how ideologies are intertwined and made explicit in fictional texts, let us look at a key scene in Jane Austen's *Emma* (1816), where Mr Knightley, whom Emma looks up to and who has watched Emma grow up and then develops an interest in her, chides Emma for her insulting behaviour towards Miss Bates, one of their acquaintances, during a picnic that was also attended by other guests. Emma ridiculed Miss Bates ironically for her dullness in front of everyone.

(8.3) *Emma* (Austen 1816), chapter VIII, Gutenberg online version, bold, italics and underlining added

1   While waiting for the carriage, she found Mr. Knightley by her side. He looked
2   around, as if to see that no one were near, and then said,
3   'Emma, I must once more speak to you as I have been used to do: a privilege rather
4   endured than allowed, perhaps, but I must still use it. I cannot see you *acting wrong*,
5   without a remonstrance. How could you be so *unfeeling* to Miss Bates? How could you be

6   so *insolent* in your wit to a woman of her <u>character, age, and situation</u>?— Emma, I had
7   not thought it possible.'
8   Emma recollected, blushed, was sorry, but tried to laugh it off.
9   'Nay, how could I help saying what I did?—Nobody could have helped it. It was not
10 so very bad. I dare say she did not understand me.'
11 'I assure you she did. She felt your full meaning. She has talked of it since. I wish you
12 could have heard how she talked of it—with what *candour and generosity*. I wish you
13 could have heard her *honouring your forbearance*, in being able to pay her such
14 attentions, as she was for ever receiving from yourself and your father, when *her society*
15 *must be so irksome.'*
16 'Oh!' cried Emma, 'I know there is not a better creature in the world: but you must
17 allow, that what is good and what is ridiculous are most unfortunately blended in her.'
18 'They are blended,' said he, 'I acknowledge; and, <u>were she prosperous</u>, I could allow
19 much for the occasional prevalence of the ridiculous over the good. <u>Were she a woman of</u>
20 <u>fortune</u>, I would leave every harmless absurdity to take its chance, I would not quarrel
21 with you for any *liberties of manner*. <u>Were she your equal in situation</u>—but, Emma,
22 consider how far this is from being the case. <u>She is poor; she has sunk from the comforts</u>
23 <u>she was born to; and, if she live to old age, must probably sink more</u>. Her situation should
24 secure your compassion. *It was badly done, indeed!* You, whom she had known from an
25 infant, whom she had seen grow up from a period when her notice was an honour, to have
26 you now, in thoughtless spirits, and the *pride* of the moment, *laugh at her, humble her*—
27 and before her niece, too—and before others, many of whom (certainly *some*, [italics in
28 original]) would be entirely guided by *your* treatment of her [italics in original].—This is
29 not pleasant to you, Emma—and it is very far from pleasant to me; but I must, I will,—I
30 will tell you truths while I can; satisfied with proving myself your friend by very faithful
31 counsel, and trusting that you will some time or other do me greater justice than you can
32 do now.'

In this scene, Mr Knightley frames his reprimand explicitly in light of 'manner' and thus evokes norms of conduct in a linguistic meta-comment since he reproaches Emma that her taking 'liberties of manner' was inappropriate in this context (line 21). Mr Knightley is quite explicit in what he means by this so that the extract is rich in evoking the groups of factors that were introduced in Table 8.1. Mr. Knightley is upset with Emma not only for her insulting behaviour towards Miss Bates as such (in fact, he agrees with Emma that Miss Bates is somewhat ridiculous, line 18), but because Emma behaves in this manner to a woman who is socially lower than Emma, i.e. whose status is not at the same rank as Emma's, and who is powerless to change her situation. The passages underlined all refer to Miss Bates's lower position in relation to Emma and the other members of the picnic company. Mr Knightley also explicitly defines the proper comportment of a person in a high position towards a person of lower position: Emma should have shown 'compassion' (line 24) and should have ignored Miss Bates's less attractive characteristics; she should have fulfilled her role as an example of proper conduct for others ('many of whom (certainly *some*,) would be entirely guided by *your* treatment of her', lines 27–28). In this way, he positions Emma in a responsible role that comes with obligations of setting a good example.

In this scene, Mr Knightley also makes a comment about the participation structure by pointing out that the face-loss to Miss Bates has been exacerbated by the fact that Emma's careless comments were witnessed by the picnic company ('and before her niece, too—and before others', line 27). Mr Knightley himself took care that his chiding of Emma was conducted in private ('He looked around, as if to see that no one were near', lines 1–2). This has the dual purpose of saving Emma's face in front of witnesses but also of protecting Mr Knightley's face, who is taking certain liberties in chiding her himself since he is not related to her. He justifies his doing so with his role as counsellor in the past (lines 3–4 and 28–31) and ends with tying his expectations of her future good behaviour to doing justice to him (lines 31–2).

Mr Knightley's judgements of Emma's behaviour are full of assessments that convey negative stance ('acting wrong', 'unfeeling', 'insolent', 'pride', 'laugh at her, humble her') in contrast to his assessment of Miss Bates ('candour and generosity', 'honouring your forbearance'; see passages in italics) and also function as judgements of character. This link of proper and polite conduct with the moral character of a person is an ideology that developed in the eighteenth century in England (for an overview of research about this link, see Locher 2008b). Mr Knightley's judgement culminates in 'It was badly done, indeed!' (line 24). As a result of this encounter, Emma is severely upset, introspects her past behaviour and strives to appear in a better light to Mr Knightley by becoming a better person. The reader, in turn, witnesses Emma being reprimanded and changing her behaviour so that Emma herself becomes an example for female readers at the time.

Note that the lexemes *polite*, *impolite* or *rude* do not occur in this extract. Nevertheless, the discussion can be interpreted as a meta-discussion on what proper manners and conduct were meant to be at the time because Mr Knightley draws on lexemes pertaining to the semantic field of relational work (for a history of the concept 'politeness' in English society, see Fitzmaurice 2010; Jucker 2020). Modern readers can interpret this understanding by contrasting it to present-day ideologies of conduct in relation to how women should behave. Gender and im/politeness concerns are closely intertwined in this extract. An analysis of the acts of positioning, however, allows us to see how the ideologies are transported in the text.

Ideologies on norms of im/politeness can surface in manifold ways in fictional artefacts. Extracts (8.1) and (8.2) *showed* and highlighted instances of relational work in connection with identity construction and plot advancement. Extract (8.3) can be seen in this light too, but is also *telling* about proper relational work at the time in sequences of meta-comments. Fictional texts can thus serve as fascinating data for studying how ideologies are passed on, discussed and negotiated.

8.5 Censuring and manufacturing

We have already established that frames are rarely if ever enacted in full in fiction (see Section 4.5). Evoking a frame is enough to tap into the audience's knowledge about how the activities usually unfold. The effects of cutting a frame short in real life might have repercussions for identity construction. For example, leaving without saying goodbye, receiving a gift without thanking the giver, ending a phone call without a closing sequence, etc. might all result in potentially negative assessments of the speakers. This is because they are breaking frame expectations with respect to action sequences and disrespect the roles of their interactional partners. In the case of fiction, the viewer contract will attune people to the possibility that these actions occur 'off screen' and have been cut for brevity's sake (since storylines are condensed) or because spending time on enacting full sequences would distract from the main storylines. As we have established already on numerous occasions, the fictional artefact does not have to be true to how a similar interaction in non-fictional contexts usually evolves.

Next to these time-saving, space-saving and plot composition considerations, there is, however, a further factor that might influence how fictional products are shaped and this has to do with censorship. Over time, there might be censorship that restricts citizens, journalists, authors and producers in expressing their political, societal, religious and/or sexual beliefs freely in fictional and non-fictional texts. This process is well documented, especially in totalitarian regimes. This censorship can be institutionalised in agencies that check texts for their conformity to mainstream ideologies. Once such a body is established and its parameters known, this can result in self-imposed censorship or creative ways in circumventing censorship in order to produce texts that will pass the censorship hurdles.

A well-known form of rating telecinematic artefacts for their suitability for different types of audience with respect to the inclusion of violence, sexual activity, drugs and substance abuse, and language is the US film rating system (see text box), also in place in different instantiations in other countries. This rating is not enforced by law but acts as an orientation for both viewers and cinema theatres that show movies. Especially for those fictional artefacts where the primary motivation is to become a box office hit or bestseller, taking the target audience into account is a task that influences how certain scenes are composed or what language is used. If the movie is supposed to be suitable for all age groups, this will influence the use of language no matter whether the scenes in question in comparable non-fictional contexts would be full of non-standard language and profanity, violence, explicit sexual activity and substance abuse. Artefacts which nevertheless include these aspects might be shown in fewer movie theatres, at more inconvenient times or require viewers to show age identification if the movie theatre decides to follow the rating.

> **US American movie rating**
>
> G   general audiences
> PG   parental guidance
> PG13 parents are cautioned that material might be inappropriate
> R   restricted, under 17 only with parent
> NC17 no access for people under 17
> (Cressman et al. 2009: 122)

We will focus on swearing to illustrate a linguistic aspect of potential censorship since the inclusion or exclusion of swearing has multiple effects in fictional artefacts. Stapleton (2010: 289) defines swearing as 'a linguistic practice based on taboo, or that which is forbidden; expletives, or "swear-words" can be seen as referring to areas of social or cultural taboo, such as sex or bodily functions'. Swearing can be categorised with respect to what fields the swearwords belong to: excretory/scatological lexemes (i.e. 'bodily functions and associated body parts (e.g., *shit, piss, arse*)'), sexual activity ('those which relate to sexual acts or to genitalia (*fuck, prick, cunt, wank*)') and profanity ('those which refer to religious issues (*damn, goddamn, Chrissake*)') (Stapleton 2010: 290). To what extent the swearwords mentioned carry taboo character depends on many factors, among them the time period when they are used, the particular context in which they are used, and the interactional partners. What is considered taboo, to what degree, and what swearwords are particularly taboo can change over time.

Swearing is generally associated with spoken interaction and we are less used to seeing swearing in print. Within fiction, swearing is thus associated with dialogue. Swearwords can be used quite creatively in interaction. Consider the extracts from the published screenplay *Blue in the Face* (1995), a largely improvised movie, where its characters meet in a corner shop in Brooklyn in Extracts (8.4), (8.5) and (8.6).

(8.4) *Blue in the Face* (Auster 1995: 215, italics added)
Dennis (wheeling around): Don't touch me! How about you don't touch me at all. Okay? How about you keep your greasy little diner *fucking* fingers off me? All right?

(8.5) *Blue in the Face* (Auster 1995: 220, italics added)
Dot: Well, I'm just great. I'm just great. Can I have gum? (She takes a pack from the shelf) I'm just real *fucking* great.

(8.6) *Blue in the Face* (Auster 1995: 248, italics added)
Pete: Abso-*fucking*-lutely I look.

In the extracts, we see a swearword as a modifier of a noun and adjective, and as an insertion into a modifier with the effect of intensification. It is rare to see this in non-dialogic contexts such as academic texts or newspaper articles to express intensification, where a different register choice might be made.

Swearing is multi-functional in fictional and non-fictional contexts alike. Generally, the literature distinguishes between annoyance swearing and social swearing (Montagu 2001; Stapleton 2010). Annoyance swearing can aim at insulting others by engaging in face-attack and involves tensions and stress release. For example, Erin Brockovich's swearing in court or during her interaction with Ed in Extract (8.1) is a result of being upset at the injustice she perceives. To release tension and stress, you might swear at reckless car drivers who are clearly out of earshot and are not even meant to hear the swearing. You might also swear when you hurt yourself or when you are surprised.

Social swearing does not necessarily have negative connotations and can function as a form of social glue that can create and maintain in-groups. For example, a group of friends might use swearwords regularly and without negative impact. The same people might refrain from using swearwords when they interact in different contexts with different people such as during job interviews, work, at university, at wedding receptions or in church.

As Stapleton highlights:

> The interpersonal effects of swearing, then, are shaped by both the context in which it occurs and the social stereotypes/judgments it invokes within this context.
>
> However, the link between swearing and social categories is not a simple or a straightforward one. Instead, categories such as gender, age,

status and socioeconomic class all interact to produce particular identities and effects. (Stapleton 2010: 292)

For example, in the group of friends mentioned above, women and men might use swearwords and are not negatively judged for it. If, however, a man or a woman uses offensive language at work, the woman is usually more harshly criticised than the man and is more severely judged for it (Cressman et al. 2009; Jay and Janschewitz 2008). This societal knowledge of the impact of swearing can be exploited in fictional texts to shape characters and to guide audience assessments.

A first decision might be to include or exclude swearing in order to either meet potential censor guidelines or potentially also to set examples. Children's literature usually does not include offensive swearwords, probably so as not to teach children who might take the heroes and heroines in their book as role models. This does not mean that swearing episodes as such are excluded from children's literature. More often than not, however, the characters would use non-offensive or creative swearing. A case in point is the swearwords in Rowling's *Harry Potter* book series, which are mild even once the characters grow up to be teenagers, and which often take their meaning from the magical world that is created in the books ('Merlin's beard', 'Gallopin' gorgons', 'gulpin' gargoyles'; Vuille-dit-Bille 2018).

In a study on the occurrence of profanity in ninety US teen movies in the 1980s, 1990s and 2000s, Cressman et al. (2009) found that, maybe unexpectedly, the movies from the 1980s use more profanity than those in the 2000s, and in all decades they use the same swearwords. However, male characters use 'more profanity than female characters, and although both sexes frequently use mild profanity, females show a higher percentage for this type and males have a higher percentage for using the seven dirty words' (Cressman et al. 2009: 117). The gendered difference in cultural taboo of swearword usage is thus reflected in teen movies throughout the decades, and thus probably also contributes to perpetuating it.

However, the use of swearing can be unexpected, such as when a female character consistently uses swearwords and thus breaks conventional gender expectations (e.g. Erin Brockovich). It can create humour (e.g. through creative swearing), express emotions and aggression (e.g. in the case of insults or attacks) and create in-groups and out-groups (Stapleton 2010). In all cases, whether a character is made to use swearwords has an impact on character identity construction. This can be commented on, both on the intradiegetic level and the extradiegetic level. In other words, characters can comment on each other's use of swearwords and/or viewers notice their use as marked. Movies that are famous for the swearwords rolling off the tongues of their protagonists include *Pulp Fiction* (1994), *The Big Lebowski* (1998) and *Trainspotting* (1996), as are TV series such as *The Wire* (2002–2009), *The Sopranos* (1999–2007) or *South Park* (since 1997), to name just a few.

8.6 Conclusions

This chapter focused on interpersonal effects that are created in fictional artefacts. To approach this topic from a pragmatic angle, we first introduced the concept of relational work and argued that instantiations of relationship negotiation are imbued with societal ideologies of comportment as well as local community of practice norms. Just as the linguistic cues discussed in Chapter 6 (i.e. phonological, morphological, syntactic and lexical features that are associated with regional, social and ethnic varieties) function as a shorthand for character creation, these features in combination with the norms and ideologies evoked in frames (Chapter 4 and 5) can result in character judgements that are important for the stories being told.

Looking in particular at gender ideologies and im/politeness ideologies, we discussed how these ideologies are often intertwined and cannot be neatly separated. Furthermore, the fictional artefacts can raise issues of gender or im/politeness explicitly or implicitly. This observation is valid on at least two levels.

From an intradiegetic angle, characters might engage in meta-discussions of societal ideologies and thus explicitly use lexemes that evoke the issues raised and reprimand or applaud each other on social conduct. Such renditions are closest to the telling mode. In contrast, characters might be shown to behave in socially unacceptable or refined ways in contrast to other characters and thus be constructed as uncivilised or polished characters without explicitly talking about the ideologies. These would be instances of the showing mode.

From an extradiegetic angle, we can argue that the audience has access to the identity construction that is constructed to be witnessed on the intradiegetic level. In addition, however, the audience will compare what they read or see with their own values informed by present-day ideologies that they have acquired during their own ongoing socialisation. As a consequence, both present-day and past artefacts will be constantly reassessed and might add to maintaining, challenging or questioning ideologies.

We finished the chapter by looking at swearing as a linguistic practice that carries taboo and is multifunctional in its interpersonal effects. This allowed us to highlight once more that authors and producers create effects with the linguistic choices for the characters that populate the story worlds. Just as it is a decision to let a medical doctor or lawyer use technical jargon to a larger or lesser degree, the inclusion or exclusion of swearwords has an impact on character creation. By linking this topic to processes of censorship, we could show that audience design is also key. Finally, swearing can be caused by emotions in characters, can be an emotional release for the characters but can also create emotional reactions in the intradiegetic addressees and the extradiegetic audience. Since processes of judging relational work crucially entail emotional reactions, we need to learn more about emotions. This is the topic of the next chapter.

Key Concepts

Community of practice, face, frame, identity construction, ideology, interpersonal pragmatics, meta-comment, relational work

Exercises

1. Have you ever watched or read a fictional scene and wondered about im/politeness concerns? For example, did you wonder whether the portrayed interaction is really how people do things? Was your assessment mirrored in the characters' uptake as well or were you, as a member of the audience, alone in your assessment? How do such scenes make you reflect on your own expectations about norms of interaction?
2. Do you watch telecinematic artefacts and written fiction from cultures not your own? Find a scene where you noticed issues of relational work that made you realise that different cultural norms are in place. Discuss your interpretation with your colleagues. What did you discover about your own culture and the culture portrayed in the artefact? For example, if you consume Japanese anime, do you think you learn something from it about appropriate Japanese rules of conduct and use of address terms?
3. Interaction sequences in movies and written fiction are often not portrayed in full. For example, a telephone call might be presented as only giving the gist relevant to the plot, leaving out the often quite lengthy sequences of greetings and farewells. Have you ever noticed characters just hanging up without leave-taking words? Does this

AVERAGE TIME SPENT COMPOSING ONE E-MAIL

PROFESSORS: 1.3 SECONDS	GRAD STUDENTS: 1.3 DAYS
YES. (SEND) DO IT. (SEND) SEE ATTACHED. (SEND) NO. (SEND)	DEAR (?) PROF. SMITH, I WAS WONDERING IF PERHAPS YOU MIGHT HAVE POSSIBLY GOTTEN THE CHANCE TO POTENTIALLY FIND THE TIME TO MAYBE LOO... DRAFT PAPER THAT... AM AT... N JUST IN CASE). I... ARE V... F YOU HAVE ANY QU... WHATS... ON'T HESISTATE TO...

JORGE CHAM © 2008   WWW.PHDCOMICS.COM

Figure 8.1 PhD Comics by Jorge Cham (2008). 'Average time spent composing one e-mail'. (Piled Higher and Deeper Publishing. Reproduced with permission)

have any impact on judgements of politeness concerning the characters on your side or do you allow the fictional contract to take over?

4. Looking at the fictionalised rendition in Figure 8.1 of how a supervisor and a PhD student typically correspond, assess the cartoon with the help of Table 8.1. What factors might influence the different writing styles?

Further reading

In this chapter we draw on insights from interpersonal pragmatics and im/politeness research. For recent overviews of the field, see Culpeper et al. (2017), Locher (2018) and Locher and Graham (2010). For frames (Chapters 4 and 5) and characterisation cues (Chapter 6), we direct the reader to literature pointers in the respective chapters. The combination of fiction and im/politeness concerns is reviewed in Dynel (2017), Kizelbach (2017) and McIntyre and Bousfield (2017). Studies on past relational work norms can be found in numerous publications such as work on Medieval English texts (Jucker 2010, 2020), English Renaissance plays (e.g. Kizelbach 2017; Kopytko 1995; Jucker 2020; Rudanko 2006) and texts from the eighteenth (see Jucker 2018, 2020) or nineteenth centuries (e.g. Davidson 2004), to name just a few.

9 The language of emotion

9.1 Introduction

Emotions are one of the basic ingredients of fiction. Probably all of us have been moved emotionally at one time or another, or perhaps even regularly, by the events depicted in fictional contexts. We may have experienced joy and delight about the happy outcome of a romantic love story after a rollercoaster of emotions of anxiety, anticipation and relief as the events were unfolding. We may have felt despair and grief about the distressing events experienced by characters in sad and tragic movies like *Brokeback Mountain* or *Still Alice*, or dread and fear about the sinister and supernatural events of horror movies, such as *It*, *Godzilla* or *Jaws*.

What is truly extraordinary about such emotions that we as viewers experience is the fact that they are based on what we know to be fictitious events experienced by fictitious characters. The events that we are witnessing are performed by actors in front of a camera or on a stage in a theatre, or we may, in fact, just read about them in a printed book or an e-book on some handheld electronic device. In movies, the events may appear to be particularly real because of the naturalistic depiction on the screen, but similar emotions may, of course, also be experienced in the narrative form of a book.

In Chapter 2, we introduced the notion of the fictional contract, i.e. the silent agreement between the producer and the recipient of fictional artefacts that the depicted characters and events are not real but fictitious, and in spite of this, the experienced emotions that we undergo can be very real. This poses some interesting challenges for a pragmatic approach to fiction. The two most important of these are the following questions:

- How do fictitious characters communicate their emotions or how are these emotions depicted by the narrator? How is language used to display emotions and what other means of communication are employed to transmit emotions?

- How do the emotions of characters and the depicted fictitious events combine to create emotions for the viewers or readers?

These questions immediately give rise to some additional questions that also need to be tackled if we want to reach a better understanding of the above problems. First and foremost, we need to find out something about the nature of emotions. We may have a fairly clear idea of what they are in a pre-theoretical sense, but it is more difficult to describe them in such a way that they become empirically observable. In addition, if we want to find out how actors display (fictitious) emotions, we need to know how emotions are communicated in non-fictitious situations. How do people show their emotions, and how do other people perceive emotions?

We are concerned both with the emotions that are part of the fictitious world, i.e. emotions experienced by the depicted characters, and with the emotions experienced by the viewers or readers. In some cases, the recipients may feel similar emotions to those experienced by the characters. We rejoice or commiserate with the success or failure of our hero. We are sad when something sad happens to the characters we sympathise with. In other cases, our emotions clearly diverge from those of specific characters. We might take delight in the agony undergone by the evil villain, or we are amused and entertained by the distress and anguish suffered by a particularly clumsy and awkward character who gets caught up in comical situations.

There is a large body of research on emotions from a psychological perspective. In pragmatics, on the other hand, such research is still relatively scarce (but see Bednarek 2008; Langlotz 2017 for an overview; and Mackenzie and Alba-Juez 2019 for a recent collection of relevant papers). In this chapter, we want to tease out how emotions are communicated in fictional contexts. In particular, we want to show how language is used to reflect the depicted emotions and how this relates to the emotions that we as the recipients of fictional artefacts experience. We start this endeavour by looking at the nature of emotions in general and how they are communicated in real life (Section 9.2). In Section 9.3, we argue that in fiction emotions are discursively constructed. In written fiction, the author creates them in the narrative and in the interactions between the characters, and in performed fiction, they are performed by the actors. In Section 9.4, we then focus on the specific verbal and non-verbal cues that are used to display emotions and discuss these first with a *Calvin and Hobbes* cartoon, in which emotions are somewhat stylised and exaggerated, and then in an extract from the movie *My Life Without Me* by Isabel Coixet in which emotions are more complex and communicated not only through verbal and facial cues of the actor Sarah Polley, who plays the main protagonist Ann in the movie, but also through the entire mise en scène of the extract. In Section 9.5, we focus on the fictional paradox, i.e. the question of how the audience is affected by events and emotions that are known to be fictitious.

9.2 The nature of emotions

Emotions are not easy to define. So, instead of a clear-cut definition, we want to describe them in terms of their components, and in this we follow what psychologists call 'process theories of emotion' (see Planalp 1999: 11–34; see also Langlotz 2017: 518). Planalp (1999: 11) distinguishes five specific components that are essential for emotions:

- objects, causes, precipitating events
- appraisal
- physiological changes
- action tendencies, action, expression
- regulation.

Let us have a look at each of these components in turn. First of all, emotions generally are about something. They are about some object or precipitating event that caused them. In Chapter 5, we conjured up an upsetting and emotional experience that formed the core of a personal narrative. The incident involved a cyclist, let us call her Emma, who on the way to work got car-doored. A careless driver parked his car and opened its door into the street without checking the rear mirror or looking back, and Emma on her bike ran into the car door, fell and suffered some minor injuries. As a result, Emma is upset. She also gets angry because the driver does not apologise and instead blames her for the accident. Only a moment ago, she was perfectly content and looking forward to her day's work at university. But the incident changed all that.

Her emotions, thus, have two very specific *causes*: the car driver and his carelessness as well as his blaming the accident on the cyclist instead of acknowledging responsibility. In real life, things are often more complex than this. Emma might be especially angry because this is already the third time this week that a careless driver has put her in a dangerous situation. She might have had a rough morning already because one of her dogs had ruined a carpet and there was no milk left in the fridge for her breakfast. Or on the way to work she was already late for an important appointment and has now lost even more time through this incident. In all these cases, being car-doored was not the sole cause of her emotion. Causes of emotions are often difficult to determine because almost anything can create an emotional response. Even emotions themselves, either somebody else's or your own, can be the cause of emotions, such as when you feel angry about your partner's jealousy or guilty about enjoying an ethnic joke (Planalp 1999: 17).

While more or less anything can be the cause of emotions, not everything is. Life would probably be unbearable if it were. There has to be a process of *appraisal* to give certain events emotional meaning. We feel strongly about events and objects that concern us in some way and that affect our well-being (Planalp 1999: 19). The minor bike accident is an obvious example. Emma suffered some injuries, she lost time on her way to work and she realised that the accident could have been much worse. If an approaching tram had already reached them when the collision took place, the accident would have been much more severe. The ways in which events concern us and affect our well-being can be small or large. If you lose a cheap ball-point pen, it may not affect you very much, but if that object is connected with important memories of who had given it to you, you may feel much more strongly about it. The object has emotional value for you. If you fail an exam for which you did not prepare very much because it does not really matter very much in the further course of your studies and you did not invest any great pride in doing well, your emotional reaction may be limited. If, on the other hand, you spent a lot of time preparing for the exam because of its importance for the future course of your studies and because you really wanted to do well in this exam, your emotions are likely to be much stronger.

Emotions often produce *physiological changes* in the body. After the accident, Emma's heart rate and blood pressure are affected, and she may still be trembling half an hour later when she arrives at her place of work. But such physiological changes do not occur in all situations in which we experience emotions, and different people may undergo different levels or even different types of physiological changes. Some of these changes may be indistinguishable from the effects of exercise, drugs or sex (Planalp 1999:26), and there is no direct correspondence between specific emotions and specific types of physiological changes.

Emotions urge us to *act* in certain ways, to give expression to the emotions, or perhaps, in the case of sadness for example, to abstain from action, but they may also be *regulated*. Emma, for instance, may have the immediate urge to share a sense of relief that nothing more serious has happened with the driver who was at first startled and asked about her well-being. Once the first emotional reaction to the incident has passed, the frame of how to deal with accidents is activated also on a cognitive level (see Chapters 4 and 8). This entails establishing who is at fault, acknowledging blame and apologising in an adequate manner. Showing remorse and indicating non-intentionality might be expected actions from the driver. This 'display rule' for emotions (Ekman and Friesen

> **Display rules** are 'products of emotional socialization' that 'involve a learned response that modifies spontaneous emotional displays to be socially appropriate' (Andersen and Guerrero 1998: 54).

1975) would be expected even if the driver is not entirely convinced of his own fault (see text box). He, however, rejects this role and instead shifts blame to the cyclist. Emma perceives this as unfair and as adding insult to injury because she is assigned the offender's role rather than the victim's role. Realising that shouting at the careless car driver or perhaps even physically attacking him or his car would be futile actions to vent her anger, she retrieves her bike and cycles off to university where she can vent her emotions by telling her colleagues. Emotions can thus also be regulated.

Emotion regulation is not just the last component of a process description of emotions; it is, in fact, an integral part of the entire process. While Emma actively acknowledges how lucky she was to suffer only minor injuries and feels relief because of this, being wrongly accused of being the cause of the accident makes her feel anger and frustration, which she chooses not to display. Throughout this experience, Emma might also have tried to regulate her physiological reaction by forcing herself to calm down and take some deep breaths. Appraisal and regulation were active in both phases of the accident incident.

The accident frame evoked in the example entails the construction of identities. We have seen in Chapter 8 that emotions play a crucial role in assessing the appropriate level of relational work and how this is tied to identity construction. A further example where socially constructed display rules help us to deal with emotions and to choose a socially adequate display would be expressing condolences. In other contexts, we learn to intensify our emotions (e.g. when small children want something) or to hide them (e.g. public displays of affection might be toned down) (Anderson and Guerrero 1998: 54).

9.3 Two modes of presenting emotions in fiction

In fiction, emotions are discursively constructed (Langlotz 2017: 518). They are created and put on display for an audience, and there are two ways of doing this. In Chapter 7, we introduced the distinction between a showing mode of presentation, in which the reader experiences the fictitious events as an observer, and a telling mode of presentation, in which the narrator is in control and tells us what is happening. In performed fiction, actors make use of their art to display emotions. They perform characters and show us how these characters experience and display emotions. For this they can make use of more or less the same resources as people in real life. They can vary their voice quality from bashful whining to boisterous shouting, from a sad whisper to an angry roar and so on. They can use their bodies to indicate disgust or fear, and their faces to indicate joy or sorrow and so on. In Section 9.4 below we will give an outline of such resources, which in the context of fiction we call 'emotion cues'. Different art forms obviously rely on different sets of cues. Movies can use close-ups to focus in great detail on facial cues including the eye movements and even tears. On a stage with a large auditorium, such details would be lost on the audience and the actors have to rely more exclusively on those cues that carry over larger distances, for instance their voice and their body posture. Written fiction, on the other hand, relies heavily on the telling mode. Emotions and all their individual components as introduced in Section 9.2 can be made explicit. Narrators can explicitly name the emotions experienced by some characters, and they can explicitly describe specific physiological changes, e.g. that a character's voice was shaking with anger.

Bednarek (2008) draws the same terminological distinction when she talks of 'emotional talk' and 'emotion talk'. She defines 'emotional talk' as 'including all sorts of human behaviour that signal emotion *without* the recourse to linguistic expressions that explicitly denote emotion (*emotion talk*)' (Bednarek 2008: 11, italics in original). In her corpus study of the language of emotion, she is interested in the verbal level of expressing and describing emotions. And accordingly, emotional talk *signals* emotions ('Oh, hell!'). It displays emotions directly as a verbal emotion cue. Emotion talk *denotes* emotions ('I'm really angry') (Bednarek 2008: 11), that is to say it talks about emotion. Langlotz (2017) uses the terms 'expression of emotion' and 'description of emotion' to refer to the same distinction.

Figure 9.1 shows the two modes of presenting emotions in fiction and how they overlap. Both modes can be used both in performed fiction and in written fiction, but typically, as just pointed out, performed fiction relies more on the showing mode and written fiction on the telling mode. In the showing mode, characters produce appropriate emotion cues (see Sections 9.2 and 9.4), while in the telling mode the narrator or a character talks about emotions and makes use of emotion

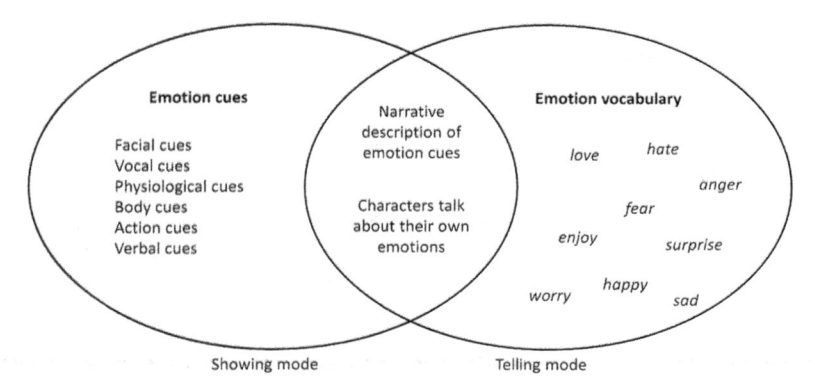

Figure 9.1 Two modes of presenting emotions in fiction

vocabulary (see Bednarek 2008). There is a significant overlap between the two circles to represent those cases in which the narrative voice, for instance, describes specific emotion cues or characters display their emotions by explicitly talking about them.

The following three extracts are retrieved from the fiction section of the Corpus of Contemporary American English (COCA). They illustrate how narrative fiction can describe the different components of feelings outlined above. And they illustrate both the showing mode and the telling mode. The words in italics all point to cues that index emotions.

(9.1) Frederik Pohl, *O Pioneer*, COCA, Fiction, 1997 (italics added)
1   He *shook his head*. 'The damage is just unbelievable, but you know what is the
2   worst part of it? It's the way he left his *poor widow* and their unborn child–' That
3   was *more than Rina could take*. 'Turn the *bastard* off,' she said, her *voice*
4   *shaking with anger* at the man. But *the fury she felt* had one good quality. It told
5   her that she did have one definite thing to go on living for.

(9.2) Mary T. Burton, *Senseless*, COCA, Fiction, 2011 (italics added)
1   Absently, Eva rubbed the scar on the back of her shoulder. *God*, she'd been *so*
2   *very* wrong. *Shaking off anger and sadness*, she pushed on the gas and slowly
3   drove away. No more memories. *No more sadness.*

(9.3) Stephen Goodwin, *We Can't Make You Whole Again*, COCA, Fiction, 2018 (italics added)
1   'You're *cruel* when you drink.'
2   'I think I'm entitled to a drink on the day I have to give up my *happy place*.'
3   'I should go,' she said. 'I can't talk to you now.'
4   'I'd say it's a very good time to talk. You've caught me at a moment when I have

5 a lot to say.'
6 Mary Mac's eyes were *cloudy with tears*. 'I have to tell you *I'm mad* – yes, I am.
7 *I'm angry*. Not because you won't stop drinking, even though I pray every day
8 that you will stop. *I'm angry* because you don't talk to me. You leave me out. We
9 should make decisions like this together.'

Strong emotions are described both by the narratorial voice and through the utterances of the characters. The extracts present different emotions and focus on different aspects of them. In Extract (9.1), the character Rina's emotions are anger and fury. Together with some other characters she watches an interview on television in which the interviewee relates some details of an accident in which – allegedly – her husband has died and in which she herself is described as 'poor widow' (line 2). The narrative focuses on the physiological changes – her voice is shaking because of her strong emotion. Her use of the expletive 'bastard' is an example of a verbal emotion cue (line 3). It shows her strong emotion directly. And her utterance shows her action tendency. She takes action to get somebody to switch the television off.

Extract (9.2) focuses on the regulation process. Eva re-evaluates the cause of her emotions of sadness and anger. She changes its appraisal. In fact, she decides to shake off the emotions that she now deems to be inappropriate and resolves to ban them from her memory.

Extract (9.3) presents the emotions both in the showing mode and in the telling mode. They mostly appear in the interaction between Mary Mac and her interlocutor. She calls him 'cruel' (line 1), and he talks about his 'happy place' (line 2). The narrator picks out one noteworthy component of Mary's emotion, the physiological change that leads to her eyes becoming cloudy with tears (line 6). At this point, Mary's emotion is not explicitly mentioned but to some extent inferable through the narrator's description of the physiological changes that it causes. Immediately afterwards, in her utterance, Mary very explicitly talks about this emotion (lines 6–8). Thus, we see two ways in which the showing mode and the telling mode can be combined (the intersection in Figure 9.1). The narrator tells us about how characters display their emotions, or characters show us their emotions by explicitly talking about them.

9.4 Emotion cues in fiction

Without a narratorial voice, performative fiction relies to a large extent on the characters' display of emotions, and in this section, we are concerned with the repertoire of cues that are used for this purpose. Let

THE LANGUAGE OF EMOTION   181

Figure 9.2 CALVIN AND HOBBES © 1990 Watterson. (Reprinted with permission of ANDREWS MCMEEL SYNDICATION. All rights reserved)

us start with a *Calvin and Hobbes* comic strip by Bill Watterson (Figure 9.2). In this strip, strong emotions appear on several levels and they are displayed both in the drawings and in the words (see also Langlotz and Locher 2013). Cartoons are, of course, very stylised in their representation of emotions. They magnify and exaggerate. Some of the emotion cues relate to the physiological changes mentioned in Section 9.2. But even in their exaggerated form, it is not a straightforward task to actually identify specific emotions on the basis of individual cues; in fact, individual cues often combine into a 'composite signal' (Clark 1996: 185). However, the simplifications and exaggerations of a cartoon also help us to disentangle the different levels of these cues.

The cartoon depicts the interaction between six-year-old Calvin and his classmate, neighbour and favourite playground adversary, Susie. Bill Watterson describes their relationship as follows: 'I suspect Calvin has a mild crush on her that he expresses by trying to annoy her, but Susie is a bit unnerved and put off by Calvin's weirdness. This encourages Calvin to be even weirder, so it's a good dynamic' (Watterson 2020: n.p.). Preceding this particular strip, Calvin pinched Susie's favourite doll, Binky Betsy, in order to upset and blackmail Susie. In retaliation, Susie has kidnapped Calvin's stuffed pet tiger, Hobbes. In this strip, Calvin wants to return Binky Betsy in order to retrieve Hobbes, but things get very emotional.

Emotions are presented both in the telling mode and in the showing mode. Susie explicitly talks about her preference for Hobbes ('I'm thinking I might rather have your tiger', panel 2), about Calvin's feelings for Binky Betsy ('You'll grow to like her', panel 3), and about Hobbes' feelings for her ('I think Hobbes likes it better here with me', panel 4). But the really strong emotions are not talked about. They are displayed, in particular by Calvin, who moves from irritation and disgust to anger and frustration, and they are mainly displayed through his voice quality, body posture and facial expression. Calvin's voice quality is represented by increasingly large and bold letters which invite us to infer an increase in the intensity of his voice. In panel 2, 'AAHH' and 'doll' stand out to express his disgust at Susie's doll, and in panel 4, he shouts 'HE DOES NOT!' (note the capitalisation and bold print to index intensity) in his frustration and anger at Susie's suggestion that Hobbes might like her more than him. The cartoon also depicts some of the physiological changes that the emotions are causing for Calvin. His eyes and mouth are wide open in disgust, he is sweating visibly and in the last panel his large open mouth signals his screaming. In panel 2, he holds Binky Betsy with outstretched arms to keep her as far away from him as possible (embodying the gender stereotype that boys do not play with dolls). And in panel 3, his body bends backwards to get away from Susie, who encouragingly leans forward. According to her, Calvin will come to like Binky Betsy, and Hobbes likes her better than Calvin, which the reader easily recognises as a strategic and highly successful way of enraging Calvin and punishing him for his previous misdemeanour. Readers are very likely to interpret her smile in the third frame as smug satisfaction at having taught Calvin a lesson. In panel 4, her posture changes. She crosses her arms and turns her back to Calvin in order to demonstrate how, in her opinion, Hobbes feels about Calvin. In the process of reading and interpreting this cartoon, the reader will take into account all the available emotion cues to combine them to a composite signal (Clark 1996).

Thus, the telling mode of presenting emotions relies on the verbal level. The characters explicitly talk about how they feel about things and how they suspect others are feeling, or ought to be feeling, about things. The showing mode, on the other hand, uses a combination of modalities to display emotions. Characters show their emotions through their facial expression, their tone of voice or physiological cues. They show them through their posture and through the way they act, and, last but not least, they show them through the words they utter. In the case of the written cartoon conventions, the size of letters, use of bold and capitalisation also carry emotional cues. Table 9.1 gives an overview of the different modalities and cues that are used to display emotions. Emotion cues do not unambiguously stand for specific emotions. The bold font and the large letters clearly indicate shouting, but they do not tell us directly what kind of emotions they index. Susie's smile and Calvin's wide-open mouth likewise can stand for a whole range of emotions. It is only in the larger context and in cooperation with all the different levels that the reader can assess the emotions that are involved.

Table 9.1 Overview of emotion cues (based on Planalp 1998: 31–37 and Langlotz and Locher 2013: 94)

Class of cues	Forms of realisation	Examples in Figure 9.2
Facial cues	– Facial expressions of emotion through forehead and eyebrows, eyes and eyelids, and the lower face (mouth, lips, nasolabial folds)	C's wide-open mouth (P2, P3, P4) S's smug smile (P3)
Vocal cues	– Voice quality: low, loud, slow, fast, trembling, high-pitched, monotonous, animated voice	C's loud voice (P2, P4)
Physiological cues	– Blushing, pupil dilation, heart rate, breathing, skin temperature	C's perspiration, wide eyes (P2, P3, P4)
Body cues	– Body posture: stiff/rigid, droopy, upright, leaning forward or back, turning – Hand/arm gestures: hand emblems, clenching hands or fists – Animated, energetic movement – Gait: walking heavily, lightly, arm swing, length/speed of stride	C's outstretched arms (P2) C's leaning back (P3) S's leaning forward (P3) S's turning her back to C (P4)
Action cues	– Throwing things, making threatening movements, kissing, caressing	S's leaning forward (P3)
Verbal cues	– Language-specific emotion vocabularies – Interjections, repetitions – Metaphors – Speech acts – Emotional discourse practices	*Dumb doll* (P1) *Aahh!* (P2), *No! No!* (P3)

Note: C: *Calvin*, S: *Susie*, P: *panel*

Let us now turn to a performed example, an extract from the movie *My Life Without Me* (2002) by Isabel Coixet, which is based on the short story by Nanci Kincaid 'Pretending the Bed is a Raft' (1997). Twenty-three-year-old Ann has been told that she has only two or three more months to live. She decides not to tell her husband or her two little daughters or anybody else but instead compiles a bucket list of all the things that she still wants to do before she dies. She tries to arrange as much as she can for the time after her death so that those that are dear to her will continue to have a good life, but she also indulges in a few secret desires as long as she still can. One of the items on her list is a series of tapes that she wants to record for every one of her daughters' birthdays until they are eighteen. In Extract (9.4), she records the first one for her older, six-year-old daughter, Penny. She uses a portable cassette player for the purpose, a so-called Walkman, which was a popular device in the 1980s and 1990s.

(9.4) *My Life Without Me*, 2002, at 42.24

((Ann sits in her parked car. It is night. She talks into a Walkman and records a birthday message for her six-year-old daughter, Penny. No background music; there is just a faint idea of traffic noise outside the car. (*): position of screenshots of Figure 9.3, p. 186.))

1 'hey my buddy 'Penny. (*1)   ((bravely cheerful smile))
2 .. I'm ^not going to be at your 'birthday party,
3 but there's ^nothing I'd like more=
4 =in the ^who=le, wide world.   ((deep breath; wistful smile))
5 I bet 'Grandma's made a special 'birthday cake just for=   ((fast))
6 ='you with your name on it in big 'chocolate letters.   ((fast))
7 (3 sec)   ((bites her lips))
8 ^Penny, (4 sec)
9 I ^want you to 'know that.
10 the ^day that you were 'born.
11 .. I ^held you in my ^arms a--
12 and that was the ^happiest day in my 'whole life. ((teary voice; happy, sad smile))
13 (3 sec)   ((teary voice, shakes head, eyes glistening))
14 I was so 'happy I couldn't even ^speak. (*2)   ((happy, wistful smile))
15 (2 sec)
16 I just 'stroked your ^tiny little feet and I cried with 'happiness.
17 .. without ^you I could have never found out that lions eat=   ((factual, quick))
18 =^pancakes o=r that the bed could be a 'raft.   ((factual, quick))
19 ^try and look after Patsy 'okay?   ((serious face))
20 (4 sec)   ((closes eyes))
21 I ^know it's hard 'cause sometimes she makes you=
22 =^mad and everything, (*3)   ((creaky voice))
23 (2 sec)   ((shakes head))
24 I ^know it's not easy being a big sister, buddy=
25 =but I know that you can do it ^okay?   ((smiles encouragingly))
26 (4 sec)
27 Mommy sends you ^millions and millions of 'kisses. (*4)
28   ((kisses recorder, sniffs, switches it off and removes tape))

The scene is very emotional for the character and presumably also for many viewers, not only on the basis of what is said but also on the basis of how it is said and the speaker's facial expressions. The tape that Ann records will be played at Penny's birthday, usually a joyful occasion for a small girl, but for Penny it will also be a very sad occasion because her mother will have died by then. What the viewer witnesses here is a one-way interaction. Ann talks to her daughter, who at this point cannot respond and who will only hear her voice on the tape at a later stage in time. Ann talks about her own emotions, i.e. her wish to be at the birthday party (lines 3–4) and about her happiness when Penny was born (lines 12, 14, 16), and she talks about Penny's emotions ('sometimes she makes you mad and everything', lines 21–22). These emotions are presented in the telling mode. But in this scene, the showing mode is equally important.

Penny will not see her mother's face when, at her birthday, she will listen to the tape. Nevertheless, Ann's emotions are displayed on all the levels listed in Table 9.1. The transcription in Extract (9.4) tries to capture some of this in the marginal comments, but these notes necessarily fall short of the full complexity and interaction of the different modalities, and some of the comments already provide an interpretation and transgress beyond a mere description of the visuals.

Probably the strongest way in which the actor Sarah Polley shows Ann's emotions is in her facial expressions. Figure 9.3 provides four screenshots from this scene. Throughout the scene, we see Ann's face in a close-up from a slightly low angle perspective. It changes several times between a profile shot from the right and a portrait shot of her entire face, and we see how it reflects her emotions, which waver between love, happy memories, encouragement and sadness. The lighting is low-key and creates strong contrasts between bright and dark parts of the image. Thus, it is not only Sarah Polley's skilful use of emotion cues in this particular context of a parked car (the so-called mise en scène; see text box) which creates the emotionality of the scene but also the way in which the camera work captures these cues (see text box). Here the

---

The **mise en scène** (French for 'placing on stage') refers to the composition and arrangement of everything that is placed before the camera, including the characters, their costumes, the location, lighting and so on.

The term **camera work** refers to the different shot sizes and scales (long shot, close-up, extreme close-up, etc.), the shot angles (low, eye-level, high, etc.) and viewpoints (in relation to the character) in which a scene is filmed. 'Metaphorically speaking, the camera is like the eye through which we see the world that is staged' (Langlotz 2017: 536).

Figure 9.3 Screenshots (details) from *My Life Without Me* (2002), Sarah Polley as Ann, at 43.04 (line 1 of Extract 9.4); 43.34 (line 14); 43.54 (line 22); 44.04 (line 27). (Reproduced with permission)

viewer gets the impression of being very close to Ann in the twilight of the streetlights outside the car. A medium long shot in broad daylight would have created a very different kind of effect (see Detenber and Lang 2011; Langlotz 2017: 536–539).

Ann starts her recording with what looks like a brave and at the same time cheerful smile (screenshot 1). She is trying to put on a happy mood for what should be a joyful occasion for Penny (line 1). But Ann will not be there when Penny hears her message, and her face changes into a wistful smile of regret. She talks about her joyful memories of when Penny was born, and her face puts on a happy look tinged with a shade of sadness and nostalgia (screenshot 2). When she admonishes Penny to look after her smaller sister Patsy, Ann's face gets more serious (screenshot 3), and at the end of her emotional recording, she kisses her daughter goodbye (screenshot 4) before she switches off the tape recorder, and at the same time her facial display of emotions gives way to a matter-of-fact face that needs to tick off one more item on the list of the things she still wants to do before she dies.

The vocal quality is, of course, something that will be preserved by the recording for her daughter. In the course of the recording, it goes through several distinct stages. At several points it adopts a somewhat teary quality. Ann is not crying, even when she talks about how she cried with happiness when Penny was born (line 16), but her slightly quavering voice faintly suggests the possibility of crying, a vocal cue of her sadness. At other points, her voice changes to a much more factual quality. She also varies speed and delivers some passages noticeably faster than the rest (lines 5–6 and 17–18).

There are also some physiological emotion cues. The close-up of Ann's face shows that at some point her eyes seem to get watery and close to actual tears (line 13). This is, of course, quite a remarkable feat for the actor, Sarah Polley, who performs these emotions in such a convincing way that it triggers actual physiological changes in her body. Throughout the recording, Ann sits in her parked car. She does not move much, except for handling the Walkman. Sometimes, she shifts slightly as if trying to get into a better position for the next sequence of the recording. The different sequences conjure up somewhat different emotions, from regret at not being at the party to happy memories and to advice on looking after Patsy, and it appears that between these sequences, Ann rearranges her position and facial expression in order to get ready for the appropriate emotions for the next sequence of what she wants to record. At the end of the recording she accompanies her verbal 'millions and millions of kisses' with an actual kiss placed on the microphone of the tape recorder.

There are many vocabulary choices that might be interpreted as verbal emotion cues, e.g. the address term that she uses for her daughter, 'my buddy Penny' and 'buddy' (lines 1 and 24), her reference to the 'who=le, wide world' (line 4), the 'tiny little feet' (line 16), or her self-reference 'Mommy' and the 'millions and millions of kisses' (line 27).

Ann's recording is interspersed with many pauses of between 2 and 4 seconds (lines 7, 8, 13, 15, 20, 23 and 26). Silence is neither a vocal nor a verbal cue per se and as such is not listed explicitly in Table 9.1, nor can it always be linked to the display of emotions. From a pragmatic point of view, silence is meaningful and needs to be interpreted in its context (see Kurzon 2011). For example, if silence follows a question, the person who asked will interpret this withholding of an answer as carrying meaning and will draw conclusions (imagine the question was 'Will you marry me?'). In the case of Extract (8.1) in the previous chapter, there is

13 seconds of silence after Erin Brockovich's heated speech to get hired. During this silence, which is full of suspense as to how Ed will react, Erin switches from being angry and upset to being desperate, a process that is made accessible to the viewers by focusing on Erin's face. In the case of the silence in Extract (9.4), the silence functions in different ways but is also primarily used to stage Ann's emotions. She organises her thoughts, composes her facial expressions and emotions in order to get through the points she wants to cover and is being silenced by the sheer power of emotion as well, before she composes herself again to continue. The multimodal possibilities of a telecinematic artefact allow silence to display its full pragmatic potential. The rendition of silence in written form is restricted to being signalled as truncated sentences, ellipses or meta-comments by narrators. It still carries pragmatic meaning, but is less powerful than performed silence.

The emotional effect of this short scene depends on the interaction between the different emotion cues. Ann talks about emotions and she displays a range of different emotions with cues from all categories listed in Table 9.1. The mise en scène, the camera work and the lighting also contribute to the emotional effect. Movies often support specific emotions with appropriate music. We are probably all familiar with movie scenes that appear to be perfectly peaceful and happy when all of a sudden the music suggests a growing tension and we know that something terrible is going to happen any moment now. Alternatively, the appearance of a sweet melody rendered by violins might trigger anticipation of a romantic scene (for the role of sound and music in films, see Atencia-Linares 2019; Dyck 2019).[1] In the scene depicted in Extract (9.4), there is no music, and apart from some distant and barely noticeable traffic noise the only thing we hear is Ann's voice, which gives the scene an increased intimacy and emotionality, even though it is difficult to specify how exactly all these individual elements contribute to it. Is it mainly Ann's face full of emotions, the message itself that she records for her daughter, the way her voice delivers the message, the way the camera captures this particular scene, or the larger context of the incongruity of a joyful birthday party and Penny's loss of her mother? It is important to remember that all the elements listed so far

---

[1] The function of music in telecinematic artefacts is not restricted to the creation of emotions. Particular music can stand for characters in the sense of a leitmotif, music can place a scene in time and space or can be used to parody and create contradictions, etc. An informative overview with clips, 'What is the function of film music?' by Robin Hoffmann, can be found at <https://www.robin-hoffmann.com/tutorials/what-is-the-function-of-film-music/> (last accessed 2 October 2020). An academic discussion is provided in Atencia-Linares (2019) and Dyck (2019).

have emotional potential. They add to the emotional impact of a scene, but they do not have fixed emotional meanings (Langlotz 2017: 538). And needless to say, not everybody reacts in the same way to the emotionality of a specific scene. This is the topic of the following section.

9.5 The paradox of fiction: real and fake emotions

In the previous sections of this chapter, we have seen that emotions in fiction are discursively constructed. They are presented in a telling mode by narrators who explicitly name emotions that are experienced by their characters or who describe specific emotion cues that signal characters' emotions. Or they are presented in a showing mode by actors who play characters and who strive to display emotion cues that make the characters' emotions authentic and believable. In either case, the emotions are constructed for the reader or viewer, and in that sense, they are not real. Nevertheless, readers and viewers are regularly touched by these emotions. They may share the sadness and grief or the joy and happiness of individual characters for a while in spite of the fact that they know these emotions to be fictitious. This is the paradox of fiction. We cannot hope to solve the paradox, but in this section, we want to disentangle some of the issues that pertain to this paradox.

In Section 9.2, we presented the five components of emotions according to a process theory of emotions (following Planalp 1999), and in Section 9.4, we gave an outline of the different emotion cues that can signal emotions. The assumption behind this was that both the process components and the display cues are roughly the same in real life, where people experience real emotions, and in fictional contexts, where actors perform fictitious emotions as if they were real. How close the similarity is between the display of real emotions and the performance of fictitious emotions is, of course, an open question. To some extent it depends on the art of the actors whether their display of emotion cues comes across as authentic or not. Some cues, in particular the physiological changes that people may undergo when experiencing emotions, may be particularly challenging to perform. In Extract (9.4) above and in screenshot 2 reproduced in Figure 9.3, we have seen that Sarah Polley's eyes are glistening with tears when she plays Ann at this particular moment in *My Life Without Me*.

For the academic analysis of emotions, whether real or fictitious, it is a problem that there is no one-to-one correspondence between specific cues and specific emotions. Tears can be a cue for sadness and grief, but they can also be a cue for extreme joy and happiness. Moreover, cues are not displayed individually. They work together in highly complex composite signals (Clark 1996), which makes it even more difficult to assign specific emotional values to them. In lines 8–16 in Extract (9.4) above, Ann tells her daughter about the happiest moment in her life, the time when Ann held her newborn baby in her arms, and she talks about her happy tears of that moment, almost six years ago. The memory brings back the happy emotions, but they are mixed with the sad knowledge that she will not be there to celebrate Penny's sixth birthday with her.

A second problem concerns the way in which the fictitious emotions in fictional artefacts relate to the actual emotions experienced by the audience. There is clearly no simple one-to-one relationship in the sense that readers or viewers experience the same emotions as the depicted characters. In the case of the *Calvin and Hobbes* cartoon presented in Section 9.4, readers can easily discern Calvin's emotions of disgust, anger and frustration, but they are unlikely to share these emotions. They are more likely to be amused, or, perhaps, they can relate to the feelings in some nostalgic way if these (exaggerated) feelings relate in some way to their own painful childhood memories, even if they do not share them now. This is different in the case of *My Life Without Me*. Viewers will differ in how much they are touched by the depicted events, but here they are more likely to feel with the characters. But even in this case, viewer emotions may diverge considerably from the depicted character emotions. Perhaps the cheerful happiness of the two daughters in some of the scenes makes some viewers sad because they know about the grief that they will soon experience when they lose their mother. Maybe they are reminded of the loss of a close person of their own and project Ann's case onto their own life experience, or they imagine how it would feel to lose persons equally close to themselves as Ann is to her daughters.

But why are we drawn in at all and why do we develop emotions, sometimes very strong emotions, about fictitious characters experiencing fictitious emotions because of fictitious events? Zillmann (2011: 101) asks, 'How can the depiction of patently make-believe events exert such power over our emotions?' and Langlotz (2017: 544), 'How do fictionally staged "fake" representations of emotional processes manage to trigger "real" emotional processes in the audience? Why can we feel about fantasy?' This is what has been described as the paradox of fiction by Radford and Weston (1975) in their article 'How can we be moved by the fate of Anna Karenina?'. At a certain level, and as a result of the fictional contract, we are always aware that the actor Sarah Polley is not going to die, that Penny and Patsy are not her real daughters and that the emotion cues that we are witnessing are discursively constructed for the viewers' benefit. But this does not stop us from getting emotionally involved, albeit perhaps only temporarily until we have left the cinema or turned our attention to something else.

In Chapter 3, we introduced the notion of different recipient roles in the context of television series. This included the core recipients of regular viewers that are directly addressed and meta recipients in the form of critics and academics, incidental recipients (i.e. irregular and chance viewers) and accidental recipients (i.e. viewers who should not even be there, such as children watching a movie rated unsuitable for their age group). It is plausible to expect that these differences have some bearing on the emotional impact that they experience. *My Life Without Me* is not part of a television series but, as a drama or romance, it is clearly aimed at a different audience than that of an action thriller or a horror movie, and in this sense, it is likely that regular viewers of drama movies and romances are more deeply drawn into the emotions of this movie than aficionados of action thrillers. Professional viewers, such as movie critics and academics with a more analytical interest in the movie, are more likely to be interested in the techniques that are used to create emotions rather than the mere experience of the depicted emotions. The movie has a rating which says that it is not suitable for persons aged under fifteen years because of the use of strong language. Thus, children, in this case, would be accidental recipients, and, of course, it is very difficult to speculate on their possible emotional reaction.

Planalp (1999: 54–67) suggests a different approach to assessing the ways in which people engage with the emotions of others. She proposes different, interrelated levels that successively build on one another. Langlotz (2017: 542–543) adapts this with slight modifications to the realm of fiction. Table 9.2 presents the five levels in a somewhat simplified form. The lowest level is emotional recognition, and each successive level includes all the preceding ones.

Of course, things are not always as straightforward as this necessarily idealised picture of five interconnected levels suggests. It may well be possible that on certain occasions we feel for somebody and perhaps even with somebody even if we are unclear about the reason for their emotion and thus lack a clear understanding. But the table in its idealised form helps us to distinguish between the *Calvin and Hobbes* cartoon and the movie extract from *My Life Without Me*. In the cartoon, readers are likely to reach some emotional understanding, especially if they can relate to similar emotions in their own childhood, but they are unlikely to share Calvin's outrage or Susie's smug satisfaction. In *My Life Without Me*, on the other hand, many viewers may feel empathy for the depicted characters. We do not only feel *for* Ann, to some extent at least we may

Table 9.2 Five levels of emotional connection with fiction (based on Planalp 1999: 54–67 and Langlotz 2017: 543)

Emotional recognition	– Recipient recognises that a character is undergoing an emotional experience without being able to determine the nature of the emotion
Emotional accuracy	– Recipient accurately recognises a character's emotion but is unable to determine its cause
Emotional understanding	– Recipient recognises a character's emotion and has an understanding of its wider context including its cause
Sympathy	– On the basis of recognising and understanding a character's emotion, the recipient feels *for* the character but still keeps some distance and does not actually share the emotion
Empathy	– The recipient experiences the same emotion and feels *with* the character

even feel *with* her and share some of her deep emotions of love, her happy memories and her anxiety for the future.

The different levels in Table 9.2 do not have any predictive power. We cannot analyse a certain scene and anticipate to what extent audiences or even individual viewers will be touched by the depicted emotions of this particular scene or how long these emotions will last. But they help us to talk more systematically about different reactions. Different viewers may reach different levels of emotional connection because of their own different backgrounds and preferences. It also helps us to distinguish different emotional reactions towards villains and heroes. We may well understand a villain's dark emotions, but we do not condone them or even share them.

9.6 Conclusions

Emotions are certainly not the only reason why we read books, watch movies or attend plays. But emotional arousal is probably one of the more important motivations for us to engage with fictional artefacts, and it is clear that for many fictional artefacts the emotional arousal of the audience is central. The classic emotion themes that drive many fictional artefacts, such as happiness, excitement, love, hate, betrayal, rejection or loyalty, also play a role in people's individual lives. To find them mirrored in fiction without having to deal with any consequences and to experience them second-hand can give pleasure in its own right. This pervasiveness of an emotional core in many fictional artefacts is also mirrored in a millennia long history of developing genres to the extent that some emotions are clearly associated with forms of genres such as tragedy, comedy, satire, romance, thriller or horror. One important way of creating emotions is the presentation of character emotions. But emotions are very difficult to describe empirically, and therefore they pose a considerable challenge to a pragmatics of fiction.

On the most basic level, we encounter the problem that even in our daily lives, emotions are difficult to describe. In Section 9.2 above, we have described a process approach to the description of emotions with the five elements of causes, appraisal, physiological changes, action tendencies and regulation. But the details of these processes do not map to specific emotions. There is no one-to-one correlation between a specific emotion, let us say anger, and specific physiological changes or action tendencies. While some people may react with increased blood pressure and shouting, others may turn pale and lose their voice altogether. And any given physiological change or action tendency may have any number of different emotions as a cause. The same is true for the different cues that display our emotions in our everyday lives, such as facial expressions, voice quality, physiology, body posture, action and what we say (Section 9.4).

An additional problem is encountered in the context of fiction, where emotions are discursively constructed. They are described or performed for an audience. Here it proves useful to distinguish carefully between the showing mode and the telling mode. The showing mode obviously inherits all the difficulties of displaying and interpreting emotions in non-fictional contexts, while the telling mode can be much more explicit. It can explicitly name individual emotions ('She was very angry') and ascribe certain physiological changes or action tendencies to specific emotions ('His voice was shaking with fear'; 'She turned away in disgust'). In contrast to everyday situations, movies, for instance, make use of additional ways of communicating or enhancing emotions through carefully chosen mise en scènes, camera work and musical accompaniment.

The most vexing problem, however, consists in the question of how the depicted emotions relate to the emotions that are experienced by the audience. Why do some viewers shed heartfelt tears while watching a sad movie, when others are merely bored by exactly the same movie? And why is it that we are moved at all by emotions and events that are known to be fictitious? The answers to this paradox of fiction remain elusive. Emotional communication, by its very nature, is vague communication. And vague communication, in a more general sense, is the topic of the next chapter.

Key Concepts

Camera work, discursive construction of emotions, display rules, emotion components, emotion cues, mise en scène, paradox of fiction

Exercises

1. When did you last laugh, cry or feel angry about characters or events in a fictional artefact? Identify a scene that you recently read or saw and that you remember because of your emotional reaction. Analyse it with the help of the emotion cue categories in Table 9.1.
2. Share your analysis of the scene identified in Exercise 1 with your colleagues. Do they experience the same emotions as you did? If yes, how do you explain this? If no, are there any ambiguous cues?
3. Some stage and movie actors are famous for their art of making the characters' emotions accessible to the audience. Discuss how their renditions are powerful by choosing a scene, transcribing it including multi-modal cues and then analysing it. See the relevant transcription conventions in the list just before Part I.
4. Choose an emotional scene in a written artefact and compare it with its dramatised (staged or televised) version. In what ways are the telling and showing mode combined? What roles do background music and silence play?
5. Film music conventions can be exploited for effect. For example, in a comedy a character is daydreaming about a developing romantic relationship and this scenario is acted out and accompanied by violins. However, the character is brought back to reality by the scene flipping back to the real time of the story world. At the same time, the music comes to a screeching and abrupt end as well, which draws the viewers' attention to the indexicality of the soundtrack in a humorous way. Can you think of scenes where sound suddenly stops? Is this trope always used for humorous effect or can you think of other functions?
6. Isabel Coixet's movie *My Life Without Me* discussed in this chapter is based on Nanci Kincaid's short story 'Pretending the Bed is a Raft' (1997). Consider the extract below taken from 'Pretending the Bed is a Raft' (Kincaid 1997: 219), which corresponds to the scene in the film adaptation reproduced in Extract (9.4). The main character in the original short story is called Belinda and has three children. The first message that she records for her oldest daughter, Penny, is quite different from the one recorded by Ann in the film adaptation. How

are emotions, if any, displayed in the written version in contrast to the performed version?

```
1  Belinda sat up most of the night talking into her new tape recorder. She
2  made each of her children four years' worth of birthday messages that first
3  night, and kept it up over the next few weeks until she had them all legally
4  grown.

5  Penny,
6     I bet you're real pretty now. You'll have to ask your daddy to explain things.
7  He won't want to talk about it, but keep asking him. He knows even if he acts
8  like he doesn't. If your daddy has a new wife, then ask her instead. Women
9  always know more about the facts of life because most of the facts happen to
10 women. I love you.
```

Further reading

This chapter draws considerably on Langlotz (2017) and Langlotz and Locher (2013), who in turn use the work by Planalp (1998, 1999) as an important source. Planalp investigates emotions as social, moral and cultural processes and draws from the extensive literature on the topic in psychology. She surveys in detail what is known about the ways in which emotions are communicated, how they are displayed and how they are understood in our daily lives. Langlotz provides a very useful overview of how emotions are communicated in fictional contexts, where they are discursively constructed for an audience. Bednarek's (2008) book *Emotion Talk Across Corpora* investigates the ways in which English speakers talk about emotions in four registers of British English: conversation, news reportage, fiction and academic discourse. The handbook by Döveling et al. (2011) provides an overview of emotion research in the context of mass media and contains many useful articles that have an application in fictional contexts. Mackenzie and Alba-Juez's (2019) volume *Emotion in Discourse* provides an up-to-date selection of articles that investigate emotions from a pragmatic perspective.

10 Poetic language

10.1 Introduction

In Chapter 2, we argued that fiction and non-fiction are not distinguished by a different type of language. They are distinguished mostly by the agreement between the producers and the recipients that the artefact is to be treated as fiction, i.e. the fictional contract. But when we hear a play by Shakespeare or we read a beautiful poem, we might still think that there must be a difference between the beauty of these lines and most of our everyday interchanges, whether spoken in a face-to-face conversation during the coffee break or exchanged in written form via our mobile phones. On the formal level, plays and poems often follow a particular rhythm of stressed and unstressed syllables and include such elements as rhymes or alliteration. And on the levels of aesthetics and content, we often make value judgements. We might consider one particular poem especially beautiful and rich in meaning. Or we might favour a particular play because of its depth and breadth of human emotions. The formal features as well as the value judgements sometimes also occur in everyday interactions, but they appear to be much more common in the case of fictional language than in the case of everyday interactions.

In this chapter, we have a closer look at the difference between everyday language and the language of fiction, and we argue that the difference is a matter of degree only. In fact, the same pragmatic principles that account for everyday communication can also account for the processes that go on when we enjoy a sitcom on television, get absorbed in a play by Shakespeare, read the latest novel by Arundhati Roy or ponder over the significance and beauty of a poem. These pragmatic principles do not provide an easy method to evaluate fiction, but they provide an explanation for what is going on when we do so.

In a nutshell, we argue that all utterances, whether mundane and everyday or highly artistic and poetic, always require an interpretation process that the addressee has to go through. This process does not retrieve the exact mirror image of the message encoded by the sender. Instead, it retrieves interpretations that are similar to that message. The degree of resemblance between the message and its interpretation is the key to our understanding of the difference between everyday communication and the artistic complexity of, let us say, a poem. In the one case, the degree of resemblance will be relatively high. But in the other case, it is more tenuous. The message of a poem is often more suggestive. It may give hints and make allusions, which make the interpretation process more difficult but also more rewarding.

A pragmatic theory that spells out the mechanisms of this interpretation process in some considerable detail is relevance theory, which was developed by Dan Sperber and Deirdre Wilson in the 1980s and 1990s (Sperber and Wilson 1986, 1995). It is a cognitive theory that explains human communication on the basis of two Principles of Relevance, and it is these principles that account not only for everyday communication but also for the language of fiction. In particular, it also offers new ways of analysing metaphors and irony. In Section 10.2, we introduce some of the relevant aspects of relevance theory and in particular the distinction between strong and weak communicative effects and how this distinction helps us to see the similarities and differences between everyday communication and poetic language. Sections 10.3 and 10.4 will be devoted to two types of figurative language, metaphors and irony, and they will argue that relevance theory provides a principled way of accounting for both of them.

10.2 Poetic effects

A simplified model of communication might assume that in the process of communication a sender encodes a particular thought, and transmits it via acoustic or graphic signs to an addressee who then decodes the precise mirror image of the encoded message. But this model is clearly far too simple (see also Section 3.5). In fact, this model goes back to ideas proposed by the engineers Elwood Shannon and Warren Weaver in the 1940s, who were concerned with communication signals transmitted via telephone cables or radio waves. In such a context, it makes sense to think in terms of the identity of the signal before and after its transmission. But if we focus on the cognitive processes that are necessary for the speaker and the hearer, we get a more complex picture.

Relevance theory suggests that utterance interpretation is not a matter of simply decoding a signal but an inferential process. Hearers use the available evidence, which includes the utterance just addressed to them together with contextual information, to derive cognitive effects, i.e.

> **'Cognitive Principle of Relevance**
> Human cognition tends to be geared to the maximization of relevance.'
>
> **'Communicative Principle of Relevance**
> Every ostensive stimulus conveys a presumption of its own optimal relevance.'
> (Wilson and Sperber 2004: 610, 612, bold in original)

assumptions that are new to them or modifications of assumptions that they were already aware of. And the key to this inferential process is relevance. Sperber and Wilson distinguish between two Principles of Relevance, a cognitive one and a communicative one (see Sperber and Wilson 1995: 260; Wilson and Sperber 2004: 608–614; see text box). The Cognitive Principle of Relevance has to do with our wish to maximise the relevance of the inputs that we process. The Communicative Principle of Relevance, with which we shall mainly be concerned here, states in essence that every utterance, or in fact every act of ostensive communication, comes with a guarantee of its own optimal relevance, that is to say it promises a sufficient level of cognitive effects for the effort needed to process it. Put simply, this means that addressees will always assume that there must be a message in a signal addressed to them that makes the signal worth processing.

Let us first consider the fact that the Communicative Principle of Relevance applies not only to utterances but to acts of ostensive communication in general. This means that it applies to any act of communication in which the communicator has an intention to communicate and, therefore, also to non-verbal communication. Imagine the situation in a lecture hall in which the lecturer continues several minutes after the official end of the lecture. Some students might start to surreptitiously check the time on their watches or their mobile phones. Or they may do this ostensively with the intention to signal to the lecturer to wrap up the lecture. The lecturer might pick up the intended message in either case, but relevance theory is primarily concerned with the case of ostensive communication, which encompasses both an informative intention ('it is time to wrap up the lecture') and a communicative intention ('I am trying to tell you something').

In this situation, the lecturer is confronted with an act of ostensive communicative behaviour, which – by the Communicative Principle of Relevance – he or she takes to be sufficiently important to justify its processing. Given the situation that they are in and the background knowledge that the lecturer has at this point, the ostensive display of a student's interest in the exact time at this moment leads to a range of cognitive effects. It will alert the lecturer to the fact that he or she is already beyond the official finishing time. In addition, it might also create some other cognitive effects. The lecturer might, for instance, remember that this particular student regularly needs to run to another lecture at this time, that it will be difficult to squeeze everything into the next lecture, that he or she is already late as well for a lunch appointment, and a possibly infinite range of other things. But the Communicative Principle of Relevance suggests that the inferential process can stop once it has reached sufficient cognitive effects to justify the cognitive effort, in this case that the lecture should stop now, and this can then be taken as an approximation to the thought that the student wanted to communicate through his or her ostensive behaviour.

The student might have communicated roughly the same information by interrupting the lecturer with a verbal utterance, such as (10.1), or even more explicitly as in (10.2).

(10.1) It's five minutes past twelve.
(10.2) Professor, class time is up.

Verbal communication is always ostensive communication. In addition to the informative intention there is clearly a communicative intention. In the case of a non-verbal display of checking the time, there are degrees of ostensiveness. You can do this in a way that makes it seem that you meant to do it surreptitiously or you can do it by waving around your watch and pointing to it with your other hand, and this will be part of the message that is being conveyed.

Another important aspect of the Communicative Principle of Relevance that we need to consider in some detail is the fact that it allows for a large range of cognitive effects to result from a given act of ostensive communication. In the simplified, or indeed simplistic, model of communication that we briefly introduced at the beginning of this section, we would assume the addressee to retrieve a specific and clearly delimited set of assumptions from a given message. Relevance theory, on the other hand, proposes a scale from communicative acts that communicate a relatively narrow set of assumptions which are strongly endorsed by the speaker to communicative acts that communicate a large range of assumptions which are only vaguely endorsed by the speaker. Let us take the example of a passer-by asking for the time (see Sperber and Wilson 1995: 194). As an answer, you may say something like (10.3).

(10.3) It's five o'clock.

In this situation, you will have no specific idea of how your utterance will be relevant to the passer-by. You probably cannot even guess how your answer will be relevant to him or her and what contextual effects it will have, but you assume, on the basis of the question, that your utterance will be sufficiently relevant for him or her to process. Thus, your answer communicates a very small range of assumptions, i.e. that it is five o'clock, and this is strongly endorsed by you.

In contrast, let us now consider an example given by Blakemore (1992: 126), in which she and Barbara are listening to some music.

(10.4) DIANE: Do you like this music?
BARBARA: I've never liked atonal music.

From this, Diane most likely will draw the conclusion (10.5). This is the implicated conclusion. But in order to do so, she must also assume something like (10.6), the implicated premise.

(10.5) Barbara does not like this music.
(10.6) The music we are listening to is atonal. (Blakemore 1992: 126)

Note that Barbara's answer implicates both the premise in (10.6) and the conclusion in (10.5). Against the context of her question and following the Communicative Principle of Relevance, Diane will interpret Barbara's answer in a way that yields adequate cognitive effects with the least processing effort necessary. As a result, she will derive both the necessary premise and the appropriate conclusion, even if she was not aware of (10.6) prior to Barbara's answer. In fact, Diane will derive both (10.5) and (10.6) even if she has no clear idea of what atonal music actually is or if it is not atonal at all. If Diane believes that according to her understanding of the term, the music they are listening to is not atonal, she will additionally derive assumptions such as (10.7).

(10.7) Barbara thinks or pretends to think (perhaps humorously) that this music is atonal.

The interesting question is, of course, why Barbara produced the answer in (10.4) rather than a more straightforward answer, like 'No!' This would have been simpler and would have required less processing effort for Diane (but it might also have been too face-threatening; see Chapter 8[1]). By the Communicative Principle of Relevance this should,

---

[1] Interpersonal pragmatics and the study of relational work – the topic of Chapter 8 – go well together with relevance theory. This is because Sperber and Wilson argue in their Communicative Principle of Relevance that '[e]very act of ostensive communication communicates a presumption of its own optimal relevance' (Wilson and Sperber 2004: 612) and that this 'optimal relevance' is not only 'relevant enough for it to be worth the addressee's effort to process it' (Sperber and Wilson 1995: 270) but is also 'the most relevant one compatible with the communicator's abilities and

therefore, have been more relevant, but this is not the case. The answer is, as we have seen, that Barbara communicated quite a bit more than just 'no'. Her answer might give a reason for her dislike, it might show her own expertise in identifying atonal music, it might indicate that she dislikes all pieces by composers of atonal music, such as Arnold Schoenberg, Alban Berg and Anton Webern, not just the one that they are listening to. Or she might be implying that the music, although not atonal in the technical sense, for her is as difficult to listen to as atonal music. It is not necessary that Barbara maintains a sharply delimited set of such assumptions. What counts by the Principles of Relevance is merely that there are sufficient assumptions over and above a mere 'no' to justify the extra effort needed for Diane to process her answer. Diane might have been aware herself that they were listening to atonal music. In that case, (10.6) would not have been any news to her, but it would still be relevant because it confirms this piece of knowledge and it makes manifest that Barbara is also aware of this.

Sperber and Wilson (1995: 55) give the example of Peter and Mary, who arrive at their holiday destination, a seaside resort. Mary opens the window of their hotel and sniffs the seaside air that comes in through the window. She does this ostensively and appreciatively so that Peter realises that she wants to communicate something with this. There is no evidence to suggest that she has a blocked nose or a cold. What she communicates may include a large range of assumptions. The air smells fresh. She can smell seaweed and fish. It reminds her of their last holiday at the seaside, and she realises how happy they are away from the polluted air and the hectic lifestyle in the city. The fresh air would have been manifest to Peter, too, but perhaps he did not pay any attention to it. Mary's ostensive act of sniffing the air makes this more manifest, and it makes manifest Mary's desire to draw Peter's attention to the air. With her sniffing, Mary has communicated a large range of assumptions, but it is unlikely that she had a specific and finite set of such assumptions in mind, and an explicit verbal utterance is unlikely to have had a similarly far-reaching and suggestive effect. All these assumptions, therefore, are only weakly communicated. Mary has not endorsed any specific one of them. And the Communicative Principle of Relevance suggests that her

---

preferences' (1995: 270). It is these 'abilities and preferences' which allow us to tie relevance theory to the notion of frames, norms and societal ideologies discussed in Chapter 8, which give rise to emergent pragmatic interpretations of interpersonal effects and identity construction. For a discussion of this link, see Locher (2004: chapter 3).

sniffing the air was an optimal way of communicating exactly such a range of weakly communicated assumptions.

Thus, to summarise briefly at this point, an act of ostensive, i.e. purposeful, communication makes manifest or more manifest a set of assumptions that the addressee takes to be optimally relevant in the given situation to represent the thought that the speaker wants to communicate. Through an inferential process, the addressee derives a set of new assumptions, which comprise both implicated premises and implicated conclusions. Some of them are strongly communicated. They are strongly endorsed by the speaker. Others are somewhat less strong or perhaps only weakly communicated, and the speaker takes less responsibility for them.

We are now in a position to consider how this applies to the language of fiction. Let us take the lyrics of a famous protest song given in (10.8).

(10.8) 'We Shall Overcome'. (Song lyrics taken from <https://genius.com/Pete-seeger-we-shall-overcome-lyrics>, last accessed 2 October 2020. Melody and lyrics in public domain)
1 We shall overcome
2 We shall overcome
3 We shall overcome, some day
4
5 Oh, deep in my heart
6 I do believe
7 We shall overcome, some day
8
9 We'll walk hand in hand
10 We'll walk hand in hand
11 We'll walk hand in hand, some day
12
13 Oh, deep in my heart
14 I do believe
15 We shall overcome, some day
16
17 We shall live in peace
18 We shall live in peace
19 We shall live in peace, some day
20
21 Oh, deep in my heart
22 I do believe
23 We shall overcome, some day
24

25 We are not afraid
26 We are not afraid
27 We are not afraid, TODAY
28
29 Oh, deep in my heart
30 I do believe
31 We shall overcome, some day
32
33 The whole wide world around
34 The whole wide world around
35 The whole wide world around some day
36
37 Oh, deep in my heart
38 I do believe
39 We shall overcome, some day

These are the verses that the American folk singer Pete Seeger used at his legendary concert at Carnegie Hall, New York City, on 8 June 1963, at the height of the American civil rights movement to end racial discrimination. The order of the verses was slightly different, and he repeated some of the verses, which he sang together with his audience. A live recording of the event is still available. Pete Seeger's version of the song goes back to a protest song that was used during a strike of African American tobacco workers in the 1940s, which in turn goes back to a church hymn published in 1901 by Charles Albert Tindley; parts of it were also used in Martin Luther King's famous 'I Have a Dream' speech in August 1963 (Boyer 1983: 131; but see Bobetsky 2014 for a more detailed history of the complex ancestry of both the lyrics and the music of the protest song that we know today).

'We Shall Overcome' is at the same time simple and powerful. Watts and Andres Morrissey (2019: 327) call it 'the greatest protest song of all time, effective in the simplicity of its lyrics and tune', and Lynskey (2011: 34) describes it as 'protest music boiled down to its quintessence: *we* – the power of community – *shall* – the promise of a brighter future – *overcome* – defiance and endurance'. The lyrical I is here turned into a plural to create a community with the audience, who is invited to sing along and to share the same confidence in a bright future, free of today's struggles. Significantly, the song does not state what exactly we shall overcome. It has generally been understood to mean that we shall overcome oppression and segregation, but it can be read in other ways, too. In fact, in Tindley's version the corresponding line reads 'I'll overcome some day', and from the remainder of Tindley's text it is clear that in his hymn the meaning was more religious than political. It suggests that the line is a prayer for help to overcome personal weaknesses and failings on the way to salvation. In Seeger's version, the explicit religious allusions have disappeared. The line 'We shall overcome, some day' is reinforced by additional verses expressing confidence in a future of peace and community ('hand in hand'). Seeger added a verse about not being afraid which he explicitly introduced and emphasised in the live performance at Carnegie Hall, and in contrast to the other lines, this is not a hopeful claim for the future but a proud and emboldening assertion about the present.

So, how does the interpretation process of this song work, and how is it possible that it has been used in many different contexts? The search for relevance for all readers or listeners involves the attempt to find ways in which the details of the song, or poem, can be contextually enriched. What exactly is it that we shall overcome some day? What does it mean for us to walk hand in hand? What potential threats are there that we want to face without being afraid? And how do we interpret the 'overcome' and 'believe'? Do they still resonate with some religious connotations or are only political and societal connotations evoked? How exactly will we 'overcome' whatever obstacles we are faced with? Will it be our patience to wait for inevitable change or will it be a violent struggle to achieve our aims with force? Interpretations will vary from singer to singer, from listener to listener or from reader to reader. However, the interpretation is not unrestricted. The lyrics constrain the interpretation process in specific ways. Even if some of the lexical items may be fuzzy and connected to somewhat different mental lexicon entries for each listener, they are not arbitrary. And the gaps in the lines 'We shall overcome [what?]' and 'We are not afraid [of what?]' are semantically constrained. They allow a broad range of interpretations, but in the one case it has to be some sort of obstacle and in the other some sort of threat. The interpretation process leads to a large range of weakly communicated assumptions. It is not possible to specify any precise range of such assumptions as either directly intended by the author or as retrieved by any specific listener.

In addition, the song is further enriched by its musical form. In the Carnegie Hall concert, Seeger accompanies himself on an acoustic guitar and gives it a strong pulse in triple time which makes it easy for the audience to sing along. However, it is difficult to specify precisely how this influences the interpretation process in detail. The music is even weaker in its specificity than the text and more akin to forms of non-verbal communication, such as the appreciative and ostensive sniffing of fresh air mentioned above (for the role of music in films, see Section 9.4; Atencia-Linares 2019; Dyck 2019).

It is also instructive to examine how a song can become richer in meaning in new contexts. In the 1960s, it was an important song of the US civil rights movement made popular not only by Pete Seeger himself but also by the young Joan Baez and by other folk singers at political rallies and protest marches. Over the years, it was adopted by political movements not only in the United States but in many different countries, which all enriched the text with their own specific obstacles that needed to be overcome. On 9 February 2010, Joan Baez performed the song in front of the newly elected 44th US President Barack Obama at a celebration of music from the period of the civil rights movement. In this context, many people will have reinterpreted the lyrics in the hopeful belief that with the inauguration of the first African American President of the United States an important milestone had been reached on the way to overcome oppression and segregation of African Americans in the United States and elsewhere.

From a pragmatic perspective, the possibility of multiple interpretations is not problematic. As Pilkington (1991: 59) has pointed out, a poem is not a cryptic crossword which will yield exactly one correct solution. It is a form of communication that gives rise to a large range of weak implicatures. According to relevance theory, as we have seen above, acts of ostensive communication can be produced with a very clear expectation that the hearer recovers a specific and clearly delimited set of propositions/assumptions (strong communication). Or they can be produced with little or no expectation about the way in which they will be understood (weak communication). And there can be any number of intermediate cases between these two extremes.

> When discussing the ambiguous nature of poetry it is important to point out that it is not the case that a poem offers a set of determinate alternative meanings to choose from. Images, symbols, metaphors within the poem interact to make manifest a vast range of weak implicatures. Individual readers will not access all the same implicatures or the same number of implicatures. But if they were responding to the poem in the most appropriate way, they would not isolate one or a small set of these implicatures and privilege them above the others. (Pilkington 1991: 59–60)

In this sense, a poem offers a broader range of weak implicatures than everyday language normally does, and it is a good poem to the extent that these implicatures resonate for a specific reader and give rise to rich cognitive effects. This makes it worthwhile to spend time and effort in trying to understand a poem and uncover some of its

> 'A speaker who constrains the interpretation of his utterance so that the hearer takes very little responsibility in the choice of contextual assumptions and contextual effects is said by Sperber and Wilson to be engaging in *strong communication*. The greater the responsibility the hearer has in the selection of contextual assumptions and effects, the **weaker** the communication.' (Blakemore 1992: 157, italics in original, bold added)

richness. Everyday language, on the other hand, often relies on 'strong communication', i.e. communication that has a small range of cognitive effects for which the speaker takes most of the responsibility (see text box). But both poetry and everyday conversation work according to the same principles. Communication is a cognitive process in which the speaker makes manifest or more manifest a set of assumptions that the hearer recovers in order to retrieve cognitive effects on the premise that the ostensive communicative act produced by the speaker (or communicator) comes with a guarantee of its own optimal relevance (according to the Communicative Principle of Relevance).

As pointed out above, it is important to realise that poems, as forms of verbal communication, constrain the interpretation process at least to some extent. In spite of the personal responses by individual readers, there is still the text, which limits the interpretation process. In the case of 'We Shall Overcome', there is not only the text but also the music, and in addition there is the history of the song in the civil rights movement of the 1960s and its origin as a gospel song with religious sources. Some of this history is likely to resonate with every new performance of the song for at least some of the listeners. The result is what Sperber and Wilson have termed a 'poetic effect' (see text box). In this case, it is a rich experience that leads to a large range of weak implicatures. A relatively clear text, which however still leaves room for different interpretations, combines with the music and its history to create something that is richer than the text on its own.

> 'Let us give the name *poetic effect* to the peculiar effect of an utterance which achieves most of its relevance through a wide array of weak implicatures.' (Sperber and Wilson 1995: 222, italics in original, bold added)

10.3 Metaphors

Let us now turn to metaphors and – in Section 10.4 – to irony. They have in common that they are usually described as forms of non-literal language use, that is to say the speaker says one thing but actually means something different. For this reason, we first look at the distinction between literal and non-literal language use and, in fact, we argue that the distinction should be rejected. Relevance theory suggests that the relation between an utterance and its interpretation is always one of resemblance, not of identity, and literalness in the traditional sense, therefore, can be seen as a case of maximal resemblance.

Let us illustrate this idea with some observations about everyday conversations. As we have seen above, utterances come with a guarantee of their own optimal relevance, that is to say that the speaker has produced them with the belief that they will yield a sufficient number of contextual effects for the hearer to make it worth their while to process this utterance (by the Communicative Principle of Relevance). Thus, if you are asked by somebody where you live, you will answer in a way that will satisfy what you think will be sufficient contextual effects for the addressee. If you are on holiday, your country of residence might yield sufficient contextual effects for your addressee, who can connect what he or she already knows about you with additional assumptions that he or she has about your country, let us say, about its political system, weather, food and sports. If the question comes from a new fellow student, you might indicate the town where you live because that is likely to yield some cognitive effects about the commuting time and the type of life you lead. If the question comes from a university administrator, a much more precise answer will probably be required, including the street address and the postal code. In all these cases, your answer is geared towards what you think will be optimally relevant to your addressee. If you give more specific information, e.g. if you give a precise street address to your new holiday acquaintance, the information would not yield additional cognitive effects, but it would require more processing effort. Or it could lead to unwanted assumptions. Your precise address might be interpreted as an invitation to stay in touch, which might be perceived as inappropriate at a first encounter. You might come across as somebody who does not know what social conventions apply or who is inept, etc. Since information is valuable, your sharing this early on might be considered inappropriate. If you do share it, you might claim levels of intimacy that have not been reached yet (see Chapter 8 on the relational side of communication). It can easily happen that your first estimation about the possible cognitive effects for your addressee is mistaken. If your new fellow student happens to live in the same town or knows it well, he or she might be interested to have a more precise answer because that would yield additional cognitive effects.

Sometimes the most relevant utterance might even be one that is strictly speaking not true. If your friend asks you about the length of a movie, you might say something like 'an hour and a half', even though you have just checked the DVD cover, where it says that it actually lasts 86 minutes. But you assume that the imprecise, rounded figure will yield sufficient cognitive effects for your friend who wants to know whether he or she will have enough time to watch it. Similarly, a question about the monthly salary that you get for your student job at a supermarket may be answered with a rounded, and therefore strictly speaking inaccurate, figure, which will be more relevant to your fellow student who is considering working there as well. But for the tax office, the approximate figure would not be good enough. The precise figure would be required.

Thus, we have to reject the idea that an utterance is a literal representation of the speaker's thought (see text box). The relationship is one of resemblance, and the speaker chooses a formulation that he or she believes will be optimally relevant for the addressee, i.e. one that will yield a sufficient number of cognitive effects to make it worth the addressee's while to process the utterance.

> 'Literalness is simply maximal resemblance and enjoys no privileged status.' (Sperber and Wilson 1987: 708, bold added)

Let us now see how this can be applied to the interpretation of metaphors. Extract (10.9) is retrieved from the fiction part of the Corpus of Contemporary American English (COCA).

(10.9) Murzban F. Shroff, 'A Matter of Misfortune', COCA, Fiction, 2008
That's your civilization – designed to favor the few at the expense of many – and you, you are the pawn, not realizing that you are being moved around, shunted or shafted in the name of progress.

Here the addressee is described as a pawn, and we easily recognise this as a metaphor derived from the game of chess. Traditional approaches to metaphors would claim that this is a case of non-literal language use because the addressee is not in actual fact a pawn. In his introduction to relevance theory, Billy Clark (2013: chapter 9) describes three different pragmatic accounts of metaphors. The first approach goes back to H. Paul Grice and his Cooperative Principle. Grice (1975) proposed this principle as a first step towards developing an explanation of how people manage to read between the lines of what they hear. People systematically manage to get aspects of meaning that are only implied – or 'implicated' to use the technical term – rather than explicitly said (see text box). When you hear somebody say that so-and-so remembered most of a particular poem, you immediately assume that he or she did not remember everything. The term 'most' implicates 'not all' because the listeners assume that the speaker would have given the more informative version about the entire poem rather than most of the poem if that had, in fact, been true.[2]

> **Implicatures** are aspects of meaning that are not explicitly communicated but retrieved by readers or listeners who 'read between the lines' as it were by assuming that the speaker or writer is trying to be cooperative (informative, truthful, relevant and clear) in the sense of Grice's Cooperative Principle. The utterance 'Tim has two sisters', for instance, will usually be taken to implicate that he has only two sisters and no more because otherwise the speaker would have given the higher, more informative figure.

In the case of metaphors, Grice's approach claims that they provide information that is patently not true, which encourages the listener, who assumes that the speaker wanted to be cooperative in spite of the blatant falsehood of the information, to search for an alternative meaning that is closely related to the meaning actually expressed and might have been the one intended by the speaker. In the case of the use of 'pawn' in Extract (10.9), the listener might come up with something like (10.10).

(10.10) you are a weak person who is being pushed around by others

---

[2] Grice's Cooperative Principle consists of the four maxims of Quantity, Quality, Relation and Manner, which state that listeners assume that utterances provide an appropriate amount of information, truthful information, relevant information, and that they provide it in an orderly fashion. The example given in the text illustrates the Maxim of Quantity. The Cooperative Principle also provides an account of seeming violations (so-called 'floutings' of the maxims) when the above mentioned assumptions appear to be violated. In such instances, additional meanings are inferred, such as in the case of metaphors or irony, which are analysed as flouting the Maxim of Quality. What the speaker says is not literally true, but it is still cooperative, and, therefore, leads to specific implicatures, i.e. the implicitly communicated meaning. Sperber and Wilson's relevance theory is more general. It replaces Grice's four maxims with the Communicative Principle of Relevance, and it accounts not only for implicit meanings but for ostensive (i.e. intentional) communication in general.

But such an interpretation creates several problems. The account does not explain how the addressee manages to figure out the intended closely related proposition. It does not explain why the speaker did not use that closely related proposition which would have saved the addressee a considerable amount of processing effort. And it does not explain why we consider some metaphors to be more creative than others.

Two possible answers are suggested by relevance theoretic approaches, an older one (relying on weak implicatures) and a more recent one (relying on lexical pragmatics). The older approach goes back to Sperber and Wilson (1995; but see also Blakemore 1992: 160–164). It also takes a metaphor to be an implicature, but on this account, it is not the result of a violation of some principle of truthfulness. Instead, it is part of the inferential process and subject to the Communicative Principle of Relevance. A metaphorical utterance gives rise to a whole range of contextual effects or implications, but – based on the Principles of Relevance – the addressee accesses only those that make sense in the context. In our example, the lexical item 'pawn' conjures up for the addressee whatever associations he or she might have about pawns, which of course will be somewhat different depending on whether they are accomplished chess players or people who know the game only from hearsay, but it will likely include assumptions about the small value of pawns, the limitations to their movements and so on. This account provides an answer to the question of why the speaker has chosen a metaphor at all rather than a non-metaphoric designation like 'a weak person'. The metaphor conveys additional, weakly communicated assumptions that would be lacking in the non-metaphorical term. The result, if it is a well-chosen metaphor, is a richer, more interesting interpretation that is worth additional processing effort for the addressee.

On this account, it is also possible to integrate conventional metaphors. When we say that somebody has 'grasped' a concept, that time is 'running out' or that an argument has 'collapsed', we use verbs that in their literal sense describe a physical action. Here they are used in a metaphorical sense. However, the implicatures that derive from these metaphors are not very creative, unexpected or novel. In the context of computers, we talk of a 'desk top', 'windows', 'memory', a 'mouse' and so on, and we tend to forget that originally these were metaphors. There are many words in the English language that have a metaphorical origin which is no longer apparent to present-day speakers. In the case of 'grasp', we are aware that it may be used for physically seizing and holding an object but also for comprehending a problem or a situation. It is probably less well known that the verb 'comprehend' itself originally also had the meaning of 'grasp, lay hold of or catch'. The *Oxford English*

Dictionary gives an example from 1584 in which priests were 'comprehended' by the Spanish Inquisition (OED, 2nd edn, comprehend, *v.* I.1), that is to say they were physically arrested rather than cognitively understood.

At the other end of the scale there are highly creative literary metaphors. Clark (2013: 271) gives as an example a remark by Flaubert about the poet Leconte de Lisle (originally from Sperber and Wilson 1995: 237).

(10.11) Son encre est pâle. ('His ink is pale')

This metaphor of pale ink gives rise to a whole range of weak implicatures, which presumably include assumptions about the lack of passion and effectiveness of de Lisle's writings, lack of assertiveness and confidence, lack of durability of his arguments and so on. The list is clearly open-ended, and this is exactly what makes this a more creative metaphor. Clark concludes:

> Relatively poetic or creative metaphors give rise to a range of weak implicatures rather than strongly implicating a small number of conclusions. This open-endedness is a key feature of relatively poetic metaphors. One thing which follows from this characterisation is that hearers might spend a considerable amount of time thinking about exactly what range of implicatures are evidenced by a particular utterance. This fairly sustained interpretive process is, of course, typical of literary interpretations. (Clark 2013: 271)

The second, more recent relevance theoretic account argues somewhat differently. Metaphors are not explained as a range of weak implicatures, but they are explained in the context of lexical pragmatics. In contrast to lexical semantics, which explores what is encoded by a word, lexical pragmatics explores what a word means in a particular context. Let us first consider a non-metaphorical utterance like (10.12) and focus on the meaning of 'nobody'.

(10.12) Nobody likes that music. (COCA, Magazines, 2006)

This utterance appears in an interview with the CEO of a food processing company with a multicultural workforce, and it is his answer to a question about the open-mindedness of his workforce and whether they would listen to country music. In this situation, an ad hoc concept for 'nobody' must be constructed, which restricts it to the CEO's workforce and perhaps is not quite as exclusive as the semantics of the word would suggest. It is quite possible that out of the sixty-five employees mentioned in the article, a few have slightly different preferences and would not object to listening to country music. Whether this is the case or not is irrelevant in the context in which this utterance is used. It justifies the CEO's assertion that they have banned country music from their premises because that seems to work for everybody.

Metaphors, too, are considered to be processed as ad hoc concepts, but in this case the ad hoc concept is further removed from the lexically encoded meaning. That is to say that they are not interpreted as giving rise to weak implicatures as in the more standard relevance theoretic approach, but they are part of the explicature of a proposition, i.e. the more explicit part of what is communicated (see text box). In the case of our earlier Extract (10.9), the reader constructs an ad hoc concept of a 'pawn', for which the speaker in this case even gives specific indications. A 'pawn' is somebody who is 'being moved around, shunted or shafted in the name of progress'.

> **Explicatures** are aspects of meaning that derive from the fleshing out of the semantic representation of an utterance. They are more explicit than **implicatures**, but they still require contextual information and inferential processing to be retrieved. The interpretation of the utterance, 'It's in there', for example, is only possible if the addressee can figure out what *it* refers to and which place is intended by *there*. See Clark (2013: 171–183) for a more extensive and more technical account of the difference between implicatures and explicatures.

Extract (10.13) is taken from a novel and was also retrieved through the Corpus of Contemporary American English (COCA).

(10.13) Steve Hamilton, *Winter of the Wolf Moon*, COCA, Fiction, 2001
'Hey, ref,' I said. 'That metal thing in your hand, when you blow in it, it makes the little pea vibrate and a loud sound comes out. You should try it. And then you can send this clown to the penalty box for two minutes.'

The interaction, which is also heavily ironic (see next section), takes place in the context of an ice-hockey match, and the I-narrator, a goalie, has just got into a skirmish with an opposing player when the referee intervenes. The narrator has already described the game as very rough and the referee as incompetent and unwilling to use his whistle. So, when the referee interferes in the brawl in Extract (10.13), he wants him to penalise the other player, whom he describes as a clown. The opposing player had stopped hard in front of him when he was down on the ice to secure the puck and thus sprayed him with ice, 'the old shower trick', as the narrator calls it. The semantics of 'clown' includes a whole range of different aspects, including, for instance, that clowns are entertainers, playful and extrovert, that they behave in comical and funny ways, that they often wear traditional costumes and exaggerated make-up, that they have a licence for non-seriousness and so on. Here the ad hoc concept focuses on those elements that will enhance the relevance of the utterance. The hockey player in question certainly does not wear a traditional circus costume and exaggerated make-up. Instead, the ad hoc concept focuses on what the speaker apparently perceives as non-serious and unprofessional behaviour. For some people, the semantics of 'clown' will also include assumptions about highly professional and skilful artists who play a particular role as a circus clown or of a kind and caring person who assumes the role of a hospital clown to entertain hospitalised children. The ad hoc concept is unlikely to include these aspects. It focuses more on the slapstick qualities of the performed role rather than on the professionalism of the performer and thus belittles and insults the opposing player (see the comments on identity construction in Chapter 8). Table 10.1 gives a schematic overview of the three accounts.

To some extent the difference between the two relevance theoretic approaches to metaphors is a technical one. In both cases, the interpretation is based on an inferential process that derives a range of weak implicatures, but there are different mechanisms which lead to these. The meaning is derived on the basis of the lexical entry itself together with contextual assumptions supplied by the addressee and a search for

Table 10.1 Three pragmatic accounts of metaphors

Account	Interpretation of metaphoric expressions (ME)
Gricean account	– ME are non-literal and blatantly false – ME violate Maxim of Quality – ME force listener to search for closely related meaning
Relevance theoretic account based on implicatures	– ME give rise to a range of weak implicatures – Listeners access a range of implicatures which provide enough effects to be consistent with the Communicative Principle of Relevance – ME range from highly creative (many weak implicatures) to conventional (few relatively strong implicatures)
Relevance theoretic account based on explicatures (lexical pragmatics)	– ME are ad hoc concepts that are part of the explicature of an utterance – Features enhancing the relevance of the utterance emerge in the inferential interpretation process of ME

the optimal relevance of the utterance in which the metaphor occurs. There is no need to postulate a clear-cut distinction between a literal and non-literal level of meaning. Instead, there is a scale that ranges from conventionalised meanings to more creative, ad hoc meanings which require more processing effort from the addressee, and this explains the difference between conventionalised, dead metaphors, like 'comprehend' or 'grasp an idea', and creative metaphors, such as Leconte de Lisle's pale ink. Such a treatment has the advantage that other forms of loose use of language can be treated in the same way (see Clark 2013: 279). In the following section, we are going to turn to irony, another figure of speech that has traditionally been analysed as a non-literal use of language. Here, too, we are suggesting that a relevance theoretic approach offers a convincing account of how it should be interpreted.

10.4 Irony

Ironical utterances are traditionally understood to mean the opposite of what they say. Let us imagine a party that turns out to be horrible for Matt and Liz. They do not enjoy themselves at all and they signal this to each other by surreptitiously rolling their eyes. On their way home, Liz says one of the following.

(10.14) What an awful party!
(10.15) What a wonderful party!

In the given circumstances, (10.14) would be a truthful description while (10.15) would be untrue on a literal level and, therefore, ironic. It is likely that Liz would use a different tone of voice for either (10.14) or (10.15) but even without that Matt would be able to tell the difference. According to Grice, Matt would realise that (10.15) states something that is obviously not true because he has seen how Liz rolled her eyes. In technical terms, (10.15) flouts the Maxim of Quality (see footnote 2 above), it is not truthful and, therefore, on the assumption that Liz was cooperative, it gives rise to an implicature. Liz must have meant something that is closely related to (10.15), and that is its opposite (10.14). In an early paper, Sperber and Wilson (1981) already pointed out that such an approach is seriously flawed. It fails to explain a range of interesting facts about ironic utterances. In the meantime, their original analysis has been refined in several publications (see in particular Wilson and Sperber 2012: chapter 6; Clark 2013: chapter 10).

The first problem encountered by a traditional theory, which describes irony as meaning the opposite of the literal meaning of an utterance, is the question of why the speaker used an ironic utterance at all. If Liz intends to convey that she did not like the party, why does she use (10.15) rather than the more straightforward (10.14)? This would be easier for Matt to process, and Liz would not run the risk of perhaps being misunderstood. The second problem consists in the observation that it is much easier to imagine (10.15) as an ironic utterance about a horrible party than (10.14) as an ironic utterance about a thoroughly delightful party. And the third problem has to do with the fact that ironic utterances are often delivered with an ironic tone of voice, which appears to be a special feature of irony. Other figures of speech, for instance metaphors, do not have a specific tone of voice associated with them.

The key to these problems, according to relevance theory, lies in the analysis of ironic utterances as echoic. Ironic utterances do not describe a state of affairs, but they quote or refer to another utterance, perhaps only a potential utterance. They echo this earlier utterance and they express a distancing attitude towards it. Before we can apply this key to the three problems, we need to introduce the difference between two types of utterances. Originally, Sperber and Wilson (1981) called this the use–mention distinction, which applies in a rather obvious way to reported speech. At a certain point during the party mentioned above, Liz might say something like (10.16) to Matt. She uses the utterance to make a specific suggestion.

(10.16) Let's go home.

However, when Matt turns to Peter, who is sitting next to him and wants to know what Liz has just said, he utters (10.17), and here the utterance 'Let's go home' is mentioned, rather than used. Matt does not suggest to Peter that he and Peter should go home, he is only reporting what Liz said. He might also have used the version in (10.18) in which the original utterance is not directly quoted but only referred to.

(10.17) Liz said, 'Let's go home.'
(10.18) Liz said that we should go home.

We have to remember that according to relevance theory, an utterance is used to represent a thought that it resembles in content. In the case of (10.16), the utterance 'Let's go home' represents a thought of the speaker about an actual state of affairs, i.e. her wish to leave the party. In the case of (10.17), the same utterance represents a thought not about a state of affairs but about another thought that, in this case, is attributed to Liz. The utterance 'Let's go home' is not used but mentioned.

In their later work, Sperber and Wilson (2012: 128) capture the same distinction with the terms 'descriptive' and 'attributive', and Clark

(2013: 258ff.) uses the terms 'descriptive' and 'interpretive'. However, the terms are less important than the basic insight that some utterances represent a thought of the speaker that resembles an actual or potential state of affairs while others represent a thought of the speaker about another thought (a thought entertained either by somebody else or by herself at another time). In this framework, ironic utterances are interpreted as echoic. They are not used but mentioned, or – in the more recent terminology – they are not descriptive but attributive:

> In any genuinely linguistic act of communication, an utterance is used to represent a thought of the speaker's that it resembles in content [...]. In ordinary *descriptive* uses of language, this thought is about an actual or possible state of affairs. In *attributive* uses, it is not directly about a state of affairs, but about another thought that it resembles in content, which the speaker attributes to some source other than herself at the current time. (Wilson and Sperber 2012: 128, italics in original, bold added)

Sperber and Wilson (1995: 239) give the following example.

(10.19) (a) *He*: It's a lovely day for a picnic.
[They go for a picnic and the sun shines.]
(b) *She* (happily): It's a lovely day for a picnic, indeed.

(10.20) (a) *He*: It's a lovely day for a picnic.
[They go for a picnic and it rains.]
(b) *She* (sarcastically): It's a lovely day for a picnic, indeed.

In this situation, Peter and Mary go for a picnic after Peter predicted a lovely day. And during the picnic Mary repeats, i.e. mentions, Peter's prediction either with approval because the sun is shining or ironically because it is actually raining. Mary's utterance in this example is a precise repetition of Peter's earlier utterance.

In this interpretation, the three problems mentioned at the beginning of this section can be solved very elegantly. In (10.20), Mary's point is not so much about the weather condition itself but about the discrepancy between Peter's prediction and the actual weather condition. She crucially communicates her attitude towards Peter's prediction. In a more straightforward and unironic 'It's an awful day for a picnic', this reference to the earlier utterance and her attitude towards it would be likely to be lost. This is why an ironic utterance in this context is more relevant than an unironic one.

Ironic utterances do not always echo actual utterances. Very often they echo possible utterances. In the case of Liz and Matt's unsuccessful party, they may not have made any predictions about its success. In this case, Liz's utterance 'What a wonderful party' merely picks up a default assumption that we expect or hope parties to be successful rather than unsuccessful. If Liz and Matt share this default assumption, it is easy to utter (10.15) with irony after a horrible party, and it is more difficult to imagine (10.14) after a delightful one. However, if Matt predicted that the party will be awful before they even set off or if Liz knows that he always expects parties to be horrible, she can easily use (10.14) when – against predictions – the party turns out to be very nice. Ironic utterances, therefore, are echoic either to some actual earlier utterance or to some default expectations shared by speaker and addressee. In either case, the speaker communicates a dissociating attitude towards the original thought. Mary indicates in (10.20b), for instance, that Peter's weather prediction turned out to be ludicrously wrong. In (10.15), Liz indicates that their (possibly tacit but shared) hope for a delightful party was sadly mistaken or in (10.14), if used ironically, that Matt's pessimistic expectation of a failed party turned out to be unfounded. The ironic tone of voice, therefore, can be explained as a quotation voice quality. The speaker indicates that she is quoting somebody else and that she is making fun of that person or perhaps more generally of people who expect parties to be successful or the weather for picnics to be good.

With this background, let us now have a closer look at a famous case of literary irony. In William Shakespeare's play, *Julius Caesar* (1599), Mark Antony delivers a funeral oration for Caesar, who was assassinated by Brutus and other conspirators. Antony has been allowed to deliver a funeral oration by the conspirators on the condition that he does not blame them for Caesar's death, but before he is allowed to speak, Brutus talks to the citizens of Rome and convinces them that Caesar's ambition had made it necessary to eliminate him. They are so taken in by the argument that they cheer him and want him to take over the role of Caesar. At this point, Mark Antony addresses the citizens with his famous speech that has often been quoted as a masterpiece of political rhetoric. Extract (10.21) gives the opening of his oration.

(10.21) William Shakespeare, *Julius Caesar*, 3.2.74–108
  1 Friends, Romans, countrymen, lend me your ears:
  2 I come to bury Caesar, not to praise him.
  3 The evil that men do lives after them:
  4 The good is oft interred with their bones.
  5 So let it be with Caesar. The noble Brutus
  6 Hath told you Caesar was ambitious:
  7 If it were so, it was a grievous fault,
  8 And grievously hath Caesar answered it.

9   Here, under leave of Brutus and the rest
10 (For Brutus is an honourable man;
11 So are they all, all honourable men)
12 Come I to speak in Caesar's funeral.
13 He was my friend, faithful and just to me;
14 But Brutus says, he was ambitious,
15 And Brutus is an honourable man.
16 He hath brought many captives home to Rome,
17 Whose ransoms did the general coffers fill.
18 Did this in Caesar seem ambitious?
19 When that the poor have cried, Caesar hath wept:
20 Ambition should be made of sterner stuff.
21 Yet Brutus says, he was ambitious,
22 And Brutus is an honourable man.
23 You all did see, that on the Lupercal
24 I thrice presented him a kingly crown,
25 Which he did thrice refuse. Was this ambition?
26 Yet Brutus says he was ambitious,
27 And sure he is an honourable man.
28 I speak not to disprove what Brutus spoke,
29 But here I am to speak what I do know.
30 You all did love him once, not without cause:
31 What cause withholds you, then, to mourn for him?
32 O judgment, thou art fled to brutish beasts,
33 And men have lost their reason. Bear with me.
34 My heart is in the coffin there with Caesar,
35 And I must pause till it come back to me.

Antony carefully and step by step contrasts Brutus' argument that Caesar had been ambitious, which he does not deny, with pieces of evidence that suggest that Caesar was not at all ambitious. Instead, he reminds his audience how Caesar had provided for them: 'He hath brought many captives home to Rome, Whose ransoms did the general coffers fill' (lines 16–17); how he cared for them: 'When that the poor have cried, Caesar hath wept: Ambition should be made of sterner stuff' (lines 19–20); and how he three times declined to become king when he was offered the crown (line 25). At the same time, he keeps referring to Brutus and the other conspirators as 'noble' and as 'honourable men' (lines 5, 10, 11, 15, 22 and 27). Initially, in lines 5, 10 and 11, there is little indication that he is being ironic. He refers to a common understanding in a situation where the crowd has just cheered Brutus for his speech justifying Caesar's death. Only a moment ago, at the opening of his speech, Brutus himself has referred to his own honour: 'Believe me for mine honour and have respect to mine honour, that you may believe' (*Julius Caesar*, 3.2.14–16). Thus, Mark Antony's epithet explicitly echoes Brutus's own self-description. But with every repetition it becomes increasingly obvious that Antony dissociates himself from the epithet.

There is no point in Antony's speech where he explicitly denies that Brutus and the other conspirators are noble and honourable. A traditional theory that describes an ironic utterance as meaning the opposite of what it literally says would have to specify a certain point at which the interpretation switches from literal to ironical. But this does not capture what is going on in this speech. It is a gradual process that is more easily described in terms of an echoic use of the terms 'noble' and 'honourable'. This also helps to distinguish the reaction of the Roman citizens to whom the funeral oration is addressed and the reaction of the theatre audience. At the beginning of the speech, the citizens have only just applauded Brutus, who – in his speech – had explained why Caesar's ambition made it necessary to stop him. They cheered him, and they wanted him to become Caesar himself. At this point the designations 'noble' and 'honourable' are no more than accurate descriptions of their own feelings, while the theatre audience may already have some suspicion about Mark Antony's own feelings about these designations. Does he really mean what he says? With each repetition and with every new example that Antony provides to show that Caesar was not ambitious, it becomes increasingly clear not only to the theatre audience but also to the Roman citizens that Antony dissociates himself from the designations. He uses them attributively, not descriptively. What started out as praise turns into irony and finally into sarcasm.

It is part of the actor's art to indicate this increasing dissociation with his tone of voice, speed of delivery, hesitations, gestures, facial expressions and so on (see Exercise 4). Even at the very first two occurrences of 'honourable' in lines 10 and 11, the actor can give subtle hints that they are to be understood with a touch of irony or he can wait for later occurrences and then make the irony shine through more clearly. This can easily be accounted for in a relevance theoretic account, which stresses the echoic nature of ironic utterances. What the speaker communicates is not a description of a state of affairs but an attitude towards somebody else's description. The attitude is a dissociating one, and it is gradual. It gradually moves from an indication that this is not his description to an expression of utmost contempt for whoever might sustain such a description.

10.5 Conclusions

Relevance theory is a cognitive account of utterance interpretation. The two Principles of Relevance provide generalisations about the processes that are necessary for a hearer to understand what a speaker is saying, or, more precisely, to derive relevant cognitive effects from an utterance, which, in turn, resembles a thought that the speaker wishes to communicate. In this chapter, we have argued that this theory provides an account not only for everyday communication, including even non-verbal acts of ostensive communication, but also for highly creative acts of literary communication. Utterance interpretation is an inferential process. The listener, or reader, uses the available evidence to derive cognitive effects. The evidence includes available background knowledge and the utterance itself. By the Communicative Principle of Relevance, the inferential process can stop as soon as the addressee has derived sufficient cognitive effects. In the case of simple, everyday utterances, this process can be simple and relatively straightforward. The result of the process is a small range of strongly communicated assumptions, strongly communicated in the sense that they can safely be assumed to have been meant by the speaker. In more creative communicative acts, such as poetic communication, the result of the process is a much larger range of relatively weakly communicated assumptions. They are weakly communicated because the addressee has to take more responsibility in working out what they are. The communicative act is more suggestive and less clear-cut.

This theoretical approach also helps to explain figures of speech such as metaphors or irony. Traditionally these have been explained as forms of non-literal language use. In a relevance theoretic approach, the literal–non-literal distinction is abandoned and replaced by degrees of resemblance. Metaphors, under this interpretation, can be seen as more or less conventionalised. Highly conventionalised metaphors are usually not even recognised as metaphors while creative, ad hoc metaphors lack conventionalisation and are felt to be more poetic, as in the case of the pale ink discussed in Section 10.3. The interpretation of irony also diverges from traditional interpretations, which generally argue that ironic utterances mean the opposite of their literal meaning. In a relevance theoretic interpretation, ironic utterances are seen as expressing a specific distancing attitude. They are attributive, or echoic, rather than descriptive. The utterance does not resemble a thought about a state of affairs but it resembles a thought about another thought, possibly in the form of a more or less direct quotation but possibly in the form of echoing some standard assumptions that the speaker assumes to be sharing with his or her addressee.

Thus, we are now in a position to spell out the difference between mundane everyday language and highly poetic literary language without having to posit different types of language. The difference is gradual. It has to do with the sliding scale of strong, i.e. relatively clear and unambiguous, communication at one end to, at the other end, weak communication for which the addressee has to invest more processing effort and take a larger range of responsibility. This also explains why experienced readers generally retrieve richer interpretations from poems or other literary works. They have a larger range of background assumptions that can interact with the words and the imagery of the literary work, and, therefore, the inferential interpretation process can produce a richer range of cognitive effects.

Key Concepts

Attributive language use, Cognitive Principle of Relevance, Communicative Principle of Relevance, descriptive language use, explicature, implicature, irony, literalness, metaphor, ostensive communication, poetic effect, Principles of Relevance, relevance theory, strong communication, weak communication

Exercises

1. The following lines are the opening of the sound poem 'Catbird' by John Glassco (1971, taken from *John Glassco: Selected Poems with Three Notes on the Poetic Process*, 1997: 54).

   1   '*Airoee*...
   2   eh 'rhehu 'vrehu
   3   eh villia villia 'vrehu, eh villia 'vrehu
   4   eh velù villiu villiu villiu!
   5   'tse dàigh   dàigh   dàigh
   6   Tse-de-jay 'tse-de-jay 'tsee-'tsee 'tsìrritse-'tsìrritse
   7   'tsirao 'twitsee

   A catbird is a songbird that appears to have got its name because of its wailing calls that have some similarities to the meowing of a cat. Its scientific name is *Ailuroedus*, which is derived from the Greek *ailouros*, 'a cat', and *eidos*, 'species'. John Glassco's poem 'Catbird' shares properties of both verbal language and music. Try to give a relevance theoretic explanation of the ways in which a reader would try to derive relevant cognitive effects from this poem.

2. The following is an extract from William Shakespeare's *As You Like It* (1599: 2.7.140–148), which contains an extended metaphor.

1	JAQUE	All the world's a stage,
2		And all the men and women merely players.
3		They have their exits and their entrances,
4		And one man in his time plays many parts,
5		His acts being seven ages. At first the infant,
6		Mewling and puking in the nurse's arms;
7		Then the whining schoolboy, with his satchel
8		And shining morning face, creeping like snail
9		Unwillingly to school.

   Check the context of this extract and discuss how the three pragmatic approaches to metaphors outlined in Section 10.3 would explain it.

3. In Section 10.3, we analysed the metaphor 'clown' in Extract (10.13), repeated here for convenience.

   (10.13) Steve Hamilton, *Winter of the Wolf Moon*, COCA, Fiction, 2001

   'Hey, ref,' I said. 'That metal thing in your hand, when you blow in it, it makes the little pea vibrate and a loud sound comes out. You should try it. And then you can send this clown to the penalty box for two minutes.'

   The extract is also a great example of irony. Consider the words that the ice-hockey goalie I-narrator addresses to the referee and how they can be interpreted as echoic (attributive). Who is being echoed? And what is the attitude that the I-narrator expresses about this (imagined) source?

4. Find some video clips of performances of Mark Antony's funeral oration on the internet and watch them carefully (see Section 10.4). How do the actors playing Antony indicate his increasing dissociation from the description of Brutus and the conspirators as 'noble' and as 'honourable men'? And how does the production indicate the crowd's reaction to each repetition of Antony's assertion that Brutus is an honourable man?

Further reading

This chapter has relied heavily on relevance theory. The best relatively recent textbook on this theory is Clark (2013). It provides a careful introduction to all the necessary notions of the theory, and it also contains chapters that are specifically devoted to metaphors and to irony (Chapters 9 and 10). For an overview, see also Clark (2014). Blakemore (1992) provides a useful discussion of many literary examples. In particular, chapter 9 on implicatures and style provides a very readable introduction to a relevance theoretic approach to poetic effects, metaphors and irony with many well-chosen illustrations from literary texts.

The background to all this, is, of course, the original work by Dan Sperber and Deirdre Wilson themselves, in particular the second edition of *Relevance* (Sperber and Wilson 1995) published nine years after the first edition (Sperber and Wilson 1986). In a handbook article, Wilson and Sperber (2004) provide a very useful and succinct overview of their theory. The volume Wilson and Sperber (2012) consists of fifteen chapters devoted to specific relevance theoretic aspects. Chapters 5 and 6 are devoted to metaphors and irony respectively. The volume edited by Chapman and Clark (2014) contains excellent papers that analyse literary texts from a relevance theoretic perspective. Pilkington (2000) offers a concise and readable relevance theoretic introduction to poetic effects. Chapter 4 is devoted to metaphors. For the concept of conventional metaphor, please turn to Lakoff and Johnson's ([1980] 2003) insightful and classic *Metaphors We Live By*.

11 Fiction, pragmatics and future research

11.1 Introduction

In this textbook on *The Pragmatics of Fiction: Literature, Stage and Screen Discourse*, it has been our aim to approach fictional texts as cultural artefacts in their own right from a pragmatic perspective. We stated a twofold trajectory in our introduction:

> First, it wants to raise awareness of the complexity of fictional data for pragmatic analyses. And second, it wants to demonstrate how fictional texts can be studied from a pragmatic perspective.

Throughout the book we have, therefore, introduced key notions in pragmatics and have applied them to extracts from fictional texts, and, turning the tables, we have also started from the fictional artefacts themselves and asked what we need to better understand about the particular communication processes entailed in fiction. This dual approach has guided our discussion and allowed us to draw on previous work from both fictional and non-fictional data to increase our insights into the pragmatic meaning of fictional texts. And at the same time, it has highlighted particular areas where the complexity of fictional artefacts helps us to further develop the level of pragmatic theorising. It turned out that the complexity of fictional discourse often requires somewhat more sophisticated pragmatic models than had been available so far.

Until relatively recently, pragmatics and fictional data were considered not to be easily compatible because pragmatics was mostly interested in everyday face-to-face conversations rather than what was considered to be the artificiality of fictional data. Today, this has clearly changed, and there are many reasons why pragmatic theories can profit from being tested on fictional data and why our understanding of fictional data profits from a pragmatic perspective. Here are some of the most important ones summarised:

- Fictional data in the form of literature, plays, movies, television series and so on is pervasive in our lives. It is an important form of communication, and it is rich in depicted communication. Any self-respecting pragmatic theory with a claim to describe and explain aspects of communication must, therefore, be able to say something about fictional data if it is not to be accused of neglecting a large and important part of our daily communicative lives.
- The boundary between fiction and non-fiction is fuzzy, as we have repeatedly shown throughout the chapters of this book. Fictional and non-fictional storytelling is an intricate part of our culture. It would be highly counter-intuitive to propose an (artificial) boundary between fiction and non-fiction as a boundary for the applicability of pragmatic theorising.
- What distinguishes fictional texts from non-fictional texts is first and foremost the fictional contract, i.e. the silent agreement between the producer and the recipient of a communicative act to treat this act as fictional rather than factual. This is a fundamentally pragmatic argumentation because it deals with the larger context of the communicative situation of a fictional artefact. Thus, a pragmatic perspective is an essential ingredient of our understanding of fiction.
- In our daily lives, we constantly encounter familiar situations, or frames, that create frameworks of expected behaviour and communicative patterns, such as service encounters or doctor–patient interactions. In some cases, our knowledge of such frames may be based partly or even entirely on fictional examples, e.g. police interrogations. Such frames are also regularly exploited for effect as shortcuts in fiction. This means that – because of the fictional contract – fictional renditions can be less precise, less complete (in the case of frames) and less 'true to reality', and still achieve effects. A pragmatic theory also needs to account for the interaction between frames of expectations in fictional and non-fictional contexts.
- Figures of speech, such as metaphors or irony, are often considered to be literary devices, and indeed they are often used in fictional artefacts, but they are by no means restricted to fictional contexts. A pragmatic theory, therefore, should be able to account for such devices both in fictional and in non-fictional contexts.

In what follows we will highlight a number of issues that have surfaced throughout the chapters. In particular, we want to highlight how, on the one hand, the analysis of fiction can benefit from a pragmatic perspective and, on the other, how pragmatics in turn can also benefit from considering fictional language. In Section 11.2, we are going to focus on the fictional contract again and on how it has permeated all the chapters of this volume. Section 11.3 will then return to the distinctive features of the language of fiction and the participation structure of fiction. In fact, throughout this book we have argued that there is no fundamental difference between everyday language and the language of fiction, but this does not amount to the claim that there are no differences at all, even though the differences are mostly gradual. Section 11.4, finally, will give an outlook on further research opportunities.

11.2 Fact, fiction and the fictional contract

The current textbook starts from the very basic assumption that it is possible to distinguish between fictional and non-fictional contexts. Without this assumption, this textbook would not make sense. But this does not mean that the distinction is easy, particularly in today's world of widespread fake news, lies and deceptions, manipulated pictures and so on. Linguists do not have any special tools to distinguish between truths and falsehoods. They describe how people communicate, what kind of resources they use for the purpose and so on, but they cannot reliably assess whether people actually believe what they say, whether people want to deceive or to inform. So, how can we maintain a distinction between fiction and non-fiction? In Chapter 2, we argued in some detail that we need to make a careful terminological distinction between the fictionality of genres and text types and the fictitiousness of depicted characters, events and other entities. The fictionality of genres and text types is connected to the silent contract between the producer and the recipient of a text about how the contents are to be treated. Are the events, characters and the depicted world to be treated as the result of the producer's imagination and, therefore, fictitious? Or are they to be treated as representations of real-world entities and, therefore, as non-fictious, i.e. factual?

The answer to these questions is often complex, even in what may appear to be straightforward cases. Some works of fiction spell out this fictional contract down to the legal detail, for instance Nanci Kinkaid's (1997) collection of short stories *Pretending the Bed is a Raft*. The final story has the same title as the entire collection and was the source for the movie *My Life Without Me*, which we discussed in Chapter 9. On the copyright page of this book, the following blurb appears:

> This is a work of fiction. While, as in all fiction, the literary perceptions and insights are based on experience, all names, characters, places, and incidents are either products of the author's imagination or are used ficti-

tiously. No reference to any real person is intended or should be inferred. (Kinkaid 1997: iv)

This note makes a far-reaching claim about the fictitiousness of the contents of these stories. However, no mention is made in this blurb of the fact that the story world of the depicted events appears to be very realistic in depicting a possible world somewhere in North America in the last decade of the twentieth century with the social realities of long-term unemployment, the medical realities of a cancer diagnosis, and technical innovations, such as tape recorders.

This contrasts with Douglas Adams's mock science fiction novel, *Hitchhiker's Guide to the Galaxy* ([1979] 2005), which carries a very similar statement on its copyright page. In this novel, very little corresponds to the world that we are used to. The planet Earth is casually demolished to make way for a galactic freeway, and the characters include such bizarre figures as a paranoid and manically depressed robot and a galactic president with two heads. The story world consists of a galaxy full of outrageous improbabilities with very little resemblance to our everyday world. Or, to take a different example, the movie *Erin Brockovich* (2000), from which we discussed an extract in Chapter 8, starts with a black screen and a text in a white font, 'This film is based on a true story' (0:48), before the first scene opens. It makes a claim that in spite of the fictional context of a movie, the depicted events are not entirely fictitious. They are based on events that happened in the real world. In Chapter 2, we discussed additional examples, such as real people fiction, in which real people are put into a fictitious context, and as illustrations we mentioned Shakespeare's history plays or fan fiction, in which real-life celebrities are cast into the dream world of the writer.

In all these cases, the fictional contract is an essential ingredient. It is an agreement – whether explicitly stated or silent – between producer and recipient about the level of veracity that should be expected from a particular text genre or even a particular text. And, in fact, it is the fictional contract which is the leitmotif of the entire book. It is the cornerstone of a pragmatic explanation both for the similarities and for the differences between the language of fiction and non-fictional language.

In Chapter 4, for instance, we showed how different genres and frames create specific expectations for readers and viewers who often take such expectations as guidelines when deciding which book to read or which movie to watch. They should be seen in the larger context of frames of expectations that are associated with all sorts of everyday situations. Our experience with visits to restaurants, classroom lessons, supervisions with a professor, parties, visits to big sports events, funerals and many, many more guides our expectations for similar events in the future. Everybody has their own unique combination of such experiences, but within a given culture such experiences are also shared. They evoke patterns of behaviour and expectations. In some cases, our familiarity with particular situations might be based largely or even entirely on fictionalised representations, e.g. in the case of police interrogations, courtroom interactions or interactions in an operating theatre. Thus, there are several levels of expectations involved when we encounter a fictional artefact: expectations about the fictitiousness of the depicted events, expectations about the specifics of certain genres and expectations about the depicted situations themselves.

Often, creators play with such expectations and creatively subvert them. We have seen several such cases in the chapters of this book, for instance in Chapter 2, where we presented the case of *lonelygirl15*, the assumed video blog of a teenage girl, which later transpired to be a fictional performance produced by scriptwriters and actors. Or in Chapter 4, where we discussed the Korean drama *Meloholic*, which received countless viewer comments about the appropriateness of its genre classification, and the trailer to the movie *He's Just Not That Into You*, which plays with all the clichés of a typical chick flick movie and claims that – against expectations – they do not occur in this movie.

The fictional contract also plays an important role in the characterisation of fictitious characters (Chapter 6). Characterisation in fiction draws on the same resources that we use in everyday situations. We grouped them into explicit cues, such as self- or other-presentation, and implicit cues, such as conversational structures used by characters, their vocabulary, accent and dialect, as well as visual appearance or a character's company and setting, to pick out just a few examples. In a fictional context, however, such cues are generally understood to be purposeful in the narrative context. They are more systematically significant where some of these features in real life may turn out to be accidental and misleading without being meant to be misleading. On the level of language, the indexicality of regional, social and ethnic markers, for instance, are shortcuts for the creation of characters that – in combination with what people say, how they say it, how they comport themselves and dress, etc. – form complex and dynamic projections, and these markers do not even have to be entirely accurate. The occasional archaism may already index a character as speaking an older form of English, and a sprinkling of Cockney expressions may index a working-class London character. The fictional contract becomes even more apparent in multilingual contexts, when viewers or readers accept that a character speaks a foreign language. The possibilities here range from the untranslated use of the foreign language with limited audience comprehension, except for people who are familiar with the depicted foreign language, to the unmitigated use of the main language where audience awareness of the foreign language depends entirely on extralinguistic cues. Miloš Forman's film *Amadeus* (1984), for instance, depicts a fictitious rivalry between the composers Wolfgang Amadeus Mozart and Antonio Salieri at the court of Emperor Joseph II in eighteenth-century Vienna, but all the characters speak English. The context and the depiction of historical figures suggest that the characters are meant to speak German, except when Salieri, for instance, utters a word or two in his native Italian. But, on the basis of the fictional contract, the audience witnesses 'German' conversations in English.

The fictional contract also plays a role when assessing interpersonal aspects and the positioning of characters in light of societal ideologies, as discussed in Chapter 8. Just like the evocation of frames and characterisation cues that do not have to be enacted in full to tap into their indexical meaning, ideologies also do not need to surface in the form of explicit meta-talk in a fictional artefact in order to fulfil their full potential as a topic of fiction. Ideologies of comportment in light of gender, im/politeness, power, etc. can surface in subtle ways yet still evoke the entire breadth of the concept. In other cases, the topic of a fictional artefact might deal quite explicitly with particular ideologies (e.g. the notion of class as reflected in linguistic comportment in *Pygmalion*). We will expand on this idea in the next section. In Chapter 7, we presented features of orality which have their origin in the online planning process of utterances and in the interaction between two or more speakers. People normally plan their utterances while they speak and they react to each other in real time, which leads to hesitation phenomena, contractions, self-corrections, turn-taking signals, interruptions, overlaps and so on. In fictional contexts, apart from improvisation theatre, utterances are planned and scripted before they are performed. The actors have learned their lines by heart, but nevertheless features of orality are often present, even in written fiction. They are staged for the audience to give the impression of spontaneously produced language. As in the case of characterisation cues, these features do not need to be realistic with their frequency. A few of them may be sufficient to create the desired effect. In everyday life, a certain amount of hesitation, repetition and self-correction may go entirely unnoticed, but in fictional contexts, such features are often more noticeable and more significant if they occur at all.

Emotions, to take a last example, are particularly interesting in terms of the fictional contract (Chapter 9). Again, we argued that fiction by and large uses the same repertoire of emotion cues that we rely on in real-life situations, but in fiction, emotions are always discursively constructed for an audience. They are presented in the showing mode when we see characters who display their emotions through facial, vocal, physiological, body, action or verbal cues. Or they are presented in the telling mode when the narrator or one of the characters explicitly talks about emotions. In either case, they are fictitious emotions, but nevertheless they regularly manage to stir (real) emotions in the audience. The question of how audience emotions are related to character emotions is complex. We are probably all familiar with situations in a theatre or a movie where we did not buy the display of emotions by an actor. Clearly, sometimes we are moved, and sometimes we are not, and even if we are, our emotions may be short-lived, and soon replaced by some more analytical considerations about the actor's skill in giving a plausible presentation of the emotions of a character.

This brings us back to Coleridge's adage of the suspension of disbelief (Chapter 2). We argued that this does not adequately capture what is going on in fiction. We do not suspend disbelief in order to temporarily accept the fictional reality as true. On the contrary, we engage in the fictional contract and accept that what we witness is – to some extent at least – fictitious. We accept the depicted emotions to be fictitious, and, therefore, we are at liberty to get more or less involved ourselves. We can keep our analytical distance and admire or criticise the actors' art, and/or we can go along with the emotions and allow them to touch us, albeit perhaps only briefly.

11.3 Distinctive pragmatic features of fiction

Throughout the chapters of this textbook, we have worked from two seemingly contradictory assumptions. First, we have assumed that the language of fiction draws from the same resources as non-fictional language. They are not really different. But second, we have also assumed that fiction is nevertheless somehow special and deserves special analytical efforts, including a dedicated introductory text like this one. And both these assumptions have repercussions for the status of pragmatic theories in the analysis of the language of fiction. The same pragmatic tools that are used for non-fictional language should also be able to handle the language of fiction, and at the same time, some of the consequences of the fictional contract challenge us to further develop these tools and make them more sophisticated. Let us illustrate this with a few relevant examples from the previous chapters.

In Chapter 3, we talked about the intricacies of the participation structure of fictional artefacts, and in particular of movies and television series. Our starting point was based on the frameworks developed by Goffman (1979) and Bell (1991), who carefully distinguished different sender roles and different recipient roles. These models had been developed on the basis of everyday conversations and, in particular, on the basis of the traditional forms of mass media communication. The sender consists of the three roles of animator, author and principal, and the recipients can consist of addressees, auditors, overhearers or eavesdroppers. These distinctions turned out to be very useful when applied to fictional artefacts but not sufficiently complex. For telecinematic discourse, they need adaptations to account for the different levels of embedding. Several researchers working on telecinematic discourse have already proposed such adaptations, e.g. Bubel (2008) or Dynel (2011), who conceptualise viewers as overhearers or ratified listeners (see Messerli 2017 for an overview). In our own model, we separate the different levels (intradiegetic, supradiegetic and extradiegetic) more consistently, and use this as a basis to distinguish the different creator roles and the different recipient roles on each of these levels, such as, for instance, addressee recipients, meta recipients, incidental recipients and accidental recipients on the extradiegetic level, i.e. on the level of viewers of a movie or television series. This model is largely compatible with the models proposed by Goffman and Bell but it is also more sophisticated and able to account for the increased complexity and multi-layered nature of telecinematic discourse, where we have to account for a very large team of creators, including not only authors, but also actors, script writers, camera operators and many more. We have to account for a possibly very large and heterogeneous audience consisting of regular viewers and aficionados of a particular series or movie genre, academics and critics who view it with a more professional and analytical interest, as well as incidental recipients and accidental recipients. And we have to account for the communicative complexity of the fictional artefact itself, where we have characters communicating with each other on the intradiegetic level and perhaps even a studio audience on what we called the supradiegetic level.

Chapter 5 was devoted to the narrative core, and we introduced stories as fundamental meaning making units both in fiction and in everyday discourse. In fact, the study of narrative, story and plot has a much longer tradition in literary contexts than the analysis of oral narratives, which only gained momentum in the 1970s, in particular through the work by Labov (Labov and Waletzky 1967; Labov 1972).

In this context, the cline between fiction and non-fiction appears to be particularly blurry. Everyday storytelling regularly uses strategies that are employed in fiction, and fiction regularly draws on everyday linguistic strategies in order to tap into the knowledge that viewers, for instance, bring to the watching of a movie. When we tell a story at a party, for instance, it may be entirely fictional, as for instance in the case of jokes or in the case of fantasising about possible events in a dream world. Or a story may be partly a true account of events in the form of an anecdote that through numerous retellings has become embellished with certain elements that even if not quite true add to the drama or humour of the recounted events. Or stories may be more or less accurate accounts of actual events, such as the story of the bike accident that happened on the way to work, for example. But even in this last case, the narrator has to carefully select the individual elements that add up to make the story tellable, which leads to the prototypical structure of narratives of personal experience, which include an optional abstract followed by the story itself which contains orientation, complicating action, evaluation and result or resolution, and finally a coda, which is again optional.

Using and interpreting characterisation cues as well as relational work and the evocation of ideologies are all-pervasive processes in human interaction. It is therefore not surprising that fiction also makes use of such cues. As discussed in the previous section and in Chapters 6 and 8, the cues to evoke judgements about characters as behaving in, for example, an unacceptable/acceptable manner, or polite/impolite way are tied to complex and intertwined expectations about manifold ideologies. The judgements will then be linked to making assumptions about the identity of the person ('this is an impolite woman/character', 'this is a polite man/character'). The cognitive processes of how indexicalities are evoked and interpreted is not different in fictional and non-fictional texts. However, what can be stated is that many forms of fiction represent a *persistent* locus of the transportation of ideologies, i.e. a locus where ideologies are challenged, maintained and perpetuated. With the exception of unrecorded live performances, fictional texts such as novels, poetry, written drama, telecinematic artefacts, cartoons, etc. can be reread and reviewed and continually reassessed. This is why we can read the Greek classics and their adaption to English works of fiction and peruse the ideologies that they raise for discussion, or turn to Jane Austen's novels and learn something about the values of comportment in the nineteenth century and see how the characters negotiate these gender and im/politeness expectations within the novels. Or we can read a contemporary novel and compare the behaviour of its characters with what we know from our own socialisation to be either the norm or exceptional behaviour.

It is of course true that non-fictional texts also carry ideologies. For example, in business correspondence, ideological values of positioning surface (the choice of correct address terms, the right register, etc.), but it is maybe less expected that business correspondence contributes to the societal discussion of ideologies in the same way as these expectations exist for fiction. In this way, fictional texts also deal with ideologies differently than, say, academic treatises on the development of ideologies or etiquette books since fictional texts rely to a larger extent on the showing than the telling mode. The differences between how fictional and non-fictional text types evoke ideologies are thus fuzzy. However, fiction can be argued to raise more expectations about the texts being carriers of ideologies because literature is often associated with transporting culture.

When discussing the features of orality presented in Chapter 7 in light of the fictional contract, we stated that the frequency with which oral features occur in spoken interaction often goes unnoticed in the sense that they are 'edited out' in the comprehension process and do not distract from the message. They are also largely expected to occur and do not appear as particularly marked. However, when the same features appear in fiction in print, they are much more noticeable, even in small quantities. This is because the written register is associated with standard spelling and standard varieties of English. As a consequence, even a small or incomplete list of cues of orality will catch the reader's eye and be able to contribute to characterisation and to the flavour of the scene as performing dialogue. In performed fictional artefacts, too, features of orality can be marked. Let us compare a non-fictional with a fictional example. When a politician delivers a speech, we expect a rhetorically sound text with few hesitation markers, false starts and repetitions. The speech text has been carefully composed and the politician has experience in delivering such speeches either by heart or reading the text from a teleprompter. The same kind of delivery would be expected from an actor who plays a president competent in delivering speeches in a live drama. If the actor hesitates, is looking for words, or has to self-correct, the interpretation could indeed be that the president in the play delivers speeches badly, but it could also be that the audience assigns this lack of skill to the actor rather than the character. A live performance cannot be repeated in the exact same ways since it is ephemeral. Once the actor's performance is recorded, however, the directors can decide to repeat the recording until the right amount of oral features is present so as to evoke the desired characterisation of the president.

Chapter 10 was most explicitly concerned with the question about some potentially unique features of the language of fiction and whether special theoretical tools are needed for them. Clearly, poems, song texts and plays are often written in a way that seems special both on the formal level and on the level of content. On the formal level, there may be particular rhythmic patterns of stressed and unstressed syllables, and there may be rhymes, alliteration and similar devices, while on the content level, the communicated meaning may not reveal itself as easily as in other contexts, or – put more positively – meanings may be much richer than in the case of everyday utterances. We introduced relevance theory in order to account in more detail for the interpretation processes that are at work both when we are engaged in an everyday conversation and when we try to understand the complex levels of meanings in a beautiful poem. Relevance theory is a cognitive theory. It tries to explain this interpretation process, and it claims to account for all forms of ostensive communication, which by implication, of course, also includes all forms of fictional communication. A crucial element in the workings of relevance theory when applied to the language of fiction is the distinction between stronger communication, in which the speaker makes manifest for the listener a small range of assumptions that can be safely assumed to have been intended by him or her, and weaker communication, in which the hearer has to take more responsibility in working out a possibly large range of assumptions. We have provided the examples of telling the time for the former and Mary's ostensively sniffing of the seaside air for the latter. Poems share aspects of both. They constrain the interpretation process in certain ways through the actual words that are used, the imagery and the cultural context in which they were written, but they also leave a lot of responsibility to the reader who has to ponder over possible ambiguities, levels of meanings, allusions and so on.

Relevance theory has also suggested specific ways of dealing with metaphors and irony. Both of them are important literary devices but they are, of course, not unique to literary contexts. They are pervasive in everyday language, too. In contrast to many traditional accounts, relevance theory does not consider metaphors or irony to be cases of non-literal language use. In fact, it abandons the distinction between literal and non-literal altogether and replaces it by degrees of resemblance. This provides for the interpretation of metaphors as ad hoc concepts that are either conventionalised (in the case of dead metaphors) or innovative (in the case of creative metaphors). And irony is seen as a case of attributive, or echoic, language use, which includes a distancing attitude towards the thought that is communicated. Relevance theory, thus, is a pragmatic theory that from its very beginning has been tested and developed also on the basis of the language of fiction (see in particular Sperber and Wilson 1981, 1995: 231–243; Blakemore 1992; Pilkington 1991, 2000). It replaces clear-cut dichotomies with sliding scales. There is no clear-cut distinction between the language of fiction and non-fictional language, but we can specify more precisely why some uses of language strike us as more poetic and creative than others. Poetic and creative language use is not restricted to the language of fiction, but it is perhaps significantly more frequent in such contexts.

11.4 Outlook and future research

In this chapter, we have brought together lines of thought that permeated the book and now we have come to the end of this journey and can look ahead. When we planned the textbook, we had to make decisions as to what was central to our argument and what could be left out for the purpose of an introductory textbook due to space constraints. In other words, not every aspect that deserved to be looked at in its own right could be given equal attention. Promising areas of further pragmatic analysis of fictional texts are therefore briefly mentioned here but this list of areas is clearly open-ended.

Since pragmatics is about studying language in use and narratives represent a fundamental discourse unit both in fictional and in non-fictional instantiations, the interconnectedness of how narratives shape our understanding of face-to-face interaction and how face-to-face interaction shapes our understanding of narratives deserves further scrutiny. Klapproth (2004), for example, compares storytelling in Aboriginal culture in Australia with traditional Anglo-Western fairy stories in English. In doing so, she worked out that the different combinations of story modes (oral, painted and performed versus written, read and performed) have an influence on how people recognise and understand their cultural contexts. The Aboriginal stories are carriers of cultural understanding of the self and their people per se but also the self and the people within the landscape of Australia. The stories represent history and the present at the same time and are not perceived as fictitious but as instantiations of world understanding. The Anglo-Western fairy tales are carriers of educational moments of moral understanding and form a repertoire of narratives that a large part of the population grows up with and learns from. While one could argue that such findings pertain more to the field of cultural studies than linguistics, our understanding of pragmatics in the Continental European traditions means that we can also give the narratives in their cultural context centre stage and study how they are passed on and negotiated in meaning making processes.

In this textbook, we have mentioned the possibility of the back and forth between the fictional and non-fictional on a number of occasions. The list of issues in the introduction to this chapter summarises some of them. A further point worth exploring is the notion of intertextuality that can be widened in scope to refer not only to 'the interdependence of literary texts, the interdependence of any one literary text with all those that have gone before it' (Cuddon 2013: 367) but to the interdependence of all types of text. This widening in scope does not make the topic unruly since we have a set of concepts, such as frames of face-to-face encounters, text genres and ideologies, that helps us in exploring intertextuality in our data from a pragmatic perspective. In doing so, it is beneficial to combine insights from pragmatics with linguistic anthropology, sociology and culture studies.

A further area we touched upon is the engagement of readers and viewers with the fictional artefacts beyond simply reading or watching them as a private enterprise. In Chapter 2, we mentioned fan fiction in particular and in Chapter 4, viewer comments about a TV drama on an online streaming platform. There are also reading clubs, online cafes, and professional and lay book and movie reviews where interpretations of fictional artefacts are discussed and shared, etc. 'Talking about fiction' as a discourse practice is likely to touch on many of the concepts introduced in this textbook as well, such as genre, story world creation, characterisation cues and identity construction, intertextuality, the role of emotions and aesthetic pleasure, and the surfacing and negotiation of ideologies. It is interesting to see how spoken and written discussions about fiction develop and how the transitions from the 'world of the talk' (or the 'world of discussion') and 'the world of the story' (see Figure 5.1) are negotiated in this practice of meta-talk. Furthermore, interactive new ways of jointly appreciating fiction, such as online streaming platforms, allow for simultaneous viewing (as in the practice of *Danmaku* in China or Japan, where viewers post comments on the screen) or for non-synchronous, joint viewing (as in the case of timed comments in Viki; see Locher and Messerli 2020) where people can share their emotional reactions to the fictional artefact and muse about the continuation of the plot, among other things.

It has been the aim of this textbook to focus on pragmatic theorising in light of fictional data and to look at fictional data with a pragmatic lens. Therefore, we have not given any particular fictional text type or genre special attention. Instead, we have drawn eclectically on a number of fictional sources ranging from novels, poems, cartoons, song lyrics, written and performed drama to TV series and movies in order to illustrate our theoretical points, and have made some comparisons between genres to highlight differences. For example, in Chapter 7 on the performance of fiction, we explored how some of these genres differ with respect to orality features. More explorations on how particular genres work from a pragmatic angle, how pragmalinguistic effects are created and exploited by particular authors, or how other modes interact with linguistic features could be pursued (e.g. the role of silence and music in performed fiction or the conventions of the drawn pictures in cartoons and mangas). Song lyrics, too, deserve more attention from a pragmatic perspective, for example with respect to establishing the presence or absence of a narrative core and the exploitation of poetic language (see Watts and Andres Morrissey 2019).

Further issues to explore are the ludic element of creating new worlds through the invention of entirely new languages, such as Klingon or Dothraki, and the alienation effects through the invention of new words for old concepts or the invention of new words for entirely imaginary new concepts that are part of the story worlds. We also see wide-open research avenues in the pragmatics of translation of fiction in all its forms. The challenges of translating pragmatic effects of, say, im/politeness ideologies or regional, ethnic and social linguistic characterisation cues to name just a few, into other languages are substantial and demand creativity on the side of the translators, be it in translation from written text to written text or from audiotext to subtitling and dubbing.

Rather than offering a closed picture of what the pragmatics of fiction as a research field has to offer, we tried to provide an introduction to the field that paves the ground for future research endeavours and provides instruments and concepts that help approach fiction from multifaceted, pragmatic angles. We hope that this textbook will inspire some of its readers to develop research questions on this exciting research interface between pragmatics and fiction.

Exercises

1. Has engaging with the contents of this book changed your appreciation of and/or outlook on fiction? If yes, in what ways? Can you link your insights to linguistic concepts?
2. Looking at the glossary provided, are there concepts that are unclear to you? For clarification, discuss them in groups and with your teacher and come up with examples from fiction of your own to illustrate them.

3. Are there fictional artefacts that you consume which were not covered in this book? Describe them to your peers and suggest research questions and methodological approaches of how to explore them.
4. Are you an active writer or producer of fictional artefacts yourself? How do you create story worlds? In what linguistic varieties do you let your characters speak? What ideologies are touched upon in your work? How do you exploit the fictional contract? After having studied this book, are any of the answers to these questions informed by pragmatic concepts?

Further reading

If you want to engage further with the topic of this book, we recommend the handbook *Pragmatics of Fiction*, edited in 2017 by the present authors, which brings together scholars who give scholarly overviews of many of the topics raised here. Further inroads can be gained from the stylistics approach to fiction such as the collections of studies in Giovanelli and Mason (2018), Burke (2014), Chapman and Clark (2014, 2019) or Stockwell and Whiteley (2014). Watts and Andres Morrissey (2019) bring a sociolinguistic framework that is in many respects similar to ours to bear on performances of folk singers. See also the literature pointers in Chapter 1.

Glossary

> **Key concepts mentioned in each chapter at a glance**

Chapter 1 Fiction and pragmatics

Anglo-American pragmatics, Continental European pragmatics, diegesis, extradiegetic, fiction, intradiegetic, performed fiction, pragmatics, spontaneous fiction, written fiction

Chapter 2 Fiction and non-fiction

Fan fiction, fictional, fictional contract, fictitious, spin-offs

Chapter 3 Literature as communication

Accidental recipients, addressee recipients, asynchronous, audience design, communicative act, core recipients, incidental recipients, illocutionary force, meta recipients, participation structure, perlocutionary effect, quasi-synchronous, supradiegetic, synchronous

Chapter 4 Genres of fiction

Common ground, fictional contract, film, frame, genre schema, gothic novel/fiction, ideology, lyric, novel

Chapter 5 The narrative core

Audience design, deixis, external focalisation, focalisation, foregrounding, heterodiegetic narrative, highpoint story, homodiegetic narrative, internal focalisation, intertextuality, meta-comment, mind style, narrative, narrator, plot, small story, stance, story, story world, target audience, tiny story, voice, zero focalisation

Chapter 6 Character creation

Alienation effect, characterisation cues, dialect, ethnolect, functions of multilingualism (elimination, signalisation, evocation, presence), identity construction, ideology, idiolect, index and indexicality, linguicism, meta-comment, regional variation, sociolect

Chapter 7 The performance of fiction

Adjacency pair, dialogue, discourse marker, features of orality, improvisation, offline and online planning, planners, showing mode, telling mode, voice-over narrator

Chapter 8 Relational work and (im/politeness) ideologies

Community of practice, face, frame, identity construction, ideology, interpersonal pragmatics, meta-comment, relational work

Chapter 9 The language of emotion

Camera work, discursive construction of emotions, display rules, emotion components, emotion cues, mise en scène, paradox of fiction

Chapter 10 Poetic language

Attributive language use, Cognitive Principle of Relevance, Communicative Principle of Relevance, descriptive language use, explicature, implicature, irony, literalness, metaphor, ostensive communication, poetic effect, Principles of Relevance, relevance theory, strong communication, weak communication

Definitions of key concepts in alphabetical order

accidental recipients (Ch. 3) In an →audience design framework, **accidental recipients** are those members of an audience who are not intended to be audience members at all by the creators of a fictional artefact, e.g. children watching movies not suitable for their age group. Compare →core recipients, →incidental recipients and →meta recipients.

addressee recipients (Ch. 3) In an →audience design framework, **addressee recipients** are those →core recipients of the audience who are directly targeted by the creators of a fictional artefact. In the case of a television series, for instance, they are those viewers who watch the series regularly and who know the characters of the series, are familiar with previous episodes and so on. The production crew will make sure that for these viewers the characters are sufficiently consistent that allusions to earlier events in the series are understandable and so on. Compare →meta recipients.

adjacency pair (Ch. 7) **Adjacency pairs** are sequences of utterances that are produced by two different speakers, usually in adjacent position. The nature of the first utterance specifies the expectation of what type of utterance is required in response. A question, for instance, requires an answer, a greeting requires another greeting, an invitation requires an acceptance or rejection and so on.

alienation effect (Ch. 6) To create an **alienation effect** by using linguistics cues means that a (usually small) number of linguistic features are used to evoke a setting in the past, future or any other contrast that serves the narrative.

Anglo-American pragmatics (Ch. 1) **Anglo-American pragmatics** is the more theoretical branch of →pragmatics which focuses on utterance interpretation in all its complexity. It studies the principles of language use that account for meaning in context, and it often has a cognitive dimension, that is to say it asks questions about the way in which speakers and listeners cognitively process language.

asynchronous communication (Ch. 3) Interactions are described as **asynchronous** if there is a time lag between the production of a message and its reception, which is typically the case for email messages, newspaper articles or books. Compare also →synchronous communication and →quasi-synchronous communication.

attributive language use (Ch. 10) 'In any genuinely linguistic act of communication, an utterance is used to represent a thought of the speaker's that it resembles in content [...]. In ordinary →*descriptive* uses of language, this thought is about an actual or possible state of affairs. In *attributive* uses, it is not directly about a state of affairs, but about another thought that it resembles in content, which the speaker attributes to some source other than herself at the current time' (Wilson and Sperber 2012: 128, italics in original, bold added).

audience design (Ch. 3) 'In **audience design**, speakers accommodate primarily to their addressee. Third persons – auditors and overhearers – affect style to a lesser but regular degree. Audience design also accounts for bilingual or bidialectal code choices' (Bell 1984: 145, bold added).

camera work (Ch. 9) The term **camera work** refers to the different shot sizes and scales (long shot, close-up, extreme close-up, etc.), the shot angles (low, eye-level, high, etc.) and viewpoints (in relation to the character) in which a scene is filmed. 'Metaphorically speaking, the camera is like the eye through which we see the world that is staged' (Langlotz 2017: 536).

characterisation cues (Ch. 6) A cue points to a feature of a character which identifies or creates this character. **Characterisation cues** can be linguistic (indexing social, ethnic, regional or idolectal belonging) or pertain to appearance and action. They can be explicit, implicit and authorial. Compare →index and indexicality.

Cognitive Principle of Relevance (Ch. 10) The **Cognitive Principle of Relevance** states that '[h]uman cognition tends to be geared to the maximization of relevance' (Wilson and Sperber 2004: 610). Compare →Principles of Relevance and →Communicative Principle of Relevance

common ground (Ch. 4) The **common ground** between a speaker and an addressee consists of all those assumptions, or pieces of information, that they share and that they assume to share. Typically, they are more confident about some assumptions and less confident about some others. These assumptions also include higher level assumptions, e.g. the speaker's assumptions about what the addressee might assume about the speaker's assumptions and so on.

communicative act (Ch. 3) The term **communicative act** is a cover term for units of communication that are exchanged between interlocutors. Such units range from the very simple and short to the highly complex and very long. It includes one-word utterances, such as, 'Hi!', as well as long letters, status updates on social media and artistic productions, such as poems, plays or even novels with hundreds of pages (see Jucker and Dürscheid 2012).

Communicative Principle of Relevance (Ch. 10) The **Communicative Principle of Relevance** states that '[e]very ostensive stimulus conveys a presumption of its own optimal relevance' (Wilson and Sperber 2004: 612). Compare →Principles of Relevance and →Cognitive Principle of Relevance.

community of practice (Ch. 8) A **community of practice** is defined as 'an aggregate of people who come together around mutual engagement in an endeavour. Ways of doing things, ways of talking, beliefs, values, power relations – in short, practices – emerge in the course of this mutual endeavour' (Eckert and McConnell-Ginet 1992: 464).

Continental European pragmatics (Ch. 1) **Continental European pragmatics** studies the use of language in its broader social and cultural context. It focuses on the ways in which people interact with each other, including societal ideologies of what appears to be polite or impolite in a particular culture.

core recipients (Ch. 3) In an →audience design framework, **core recipients** are those members of the audience who are known, ratified and addressed by the creators of a fictional artefact, e.g. a television series. They can be →addressee recipients or →meta recipients, and they are distinguished from →incidental recipients and →accidental recipients.

deixis (Ch. 5) '**Deixis** is generally understood to be the encoding of the spatiotemporal context and subjective experience of the encoder in an utterance. Terms such as *I, here, now*, and *this [. . .]* are heavily context dependent and represent a kind of cognitive center of orientation for the speaker' (Green 2006: 415, italics in original, bold added).

descriptive language use (Ch. 10) 'In any genuinely linguistic act of communication, an utterance is used to represent a thought of the speaker's that it resembles in content [. . .]. In ordinary *descriptive* uses of language, this thought is about an actual or possible state of affairs. In →*attributive* uses, it is not directly about a state of affairs, but about another thought that it resembles in content, which the speaker attributes to some source other than herself at the current time' (Wilson and Sperber 2012: 128, italics in original, bold added).

dialect (Ch. 6) A **dialect** is a variety of language that shares lexical, phonological and grammatical features according to the geographical distribution of its speakers.

dialogue (Ch. 7) Bednarek (2017: 130) defines **dialogue** in fiction as 'shorthand for all character speech, whether or not this speech is by one character (monologues, asides, voice-over narration, etc.), between two characters (dyadic interactions) or between several characters (multi-party interactions)'.

diegesis (Ch. 1) **Diegesis** has a Greek origin and means, according to the *Oxford English Dictionary*, '[t]he narrative presented by a cinematographic film or literary work; the fictional time, place, characters, and events which constitute the universe of the narrative.'

discourse marker (Ch. 7) **Discourse markers** are stand-alone words or short phrases, such as *well, right, now, you know, I mean* or *I see*. They often occur at the beginning of an utterance and generally they can function as structural devices that help to segment discourse units or as interactional devices that signal something about the relationship between the speaker, the addressee and the message (see Biber et al. 1999: 1086).

display rules (Ch. 9) **Display rules** are 'products of emotional socialization' that 'involve a learned response that modifies spontaneous emotional displays to be socially appropriate' (Andersen and Guerrero 1998: 54).

elimination (Ch. 6) In the context of multilingualism, **elimination** refers to situations in which 'any speech that would have been in another language is completely replaced with an unmarked standard variety of the base language' (Bleichenbacher 2008: 24). Compare →signalisation, →evocation, →presence.

emotion cues (Ch. 9) The repertoire of **emotion cues** refers to all those non-linguistic and linguistic ways in which people display their emotions, including facial cues (facial expressions), vocal cues (voice quality), physiological cues (e.g. blushing), body cues (body posture and gestures), action cues (e.g. throwing things or kissing) and verbal cues (e.g. the use of emotional vocabulary). However, they are often difficult to interpret both for conversationalists and for academic analysts. They do not unambiguously stand for specific emotions.

epic (Ch. 4) Following Cuddon (2013: 239), an **epic** is a 'long narrative poem, on a grand scale, about the deeds of warriors or heroes, incorporating myth, legend, folk tale [...] and history. Epics are often of national significance in the sense that they embody the history and aspirations of a nation in a lofty or grandiose manner.'

ethnolect (Ch. 6) An **ethnolect**, or **ethnic variety**, is a variety of language that shares lexical, phonological and grammatical features according to the ethnic background of its speakers.

evocation (Ch. 6) In the context of multilingualism, **evocation** refers to situations in which 'characters speak a variety of the base language that is characterized by interference (transfer) from the language they would really be speaking'; e.g. accent, short code-switches (Bleichenbacher 2008: 24). Compare →elimination, →signalisation, →presence.

explicature (Ch. 10) **Explicatures** are aspects of meaning that derive from the fleshing out of the semantic representation of an utterance. They are more explicit than →implicatures, but they still require contextual information and inferential processing to be retrieved. The interpretation of the utterance, 'It's in there', for example, is only possible if the addressee can figure out what *it* refers to and which place is intended by *there*.

external focalisation (Ch. 5) Following Hoffmann (2017: 164): '[E]**xternal focalisation** describes a (character-)external narrative viewpoint on the story world and its events. In contrast to internal focalisation, external narrators are unable to elicit the internal, mental state and thoughts of story characters.' Compare →internal focalisation and →zero focalisation.

extradiegetic (Ch. 1) The term **extradiegetic** derives from the noun →diegesis. It refers to the outside of the fictional text, such as its author and audience, who communicate on an extradiegetic level. Literary scholars often use the terms in a slightly different way and reserve the term 'extradiegetic' for the fictitious narrative level outside of the main story world, i.e. for a narrator who tells the main story.

face (Ch. 8) **Face** is a metaphor that describes 'the positive social value a person effectively claims for [her/himself] by the line others assume [s/he] has taken during a particular contact' (Goffman 1967: 5).

fan fiction (Ch. 2) **Fan fiction**, like →spin-offs, is a form of →fiction based on another piece of fiction using some of its characters, events or aspects of its story world. Sometimes it takes the form of prequels or sequels and considers different beginnings or endings of the narrative. But it may also put the →fictitious elements of the original piece of fiction into entirely new contexts. The term 'fan fiction' is also sometimes used in a wider sense, e.g. for fiction based on real-life celebrities. Fan fiction is typically published on dedicated websites.

features of orality (Ch. 7) **Features of orality** are linguistic features that are particularly frequent in spontaneous spoken language because they are part of the →online planning process, such as fast speech processes, self-repairs, hesitations, pauses and repetitions, or because they are part of the interaction between the conversation partners and the way in which they organise speaking rights, such as adjacency pairs, address terms, turn-taking signals or interruptions and overlaps. Such features also occur in written texts where they are not the result of the online planning process but may be used to imitate such a process for special effects.

fiction (Chs 1, 2) **Fiction** is a cover term for a broad range of genres and text types which are conventionally understood by a silent agreement (→fictional contract) between their creators and their audience to typically depict →fictitious characters and events.

fictional (Ch. 2) The term **fictional** describes texts, literary genres or media which typically depict →fictitious characters and fictitious events. Thus, movies and plays are fictional. They can be distinguished from non-fictional, or factual, genres, such as newspaper articles or academic research papers. Notice that a newspaper article is a factual genre even if in some cases not everything is true that is being reported in them. In this sense, a factual text can also assert falsehoods.

fictional contract (Chs 2, 4) We use the term **fictional contract** to refer to the silent agreement between the author of a book or the producers of a film and the readers and audiences that this particular artefact is to be taken as a piece of →fiction. Depicted characters, locations and events should generally be expected to be →fictitious even if some aspects of the depicted world may well correspond to our real world. In contrast to Coleridge's dictum of the 'willing suspension of disbelief', such a contract does not require the audience to 'suspend disbelief' but merely to understand and accept the fictitious basis of the depicted worlds.

fictitious (Ch. 2) The term **fictitious** is applied to characters, events and other entities that do not exist in our real world. Hamlet, for instance, is a fictitious character in a play by Shakespeare, who is confronted with fictitious events within a world which is mostly fictitious in spite of the fact that it includes some real place names (Denmark or Wittenberg) and in many respects seems to function like the real world at the time (in terms of physical laws, social relations, cultural contexts and so on).

film (Ch. 4) 'A **film** is a multimedial narrative form based on a physical record of sounds and moving pictures. Film is also a performed genre in the sense that it is primarily designed to be shown in a public performance. Whereas a dramatic play is realized as a live performance by actors on a stage, a film is shown in a cinema (a "film theater"), is not a live event, and can theoretically be repeated infinitely without any change. Like drama, film is a *narrative* genre because it presents a story (a sequence of action units [...]). Often, a film is an adaptation of an epic or a dramatic narrative (examples: Stanley Kubrick's adaptation of Anthony Burgess's novel *A Clockwork Orange*, Milos Forman's film of Peter Shaffer's play *Amadeus*)' (Jahn 2003: F1.2, bold and italics in original).

focalisation (Ch. 5) See →external focalisation, →internal focalisation, →zero focalisation and →voice.

foregrounding (Ch. 5) **Foregrounding** means: 'Giving unusual prominence to one element or property of a text, relative to other less noticeable aspects. According to the theories of Russian Formalism, literary works are special by virtue of the fact that they foreground their own linguistic status, thus drawing attention to how they say something rather than to what they say: poetry "deviates" from everyday speech and from prose by using metre, surprising metaphors, alliteration, and other devices by which its language draws attention to itself' (Baldick 2015: 144).

frame (Chs 4, 8) A **frame** is an umbrella term for a number of actions that belong together, and, importantly, it also includes knowledge of how they are ordered into sequences and who may or may not carry them out. They are cognitive guidelines which activate expectations that are closely tied to a society's norms. Particular instantiations of frames are culturally dependent while the fact that humans orient to frames in sense-making processes is in all probability universal.

functions of multilingualism (Ch. 6) See →elimination, →signalisation, →evocation, →presence.

genre schema (Ch. 4) A **genre schema** is the 'mental construct which we draw on as we create and interpret actual text' Bax (2011: 44–45). It includes the knowledge about the typical location, length and structure, style, grammar and lexis of specific genres, such as recipes, children's books, shopping lists, tweets or status updates.

gothic novel/fiction (Ch. 4) The term **gothic novel/fiction** refers to a 'type of romance [...] very popular from the 1760s until the 1820s. It had a considerable influence on fiction afterwards (still apparent in the 21st c.), and is of much importance in the evolution of the ghost story and the horror story [...]' (Cuddon 2013: 308).

heterodiegetic narrative (Ch. 5) 'In a **heterodiegetic narrative**, the story is told by a (heterodiegetic) narrator who is not present as a character in the story. The prefix "hetero-" alludes to the "different nature" of the narrator as compared to any and all of story's characters' (Jahn 2017: N1.10, bold in original). Compare →homodiegetic narrative.

highpoint story (Ch. 5) 'A narrative of personal experience is a report of a sequence of events that have entered into the biography of the speaker by a sequence of clauses that correspond to the order of the original events' (Labov 1997: 398). Such a narrative has a clearly discernible reportable event which is referred to as the highpoint of the story. This is why this type of story is referred to as a **highpoint story**.

homodiegetic narrative (Ch. 5) 'In a **homodiegetic narrative**, the story is told by a (homodiegetic) narrator who is also one of story's acting characters. The prefix "homo-" points to the fact that the individual who acts as a narrator is also a character on the level of action' (Jahn 2017: N1.10, bold in original). Compare →heterodiegetic narrative.

identity construction (Chs 6, 8) In the postmodernist sense **identity construction** is understood as 'the social positioning of self and other' (Bucholtz and Hall 2005: 586). Identity 'is intersubjectively rather than individually produced and interactionally emergent rather than assigned in an a priori fashion' (Bucholtz and Hall 2005: 587).

ideology (Chs 4, 6, 8) Language use is shaped by **ideologies**, i.e. shared beliefs, about concepts such as age, class, gender, power, good comportment, nationality, etc. Linguistic cues can evoke an indexical

idiolect (Ch. 6) An **idiolect** is a variety of language which is characterised by lexical, phonological or grammatical features that are unique to a specific speaker.

illocutionary force (Ch. 3) The **illocutionary force** of a speech act describes the conventional value a speech act has, such as a question, an apology or a promise. It is sufficient that the addressee recognises the speaker's intention for the speech act to have this force whether or not he or she is prepared to answer the question, accept the apology or believe in the promise. Compare →perlocutionary effect.

implicature (Ch. 10) **Implicatures** are aspects of meaning that are not explicitly communicated but retrieved by readers or listeners who 'read between the lines' as it were by assuming that the speaker or writer is trying to be cooperative (informative, truthful, relevant and clear) in the sense of Grice's Cooperative Principle. The utterance 'Tim has two sisters', for instance, will usually be taken to implicate that he has only two sisters and no more because otherwise the speaker would have given the higher, more informative figure. Compare →explicature.

improvisation (Ch. 7) '**Improvisation**, in theatre, the playing of dramatic scenes without written dialogue and with minimal or no predetermined dramatic activity. The method has been used for different purposes in theatrical history' (The Editors of Encyclopaedia Britannica 2017, bold in original).

incidental recipients (Ch. 3) In an →audience design framework, **incidental recipients** are those members of an audience who are less familiar with the format of a fictional artefact than →addressee recipients. In the case of a television series, for instance, they are not sufficiently familiar with previous episodes and the depicted characters. They are known to be there, but they are not ratified. The production crew may occasionally or regularly make some allowances for them by providing contextual background or by summarising previous episodes. Compare →core recipients.

index and indexicality (Ch. 6) In linguistics, Bucholtz and Hall (2005: 594, italics in original, bold added) argue that, '[i]n its most basic sense, an **index** is a linguistic form that depends on the interactional context for its meaning, such as the first-person pronoun *I* (Silverstein, 1976). More generally, however, the concept of **indexicality** involves the creation of semiotic links between linguistic forms and social meanings (Ochs, 1992; Silverstein, 1985).'

internal focalisation (Ch. 5) Following Hoffmann (2017: 164): '[I]n **internal focalisation**, the narrator adopts the restricted, subjective viewpoint of one of the story characters (the character-as-focaliser). In this configuration, the narrator's perspective is constrained by the character's personal, spatio-temporal and emotional point of view.' Compare →external focalisation and →zero focalisation.

interpersonal pragmatics (Ch. 8) **Interpersonal pragmatics** is a perspective on language use that focuses on the interpersonal/relational side of communication in all types of data (see Locher and Graham 2010).

intertextuality (Ch. 5) **Intertextuality** is 'a term coined by Julia Kristeva in 1966 to denote the interdependence of literary texts, the interdependence of any one literary text with all those that have gone before it' (Cuddon 2013: 367).

intradiegetic (Ch. 1) The term **intradiegetic** derives from the noun →diegesis. It refers to aspects within the fictional text, and 'intradiegetic communication' refers to communication between the characters depicted in the movie or the novel or some other work of fiction. Compare →extradiegetic and →supradiegetic.

irony (Ch. 10) **Irony** is traditionally defined as a figure of speech in which a speaker means the opposite of what he or she says. In the context of →relevance theory, the concept of →literalness is rejected. Irony is analysed as a case of →attributive language use, that is to say it does not represent a thought of the speaker's about a state of affairs, but it represents a thought of the speaker's about another thought (echoic language use), and it communicates a distancing attitude towards that thought.

linguicism (Ch. 6) **Linguicism** refers to 'ideologies, structures, and practices which are used to legitimate, effectuate and reproduce an unequal division of power and resources (both material and immaterial) between groups which are defined on the basis of language' (Phillipson 1992: 47).

literalness (Ch. 10) In the context of →relevance theory, '**literalness** is simply maximal resemblance and enjoys no privileged status' (Sperber and Wilson 1987: 708, bold added).

lyric (Ch. 4) 'The Greeks defined a **lyric** as a song to be sung to the accompaniment of a lyre (*lyra*). A song is still called a lyric (the words in a song are known as lyrics) but we also use the term loosely to describe a particular kind of poem in order to distinguish it from narrative or dramatic verse of any kind. [. . .] A lyric is usually fairly short, not often longer than fifty or sixty lines, and often only between a dozen and thirty lines; and it usually expresses the feelings and thoughts of a single speaker (not necessarily the poet herself) in a personal and subjective fashion' (Cuddon 2013: 411–412, italics in original, bold added).

meta-comment (Chs 5, 6, 8) A **meta-comment** is a comment/reflection from a higher level about an issue on a lower level. We use the concept to talk about genre (e.g. a comment about the belonging of a text to a particular text type), identity construction and multilingualism (e.g. a narrator mentioning that a conversation is in French although the language used is English), and the negotiation of (linguistic) ideologies and norms (e.g. characters commenting on impolite behaviour). Compare →meta recipients.

meta recipients (Ch. 3) In an →audience design framework, **meta recipients** are those →core recipients of the audience who analyse a fictional artefact with professional skill and thoroughness, i.e. critics and academics. Compare →addressee recipients.

metaphor (Ch. 10) A **metaphor** is traditionally defined as a figure of speech in which a word or a phrase is used in a non-literal sense. In the context of →relevance theory, the concept of →literalness is rejected. Metaphors are analysed as ad hoc concepts which manifest themselves in the course of an inferential process through the connection of a lexical item with a particular context. In the case of dead metaphors like 'comprehend' or 'grasp an idea', the connections are largely conventionalised. In the case of creative metaphors, such as 'pale ink', more processing effort is required by the hearer, who must assume a greater amount of responsibility for discovering the connections. Compare →weak communication and →poetic effect.

mind style (Ch. 5) The notion of **mind style** is used to 'capture [...] a fictional individual's mental processes, including thoughts, memories, intentions, desires, evaluations, feelings, emotions, and so on' (Semino 2007: 169).

mise en scène (Ch. 9) The **mise en scène** (French for 'placing on stage') refers to the composition and arrangement of everything that is placed before the camera, including the characters, their costumes, the location, lighting and so on.

narrative (Ch. 5) A **narrative** is 'anything that tells or presents a story' (Jahn 2017: N1.2). Compare, →heterodiegetic narrative, →homodiegetic narrative, →plot and →story.

narrator (Ch. 5) In face-to-face contexts, a **narrator** of a story gains the floor and thus speaking rights to tell a story. In fiction, a narrator is 'the teller of the narrative; the person who articulates ("speaks") the narrative text' (Jahn 2017: N1.2). They can be distinguished with respect to whether the narrator is an acting character in the story

(→homodiegetic narrative) or whether the narrator is not present in the story world (→heterodiegetic narrative). See also →voice.

novel (Ch. 4) The term **novel** '[d]erived from Italian *novella*, "tale, piece of news", and now applied to a wide variety of writings whose only common attribute is that they are extended pieces of prose fiction' (Cuddon 2013: 477, italics in original).

offline planning (Ch. 7) **Offline planning** refers to situations of →asynchronous communication, in which the content and the actual wording are planned in advance and the sentences are produced some time before their transmission to the addressee.

online planning (Ch. 7) **Online planning** refers to the situation in which speakers in →synchronous communication plan their utterances more or less while they produce them with very little time to plan what they want to say and how they want to say it. Compare →offline planning.

ostensive communication (Ch. 10) The term **ostensive communication** refers to verbal and non-verbal communication in which the communicator has an intention to communicate and wants this intention to be recognised by the addressee. Verbal communication is always ostensive in this sense while gestures, for instance, can communicate accidentally without a communicative intention, e.g. when somebody surreptitiously or absent-mindedly checks their watch without any communicative intention but nevertheless communicates their impatience to some bystanders. See also →Principles of Relevance.

paradox of fiction (Ch. 9) The **paradox of fiction** describes the puzzling fact that we regularly develop emotions, sometimes very strong emotions about what we know to be →fictitious characters experiencing fictitious emotions because of fictitious events. Zillmann (2011: 101) asks, 'How can the depiction of patently make-believe events exert such power over our emotions?' and Langlotz (2017: 544), 'How do fictionally staged "fake" representations of emotional processes manage to trigger "real" emotional processes in the audience? Why can we feel about fantasy?' Compare →fictional contract.

participation structure (Ch. 3) The **participation structure** describes who interacts with whom on what levels. For fiction, this concerns the complex constellations of the creators and the recipients of a fictional artefact as well as the interaction of the participants of the fictional artefact itself. The role of creator encompasses not only the author (or authors) of a piece of fiction but also the producers, such as publishers, typesetters and printers in the case of written fiction or play or film crews in the case of performed fiction. The fictional artefact itself may consist of communicative acts in which characters communicate with other characters. The audience can be split up into the ratified (i.e. primarily addressed) →core recipients, consisting of →addressee recipients (regular viewers) and →meta recipients (i.e. critics or academics with an analytical interest in the fictional artefact), non-ratified →incidental recipients (members of the audience who are not directly addressed) and →accidental recipients (i.e. viewers who are not meant to be included, e.g. children watching a movie not suitable for their age group).

performed fiction (Ch. 1) **Performed fiction** refers to fictional genres, such as theatre plays, movies for the cinema or television, television serials and soap operas, which generally rely on actors who perform what an author, or a team of authors, has written for an audience of spectators rather than readers. This also includes music theatre in the form of operas or musicals. It might even include dance theatre and ballet which, in a way, also narrate stories for an audience.

perlocutionary effect (Ch. 3) The **perlocutionary effect** of a speech act describes the effect the speech act has on the addressee, which may or may not have been intended by the speaker and which may differ for different addressees. One and the same utterance may have the effect of insulting an addressee or complimenting him or her. The speaker is normally aware of the potential of being misunderstood and will try to adapt her language accordingly but ultimately, he or she has only partial control over such effects. Compare →illocutionary force.

planners (Ch. 7) Elements such as *uh* and *um* are variably called hesitators, filled pauses or **planners** in the relevant literature. In British English they are usually spelled *er* and *erm*. The speaker uses them to fill in time while thinking of what to say next. They fill in what otherwise might have been silence. It makes clear that the speaker still wants to continue his or her turn (see Tottie 2016).

plot (Ch. 5) A **plot** is 'the logical and causal structure of a story' (Jahn 2017: N4.7). Compare →narrative and →story.

poetic effect (Ch. 10) Sperber and Wilson (1995: 222) use the term **poetic effect** to refer to 'the peculiar effect of an utterance which achieves most of its relevance through a wide array of weak implicatures'.

pragmatics (Ch. 1) **Pragmatics** is a field of linguistics and is devoted to the study of language use. It is often subdivided into a more theoretical branch (called →Anglo-American pragmatics) and a more socially and culturally oriented branch (called →Continental European pragmatics).

presence (Ch. 6) In the context of multilingualism, **presence** refers to situations in which 'the other language is no longer replaced at all' (Bleichenbacher 2008: 25). Compare →elimination, →signalisation and →evocation.

Principles of Relevance (Ch. 10) The **Principles of Relevance** is the key proposal of Sperber and Wilson's (1995) relevance theory, which is a cognitive theory that focuses on the processes involved in communication. Sperber and Wilson distinguish between a →Cognitive Principle of Relevance, which has to do with our wish to maximise the relevance of the inputs that we process, and a →Communicative Principle of Relevance, which states that every act of ostensive communication comes with a guarantee of its own optimal relevance.

quasi-synchronous communication (Ch. 3) The term **quasi-synchronous** is used for situations in which people exchange written messages in quick succession, for instance via computer or mobile phone. In these situations, the communicators take part in the conversation at the same time (as in →synchronous communication) but they can only read a message from their interlocutor once it has been finished and sent off (as in →asynchronous communication).

regional variation (Ch. 6) See →dialect.

relational work (Ch. 8) **Relational work** 'refers to all aspects of the work invested by individuals in the construction, maintenance, reproduction and transformation of interpersonal relationships among those engaged in social practice' (Locher and Watts 2008: 96) and it includes linguistic and other modes of interaction.

relevance theory (Ch. 10) **Relevance theory**, developed by Dan Sperber and Deirdre Wilson in the 1980s and 1990s (Sperber and Wilson 1986, 1995), is a cognitive theory that explains →ostensive communication on the basis of the →Principles of Relevance. Utterance interpretation is described as an inferential process based on the information contained in the utterance together with the addressee's world knowledge and his or her expectations about the relevance of the utterance in the given situation. Relevance theory accounts not only for everyday communication but also for the language of fiction. In particular, it offers new ways of analysing metaphors and irony.

showing mode (Chs 7, 9) 'In a **showing mode** of presentation, there is little or no narratorial mediation, overtness, or presence. The reader is basically cast in the role of a witness to the events' (Jahn 2017: N5.3.1, bold added). Compare →telling mode.

signalisation (Ch. 6) In the context of multilingualism, **signalisation** refers to situations in which 'the replaced language is explicitly named in a metalinguistic comment' (Bleichenbacher 2008: 24). Compare →elimination, →evocation and →presence.

small story (Ch. 5) **Small stories** typically do not contain any resolution and constitute a sharing of small scenarios. These stories are not fully-fledged personal narratives.

sociolect (Ch. 6) A **sociolect** is a variety of language that shares lexical, phonological and grammatical features according to the social stratification of its speakers.

spin-offs (Ch. 2) **Spin-offs**, like →fan fiction, are a form of →fiction based on another piece of fiction using some of its characters, events or aspects of its story world. Sometimes they take the form of prequels or sequels and consider different beginnings or endings of the narrative. But they may also put the →fictitious elements of the original piece of fiction into entirely new contexts. In contrast to fan fiction, which is typically published on dedicated websites, the term 'spin-offs' is often reserved for texts that are published through more traditional channels, e.g. as novels in their own right.

spontaneous fiction (Ch. 1) Daydreaming or (collaborative) conversational creations of imaginary worlds are forms of **spontaneous fiction**. The term also includes the art form of improvisation theatre (also called improv theatre), in which actors do not perform a given script but improvise scenes, often on the basis of audience suggestions.

stance (Ch. 5) '[S]tance [is regarded] as the expression of evaluative, epistemic and affective attitudes. [...] In fiction, stance can be realised both in character speech and in narratorial voice, and it can be expressed verbally as well as through non-verbal means, such as gestures and facial expressions. Studying stance can provide insights into characterisation, the dynamics between characters, plot development and narrative perspective' (Landert 2017: 489, bold added).

story (Ch. 5) A **story** is 'a sequence of events involving characters' that forms a narrative (Jahn 2017: N1.2). See →narrative.

story world (Ch. 5) A **story world** is a complex net of personal, time and place →deixis created through a →narrative which creates an imagined space in which the characters interact. The created world can contain fictitious elements and/or rely on analogies to the non-fictional world. See also →focalisation for different access to the story world.

strong communication (Ch. 10) In the context of →relevance theory, **strong communication** is defined as communication in which speakers constrain the interpretation of their utterances and leave the hearer very little responsibility in the choice of contextual assumptions and effects. Compare →weak communication.

supradiegetic (Ch. 1) The term **supradiegetic** derives from the noun →diegesis. It refers to the communicative level of an audience that is part of the fictional artefact (e.g. laugh tracks). Compare →extradiegetic and →intradiegetic.

synchronous communication (Ch. 3) Interactions are described as **synchronous** if the addressee receives a message at the very same time that it is being produced. This typically applies to face-to-face communication or telephone conversations, but it also applies to written communication if the recipient can read a message keystroke-by-keystroke while it is being produced. Compare also →asynchronous communication and →quasi-synchronous communication.

target audience (Ch. 5) Fictional artefacts are usually written with a particular readership/viewership in mind, which is referred to as **target audience**. Compare →audience design.

telling mode (Chs 7, 9) 'In a **telling mode** of presentation, the narrator is in overt control [...] of action presentation, characterization and point-of-view arrangement' (Jahn 2017: N5.3.1, bold added). Compare →showing mode.

tiny story (Ch. 5) The tweets or status updates that make up **tiny stories** have a low degree of tellability and unclear narrative stance on their own but they can be read as belonging together over time and thus constituting a narrative.

voice (Ch. 5) Narrators can speak with **voices** that give different levels of access to the story world. Compare →external focalisation, →internal focalisation, →narrator and →zero focalisation.

voice-over (Ch. 7) 'There are two major meanings [of **voice-over**]: (1) Representation of a non-visible narrator's voice (voice-over narrator); (2) representation of a character's interior monologue (the character may be visible but her/his lips do not move)' (Jahn 2003: F3.2, emphasis removed).

weak communication (Ch. 10) In the context of →relevance theory, **weak communication** refers to communication in which the speaker leaves the hearer a considerable amount of responsibility in the choice of contextual assumptions and effects. This may lead to →poetic effects. Compare →strong communication.

written fiction (Ch. 1) **Written fiction**, as used in this book, subsumes such prototypical literary genres as novels, novellas, short stories and poems, which are texts written by an author, or sometimes by multiple authors, for a large audience who will consume them by actually reading them. The term also includes graphic novels and stories for children with more drawings than written text and in an extension of what is usually meant by 'written' even to picture stories without any text.

zero focalisation (Ch. 5) Following Hoffmann (2017: 164, bold added): 'In **zero focalisation**, an omniscient narrator is capable of showing events from all possible spatio-temporal and cognitive vantage points. The narrator can slip into the minds and eyes of many different story characters and describe events at different times and in different places.' Compare →external focalisation and →internal focalisation.

Bibliography

Literary sources

AceGray (2007). *The End of Jane Eyre.* <https://www.fanfiction.net/s/3334786/1/The-End-of-Jane-Eyre> (last accessed 18 February 2020).
Adams, Douglas [1979] (2005). *The Hitchhiker's Guide to the Galaxy.* New York: Ballantine Books.
Adichie, Chimamanda Ngozi (2013). *Americanah.* New York: Anchor Books.
Austen, Jane (1813). *Pride and Prejudice.* London: T. Egerton.
Austen, Jane (1816). *Emma.* London: John Murray.
Auster, Paul (1995). *Smoke and Blue in the Face: Two Films by Paul Auster.* London: Faber and Faber.
Berlitz (2006). Berlitz language commercial. <https://www.youtube.com/watch?v=0MUsVcYhERY> (last accessed 18 February 2020).
Brontë, Charlotte (1847). *Jane Eyre.* London: Smith, Elder, and Co.
Coleridge, Samuel Taylor (1817). *Biographia Literaria.* Ed. Nigel Leask. London: J. M. Dent, 1997.
Fforde, Jasper (2001). *The Eyre Affair.* London: Hodder and Stoughton.
Glassco, John (1971). 'Catbird'. In *John Glassco: Selected Poems with Three Notes on the Poetic Process*, ed. Michael Gnarowski. Ottawa: The Golden Dog Press, 1997, pp. 54–55.
Hamilton, Steve (2001). *Winter of the Wolf Moon.* London: Orion.
James, Henry (1877). *The American.* New York: H. O. Houghton & Co., and James R. Osgood & Co.
Jemisin, N. K. (2015). *The Fifth Season. The Broken Earth: Book I.* London: Orbit.
Keats, John (1815). 'To Hope'. In Miriam Allott (ed.) (1970). *Keats: The Complete Poems.* London: Longman, p. 12.
Kincaid, Nanci (1997). *Pretending the Bed is a Raft.* Chapel Hill, NC: Algonquin Books.
McEwan, Ian (2001). *Atonement.* London: Jonathan Cape.
Martin, George R. R. (1996). *A Game of Thrones.* New York: Bantam Books.
Melville, Herman (1851). *Moby Dick; or, The Whale.* New York: Harper & Brothers.
Morrison, Toni (1987). *Beloved.* London: Vintage.

Orwell, George (1945). *Animal Farm*. Harmondsworth: Penguin Books.
PhD Comics by Jorge Cham (2008). 'Average time spent composing one e-mail'. Piled Higher and Deeper Publishing. <http://phdcomics.com/comics/archive.php?comicid=1047> (last accessed 22 February 2020).
poppy.rider (2012). Milan Mary. <https://www.fanfiction.net/s/8713771/1/Milan-Mary> (last accessed 18 February 2020).
Rhys, Jean (1966). *Wide Sargasso Sea*. London: André Deutsch.
Shakespeare, William (1599). *As You Like It*. Ed. Juliet Dusinberre. The Arden Shakespeare. Third Series. London: Thomson Learning, 2006.
Shakespeare, William (1599). *Julius Caesar*. Ed. David Daniell. The Arden Shakespeare. Third Series. London: Thomson Learning, 1998.
Shakespeare, William (1600). *Hamlet*. Ed. Ann Thompson and Neil Taylor. The Arden Shakespeare. Third Series. London: Bloomsbury, 2006
Shaw, George Bernard [1914] (1983). *Pygmalion*. Repr. London: Penguin.
Sterne, Laurence (1762). *The Life and Opinions of Tristram Shandy, Gentleman*. London: T. Becket and P. A. Dehondt.
Towles, Amor (2011). *Rules of Civility*. London: Hodder & Stoughton.
Watterson, Bill (1990). CALVIN AND HOBBES © 1990 Watterson. Reprinted with permission of ANDREWS MCMEEL SYNDICATION. All rights reserved.
WolfsCub (2013). Hermione Jane Eyre. <https://www.fanfiction.net/s/9869211/1/Hermione-Jane-Eyre> (last accessed 18 February 2020).
Wong, Jennifer (2013). 'Itinerary' from *Goldfish*. <https://www.poetryfoundation.org/poems/146990/itinerary> (last accessed 18 February 2020).

Movies and television series

Details about films and television series have been taken from <https://www.imdb.com/>.

Amadeus (1984). Dir. Miloš Forman. Original stage play and original screenplay by Peter Shaffer.
The Big Lebowski (1998). Dir. Joel Coen and Ethan Coen. Screenplay by Ethan Coen and Joel Coen.
Blue in the Face (1995). Dir. Paul Auster, Wayne Wang and Harvey Wang. Written by Paul Auster and Wayne Wang.
Bride and Prejudice (2004). Dir. Gurinder Chadha. Screenplay by Paul Mayeda Berges.
Erin Brockovich (2000). Dir. Steven Soderbergh. Screenplay by Susannah Grant.
Finding Nemo (2003). Dir. Andrew Stanton and Lee Unkrich. Screenplay by Andrew Stanton.
Game of Thrones (2011–2019). Producers and screen play writers, inter alia, Dir. David Benioff and D. B. Weiss.

He's Just Not That Into You (2009). Dir. Ken Kwapis. Screenplay by Abby Kohn and Marc Silverstein. Trailer at <http://www.imdb.com/video/screenplay/vi3392537369/> (last accessed 2 October 2020).
House MD (2006). Creator: David Shore. Season 3, Episode 3. Transcription at <https://clinic-duty.livejournal.com/13589.html> (last accessed 2 October 2020).
How I Met Your Mother (2011). Creators: Carter Bays and Craig Thomas. Season 7, Episode 10.
Lost in Translation (2003). Dir. Sofia Coppola. Screenplay by Sofia Coppola.
Meloholic (2017). Dir. Hyun Wook Song.
My Cousin Vinny (1992). Dir. Jonathan Lynn. Screenplay by Dale Launer.
My Life Without Me (2002). Dir. Isabel Coixet. Screenplay by Isabel Coixet.
The Passion of the Christ (2004). Dir. Mel Gibson. Screenplay by Benedict Fitzgerald and Mel Gibson.
The Tudors (2009). Creator: Michael Hirst. Season 3, Episode 7.
The West Wing (1999). Creator: Aaron Sorkin. Season 1, Episode 6.

Dictionaries and corpora

Corpus of Contemporary American English (COCA). <https://www.english-corpora.org/coca> (last accessed 2 October 2020).
Oxford English Dictionary (OED). <https://www.oed.com> (last accessed 2 October 2020).

Websites

100 best first lines from novels. American Book Review. <http://americanbookreview.org/100BestLines.asp> (last accessed 2 October 2020).
Archive of Our Own. <https://archiveofourown.org> (last accessed 2 October 2020).
The Big Read Top 21. BBC. <https://www.bbc.co.uk/arts/bigread/vote/> (archived website, last accessed 4 July 2019).
FanFiction. <https://www.fanfiction.net/> (last accessed 2 October 2020).
Viki. <https://www.viki.com> (last accessed 2 October 2020).
What is the function of film music? Robin Hoffmann. <https://www.robin-hoffmann.com/tutorials/what-is-the-function-of-film-music/> (last accessed 2 October 2020).

References

Agha, Asif (2003). The social life of cultural value. *Language and Communication* 23(3–4): 231–273.
Andersen, Peter A. and Laura K. Guerrero (1998). Principles of communication and emotion in social interaction. In Peter A. Andersen and Laura

K. Guerrero (eds), *Handbook of Communication and Emotion: Research, Theory, Applications, and Contexts.* San Diego: Academic Press, pp. 49–96.

Androutsopoulos, Jannis (2012). Introduction: Language and society in cinematic discourse. *Multilingua* 31(2–3): 139–154. <doi:10.1515/multi-2012-0007>.

Atencia-Linares, Paloma (2019). Sound in film. In Noël Carroll, Laura T. Di Summa and Shawn Loht (eds), *The Palgrave Handbook of the Philosophy of Film and Motion Pictures.* Cham: Palgrave Macmillan, pp. 189–214.

Baldick, Chris (2015). *The Oxford Dictionary of Literary Terms.* 4th edn. Oxford: Oxford University Press.

Bax, Stephen (2011). *Discourse and Genre: Analysing Language in Context.* Basingstoke: Palgrave Macmillan.

Bednarek, Monika (2008). *Emotion Talk Across Corpora.* Basingstoke: Palgrave Macmillan.

Bednarek, Monika (2010). *The Language of Fictional Television: Drama and Identity.* London: Continuum.

Bednarek, Monika (2017). The role of dialogue in fiction. In Miriam A. Locher and Andreas H. Jucker (eds), *Pragmatics of Fiction.* Handbooks of Pragmatics 12. Berlin/Boston: de Gruyter Mouton, pp. 129–158.

Bednarek, Monika (2018). *Language and Television Series: A Linguistic Approach to TV Dialogue.* Cambridge: Cambridge University Press.

Bell, Allan (1984). Language style as audience design. *Language in Society* 13(2): 145–204.

Bell, Allan (1991). *The Language of News Media.* Oxford: Blackwell.

Berman, Ruth A. (2009). Language development in narrative contexts. In Edith L. Bavin (ed.), *The Cambridge Handbook of Child Language.* Cambridge: Cambridge University Press, pp. 355–376.

Biber, Douglas (1988). *Variation Across Speech and Writing.* Cambridge: Cambridge University Press.

Biber, Douglas (1989). A typology of English texts. *Linguistics* 27(1): 3–43.

Biber, Douglas and Susan Conrad (2009). *Register, Genre, and Style.* Cambridge: Cambridge University Press.

Biber, Douglas, Stig Johansson, Geoffrey Leech, Susan Conrad and Edward Finegan (1999). *Longman Grammar of Spoken and Written English.* London: Longman.

Blakemore, Diane (1992). *Understanding Utterances: An Introduction to Pragmatics.* Oxford: Blackwell.

Bleichenbacher, Lukas (2008). *Multilingualism in the Movies: Hollywood Characters and Their Language Choices.* Tübingen: Narr Francke.

Bobetsky, Victor V. (2014). The complex ancestry of 'We Shall Overcome'. *The Choral Journal* 54(7): 26–36.

Boyer, Horace Clarence (1983). Charles Albert Tindley: Progenitor of Black-American gospel music. *The Black Perspective in Music* 11(2): 103–132.

Brown, Penelope and Stephen C. Levinson (1978). Universals in language usage: Politeness phenomena. In Esther N. Goody (ed.), *Questions and Politeness.* Cambridge: Cambridge University Press, pp. 56–289.

Brown, Penelope and Stephen C. Levinson (1987). *Politeness: Some Universals in Language Usage*. Cambridge: Cambridge University Press.
Bubel, Claudia (2008). Film audiences as overhearers. *Journal of Pragmatics* 40: 55–71.
Bublitz, Wolfram (2017). Oral features in fiction. In Miriam A. Locher and Andreas H. Jucker (eds), *Pragmatics of Fiction*. Handbooks of Pragmatics 12. Berlin/Boston: de Gruyter Mouton, pp. 235–263.
Bucholtz, Mary and Kira Hall (2005). Identity and interaction: A sociocultural linguistic approach. *Discourse Studies* 7(4–5): 585–614.
Bucholtz, Mary and Kira Hall (2008). Finding identity: Theory and data. *Multilingua* 27(1–2): 151–163.
Burke, Michael (ed.) (2014). *The Routledge Handbook of Stylistics*. Oxon: Routledge.
Chapman, Siobhan (2011). *Pragmatics*. Palgrave Modern Linguistics. Basingstoke: Palgrave Macmillan.
Chapman, Siobhan and Billy Clark (eds) (2014). *Pragmatic Literary Stylistics*. Palgrave Studies in Pragmatics, Language and Cognition. London: Palgrave Macmillan.
Chapman, Siobhan and Billy Clark (eds) (2019). *Pragmatics and Literature*. Amsterdam: John Benjamins.
Clark, Billy (2013). *Relevance Theory*. Cambridge Textbook in Linguistics. Cambridge: Cambridge University Press.
Clark, Billy (2014). Stylistics and relevance theory. In Michael Burke (ed.), *The Routledge Handbook of Stylistics*. Oxon: Routledge, pp. 155–174.
Clark, Herbert (1996). *Using Language*. Cambridge: Cambridge University Press.
Conrad, Susan and Douglas Biber (2001a). Multidimensional methodology and the dimensions of register variation in English. In Susan Conrad and Douglas Biber (eds), *Variation in English: Multidimensional Studies*. London: Longman, pp. 13–42.
Conrad, Susan and Douglas Biber (eds) (2001b). *Variation in English: Multidimensional Studies*. London: Longman.
Corbett, John (2006). Genre and genre analysis. In Keith Brown (ed.), *Encyclopedia of Language & Linguistics*. 2nd edn. Oxford: Elsevier, pp. 26–32.
Cresci, Elena (2016). Lonelygirl15: How one mysterious vlogger changed the internet. *The Guardian*, 16 June. <https://www.theguardian.com/technology/2016/jun/16/lonelygirl15-bree-video-blog-youtube> (last accessed 18 February 2020).
Cressman, Dale L., Mark Callister, Tom Robinson and Chris Near (2009). Swearing in the cinema. *Journal of Children and Media* 3(2): 117–135. <doi:10.1080/17482790902772257>.
Cuddon, J. A. (2013). *A Dictionary of Literary Terms and Literary Theory*. 5th edn. Malden/Oxford: Wiley-Blackwell.
Culpeper, Jonathan (2001). *Language and Characterisation: People in Plays and other Texts*. London: Longman Pearson Education.
Culpeper, Jonathan and Carolina Fernandez-Quintanilla (2017). Fictional characterisation. In Miriam A. Locher and Andreas H. Jucker (eds), *Pragmatics of*

Fiction. Handbooks of Pragmatics 12. Berlin/Boston: de Gruyter Mouton, pp. 93–128.

Culpeper, Jonathan and Michael Haugh (2014). *Pragmatics and the English Language*. London: Palgrave Macmillan.

Culpeper, Jonathan, Michael Haugh and Dániel Z. Kádár (eds) (2017). *Palgrave Handbook of Linguistic (Im)Politeness*. London: Palgrave.

Cummins, Chris (2019). *Pragmatics*. Edinburgh Textbooks on the English Language – Advanced. Edinburgh: Edinburgh University Press.

Davidson, Jenny (2004). *Hypocrisy and the Politics of Politeness: Manners and Morals from Locke to Austen*. Cambridge: Cambridge University Press.

Dayter, Daria (2015). Small stories and extended narratives on Twitter. *Discourse, Context and Media* 10: 19–26. <doi:10.1016/j.dcm.2015.05.003>.

Dayter, Daria (2016). *Discursive Self in Microblogging: Speech Acts, Stories and Self-praise*. Amsterdam/Philadelphia: John Benjamins.

Detenber, Benjamin H. and Annie Lang (2011). The influence of form and presentation attributes of media in emotion. In Katrin Döveling, Christian Scheve and Elly A. Konijn (eds), *The Routledge Handbook of Emotions and Mass Media*. London/New York: Routledge, pp. 275–293.

Doležel, Lubomír (1989). Possible worlds and literary fiction. In Allén Sture (ed.), *Possible Worlds in Humanities, Arts and Sciences*. Proceedings of Nobel Symposium 65. Berlin: Walter de Gruyter, pp. 221–242.

Döveling, Katrin, Christian Scheve and Elly A. Konijn (eds) (2011). *The Routledge Handbook of Emotions and Mass Media*. London/New York: Routledge.

Du Bois, John W., Susanna Cumming, Stephan Schütze-Coburn and Danae Padino (eds) (1992). *Discourse Transcription: Santa Barbara Papers in Linguistics*. Vol. 4. Santa Barbara: University of California.

Dyck, John (2019). The sonic art of film and the sonic arts in film. In Noël Carroll, Laura T. Di Summa and Shawn Loht (eds), *The Palgrave Handbook of the Philosophy of Film and Motion Pictures*. Cham: Palgrave Macmillan, pp. 801–821.

Dynel, Marta (2011). 'You talking to me?' The viewer as a ratified listener to film discourse. *Journal of Pragmatics* 43: 1628–1644.

Dynel, Marta (2012). Setting our House in order: The workings of impoliteness in multi-party film discourse. *Journal of Politeness Research* 8: 161–194.

Dynel, Marta (2015). Impoliteness in the service of verisimilitude in film interaction. In Marta Dynel and Jan Chovanec (eds), *Participation in Public and Social Media Interactions*. Amsterdam/Philadelphia: John Benjamins, pp. 157–182.

Dynel, Marta (2017). (Im)politeness and telecinematic discourse. In Miriam A. Locher and Andreas H. Jucker (eds), *Pragmatics of Fiction*. Handbooks of Pragmatics 12. Berlin/Boston: de Gruyter Mouton, pp. 455–487.

Eckert, Penelope and Sally McConnell-Ginet (1992). Think practically and act locally: Language and gender as community-based practice. *Annual Review of Anthropology* 21: 461–490.

Eco, Umberto (1990). *The Limits of Interpretation*. Advances in Semiotics. Bloomington: Indiana University Press.
The Editors of Encyclopaedia Britannica (2017). Improvisation. Encyclopaedia Britannica. <https://www.britannica.com/art/improvisation-theatre> (last accessed 2 October 2020).
Ekman, Paul and Wallace V. Friesen (1975). *Unmasking the Face: A Guide to Recognizing Emotions from Facial Clues*. Englewood Cliffs, NJ: Prentice Hall.
Fitzmaurice, Susan (2010). Changes in the meanings of *politeness* in eighteenth-century England: Discourse analysis and historical evidence. In Jonathan Culpeper and Dániel Kádár (eds), *Historical (Im)politeness*. Bern: Peter Lang, pp. 87–115.
Gavins, Joanna (2007). *Text World Theory: An Introduction*. Edinburgh: Edinburgh University Press.
Gavins, Joanna (2016). Text-worlds. In Violeta Sotirova (ed.), *The Bloomsbury Companion to Stylistics*. London: Bloomsbury Academic, pp. 444–457.
Genette, Gérard (1972). *Figures III*. Paris: Seuil.
Genette, Gérard (1980). *Narrative Discourse*. Ithaca/London: Cornell University Press.
Georgakopoulou, Alexandra (2007). *Small Stories, Interaction and Identities*. Amsterdam/Philadelphia: John Benjamins.
Georgakopoulou, Alexandra (2016). From narrating the self to posting self(ies): A small stories approach to selfies. *Open Linguistics* 2(1): 300–317. <doi:10.1515/opli-2016-0014>.
Giltrow, Janet (2017). The pragmatics of the genres of fiction. In Miriam A. Locher and Andreas H. Jucker (eds), *Pragmatics of Fiction*. Handbooks of Pragmatics 12. Berlin/Boston: de Gruyter Mouton, pp. 55–91.
Giovanelli, Marcello and Jessica Mason (2018). *The Language of Literature: An Introduction to Stylistics*. Cambridge: Cambridge University Press.
Goffman, Erving (ed.) (1967). *Interaction Ritual: Essays on Face-to-face Behavior*. Garden City, NY: Anchor Books.
Goffman, Erving (1974). *Frame Analysis: An Essay on the Organization of Experience*. Cambridge, MA: Harvard University Press.
Goffman, Erving (1979). Footing. *Semiotica* 25(1–2): 1–29.
Green, Keith (2006). Deixis and anaphora: Pragmatic approaches. In Keith Brown (ed.), *Encyclopedia of Language & Linguistics*. Oxford: Elsevier, pp. 415–417.
Greenfield, Steve, Guy Osborn and Peter Robson (2010). *Film and the Law: The Cinema of Justice*. Oxford: Hart.
Gregory, Michael (1967). Aspects of varieties differentiation. *Journal of Linguistics* 2: 177–198.
Grice, H. Paul (1975). Logic and conversation. In Peter Cole and J. L. Morgan (eds), *Syntax and Semantics 3: Speech Acts*. New York: Academic Press, pp. 41–58.
Gurlyand, Ilia (1904). Reminiscences of A. P. Chekhov. *Teatr i iskusstvo* 28(11 July): 521.

Hamilton, Heidi E. (1998). Reported speech and survivor identity in online bone marrow transplantation narratives. *Journal of Sociolinguistics* 2: 53–67.

Hellekson, Karen and Kristina Busse (eds) (2014). *The Fan Fiction Studies Reader.* Iowa City: University of Iowa Press.

Hodson, Jane (2014). *Dialect in Film & Literature.* Basingstoke: Palgrave Macmillan.

Hodson, Jane (2016). Dialect in literature. In Violeta Sotirova (ed.), *The Bloomsbury Companion to Stylistics.* London: Bloomsbury Academic, pp. 416–429.

Hoffmann, Christian R. (2017). Narrative perspectives on voice in fiction. In Miriam A. Locher and Andreas H. Jucker (eds), *Pragmatics of Fiction.* Handbooks of Pragmatics 12. Berlin/Boston: de Gruyter Mouton, pp. 159–195.

Huang, Yan (2014). *Pragmatics.* 2nd edn. Oxford: Oxford University Press.

Jahn, Manfred (2003). *A Guide to Narratological Film Analysis. Poems, Plays, and Prose: A Guide to the Theory of Literary Genres.* <http://www.uni-koeln.de/~ame02/pppf.htm#F1> (last accessed 18 February 2020).

Jahn, Manfred (2017). *Narratology: A Guide to the Theory of Narrative.* English Department, University of Cologne. <http://www.uni-koeln.de/~ame02/pppn.htm> (last accessed 18 February 2020).

Jay, Timothy and Kristin Janschewitz (2008). The pragmatics of swearing. *Journal of Politeness Research* 4(2): 267–288.

Johnstone, Barbara (1990). *Stories, Community, and Place: Narratives from Middle America.* Bloomington: Indiana University Press.

Jucker, Andreas H. (2010). 'In curteisie was set ful muchel hir lest': Politeness in Middle English. In Jonathan Culpeper and Dániel Kádár (eds), *Historical (Im)politeness.* Vol. 65. Bern: Peter Lang, pp. 175–200.

Jucker, Andreas H. (2015). Pragmatics of fiction: Literary uses of *uh* and *um*. *Journal of Pragmatics* 86: 63–67.

Jucker, Andreas H. (2016). Politeness in eighteenth-century drama: A discursive approach. *Journal of Politeness Research* 12(1): 95–115. <doi:10.1515/pr-2015-0027>.

Jucker, Andreas H. (2020). *Politeness in the History of English: From the Middle Ages to the Present Day.* Cambridge: Cambridge University Press.

Jucker, Andreas H. and Christa Dürscheid (2012). The linguistics of keyboard-to-screen communication: A new terminological framework. *Linguistik Online* 56(6/12). <https://bop.unibe.ch/linguistik-online/article/view/6584/> (last accessed 18 February 2020).

Jucker, Andreas H. and Joanna Kopaczyk (2017). Historical (im)politeness. In Jonathan Culpeper, Michael Haugh and Dániel Z. Kádár (eds), *Palgrave Handbook of Linguistic (Im)Politeness.* London: Palgrave, pp. 433–459.

Jucker, Andreas H. and Miriam A. Locher (2017). Introducing Pragmatics of Fiction: Approaches, trends and developments. In Miriam A. Locher and Andreas H. Jucker (eds), *Pragmatics of Fiction.* Handbooks of Pragmatics 12. Berlin/Boston: de Gruyter Mouton, pp. 1–21.

Kizelbach, Urszula (2017). (Im)politeness in fiction. In Miriam A. Locher and Andreas H. Jucker (eds), *Pragmatics of Fiction*. Handbooks of Pragmatics 12. Berlin/Boston: de Gruyter Mouton, pp. 425–454.

Klapproth, Danièle (2004). *Narrative as Social Practice: Anglo-Western and Australian Aboriginal Oral Traditions*. Berlin: Mouton de Gruyter.

Klauk, Tobias and Tilmann Köppe (2014). Bausteine einer Theorie der Fiktionalität. In Tobias Klauk and Tilmann Köppe (eds), *Fiktionalität: Ein interdisziplinäres Handbuch*. Berlin: Mouton de Gruyter, pp. 3–31.

Kopytko, Roman (1995). Linguistic politeness strategies in Shakespeare's plays. In Andreas H. Jucker (ed.), *Historical Pragmatics: Pragmatic Developments in the History of English*. Amsterdam/Philadelphia: John Benjamins, pp. 515–540.

Kozloff, Sarah (2000). *Overhearing Film Dialogue*. Berkeley: University of California Press.

Kuhn, Markus (2014). YouTube als Loopingbahn. lonelygirl15 als Phänomen und Symptom der Erfolgsinitiation von YouTube. *Repositorium Medienkulturforschung* 6: 1–21.

Kurzon, Dennis (2011). Editorial on silence. *Journal of Pragmatics* 43(9): 2275–2277.

Labov, William (1972). *Language in the Inner City: Studies in the Black English Vernacular*. Philadelphia: University of Pennsylvania Press.

Labov, William (1997). Some further steps in narrative analysis. *Journal of Narrative and Life History* 7: 395–415.

Labov, William (2013). *The Language of Life and Death: The Transformation of Experience in Oral Narrative*. Cambridge: Cambridge University Press.

Labov, William and Joshua Waletzky (1967). Narrative analysis: Oral versions of personal experience. In June Helm (ed.), *Essays on the Verbal and Visual Arts: Proceedings of the 1966 Annual Spring Meeting of the American Ethnological Society*. Seattle: American Ethnological Society, pp. 12–44. Reprinted in *Journal of Narrative and Life History* 7(1–4) (1997): 3–38.

Lakoff, George and Mark Johnson [1980] (2003). *Metaphors We Live By*. Chicago: The University of Chicago Press.

Lakoff, Robin Tolmach (1973). The logic of politeness, or minding your p's and q's. *Chicago Linguistics Society* 9: 292–305.

Landert, Daniela (2017). Stance in fiction. In Miriam A. Locher and Andreas H. Jucker (eds), *Pragmatics of Fiction*. Handbooks of Pragmatics 12. Berlin/Boston: de Gruyter Mouton, pp. 489–514.

Langlotz, Andreas (2017). Language and emotion in fiction. In Miriam A. Locher and Andreas H. Jucker (eds), *Pragmatics of Fiction*. Handbooks of Pragmatics 12. Berlin/Boston: de Gruyter Mouton, pp. 515–552.

Langlotz, Andreas and Miriam A. Locher (2013). The role of emotions in relational work. *Journal of Pragmatics* 58: 87–107.

Leech, Geoffrey N. (1983). *Principles of Pragmatics*. New York: Longman.

Leech, Geoffrey N. (2014). *The Pragmatics of Politeness*. Oxford: Oxford University Press.

Levinson, Stephen C. (1992). Activity types and language. In Paul Drew and John Heritage (eds), *Talk at Work: Interaction in Institutional Settings.* Cambridge: Cambridge University Press, pp. 66–100.

Linde, Charlotte (1993). *Life Stories: The Creation of Coherence.* Oxford/New York: Oxford University Press.

Lippi-Green, Rosina L. (1997). *English with an Accent: Language, Ideology, and Discrimination in the United States.* London: Routledge.

Locher, Miriam A. (2004). *Power and Politeness in Action: Disagreements in Oral Communication.* Berlin/New York: Mouton de Gruyter.

Locher, Miriam A. (2008a). Relational work, politeness and identity construction. In Gerd Antos, Eija Ventola and Tilo Weber (eds), *Handbooks of Applied Linguistics. Volume 2: Interpersonal Communication.* Berlin/New York: Mouton de Gruyter, pp. 509–540.

Locher, Miriam A. (2008b). The rise of prescriptive grammars in the 18th century. In Miriam A. Locher and Jürg Strässler (eds), *Standards and Norms in the English Language.* Berlin: Mouton de Gruyter, pp. 127–147.

Locher, Miriam A. (2017a). Multilingualism in fiction. In Miriam A. Locher and Andreas H. Jucker (eds), *Pragmatics of Fiction.* Handbooks of Pragmatics 12. Berlin/Boston: de Gruyter Mouton, pp. 297–327.

Locher, Miriam A. (2017b). *Reflective Writing in Medical Practice: A Linguistic Perspective.* Bristol: Multilingual Matters.

Locher, Miriam A. (2018). Politeness. In Carol A. Chapelle (ed.), *The Encyclopedia of Applied Linguistics.* 2nd edn. Hoboken, NJ: John Wiley & Sons.

Locher, Miriam A. and Sage L. Graham (2010). Introduction to Interpersonal Pragmatics. In Miriam A. Locher and Sage L. Graham (eds), *Interpersonal Pragmatics.* Berlin: Mouton, pp. 1–13.

Locher, Miriam A. and Andreas H. Jucker (eds) (2017). *Pragmatics of Fiction.* Handbooks of Pragmatics 12. Berlin/Boston: de Gruyter Mouton.

Locher, Miriam A. and Thomas C. Messerli (2020). Translating the other: Communal TV watching of Korean TV drama. *Journal of Pragmatics* 170: 20–36. <doi.org/10.1016/j.pragma.2020.07.002>.

Locher, Miriam A. and Richard J. Watts (2005). Politeness theory and relational work. *Journal of Politeness Research* 1(1): 9–33.

Locher, Miriam A. and Richard J. Watts (2008). Relational work and impoliteness: Negotiating norms of linguistic behaviour. In Derek Bousfield and Miriam A. Locher (eds), *Impoliteness in Language: Studies on its Interplay with Power in Theory and Practice.* Berlin: Mouton de Gruyter, pp. 77–99.

Lynskey, Dorian (2011). *33 Revolutions per Minute: A History of Protest Songs, from Billie Holiday to Green Day.* New York: Ecco.

Machura, Stefan and Peter Robinson (2001). Law in film: Introduction. *Journal of Law and Society* 28(1): 1–8.

Machura, Stefan, Stefan Ulbrich, Francis M. Nevins and Nils Behling (2001). Law in film: Globalizing the Hollywood courtroom drama. *Journal of Law and Society* 28(1): 117–132.

McIntyre, Dan and Derek Bousfield (2017). (Im)politeness in fictional texts. In Jonathan Culpeper, Michael Haugh and Dániel Z. Kádár (eds), *Palgrave Handbook of Linguistic (Im)Politeness*. London: Palgrave, pp. 759–783.

Mackenzie, J. Lachlan and Laura Alba-Juez (eds) (2019). *Emotion in Discourse*. Pragmatics & Beyond New Series 302. Amsterdam/Philadelphia: John Benjamins.

Mareš, P. (2000a). Fikce, konvence a realita: k vicejazy nosti v um leckych textech [Fiction, convention and reality: On multilingualism in artistic texts]. *Slovo a slovesnost* 61: 47–53.

Mareš, P. (2000b). Mnogojazy naja kommunikacija i kinofil'm [Multilingual communication and the movie]. In Rossijskaja Akademija Nauk (ed.), *Jazyk kak sredstvo transljatsii kul'tury* [Language as a means of translation of cultures]. Moscow: Nauka, pp. 248–265.

Mareš, P. (2003). *'Also: Nazdar!': Aspekty Textové Vícejazy nosti*. Prague: Karolinum.

Marsh, Huw (2018). Narrative unreliability and metarepresentation in Ian McEwan's *Atonement*; or, why Robbie might be guilty and why nobody seems to notice. *Textual Practice* 32(8): 1325–1343. <doi:10.1080/09502 36x.2016.1276955>.

Martínez, Matias and Michael Scheffel (2009). *Einführung in die Erzähltheorie*. Munich: Beck.

Mayer-Schönberger, Viktor and Lena Wong (2013). Fan or foe: Fan fiction, authorship, and the fight for control. *IDEA* 54(1): 1–21.

Messerli, Thomas C. (2017). Participation structure in fictional discourse: Authors, scriptwriters, audiences and characters. In Miriam A. Locher and Andreas H. Jucker (eds), *Pragmatics of Fiction*. Handbooks of Pragmatics 12. Berlin/Boston: de Gruyter Mouton, pp. 25–54.

Montagu, Ashley (2001). *The Anatomy of Swearing*. Philadelphia: University of Pennsylvania Press.

Nelson, Keith E. and Kiren S. Khan (2019). New frontiers in facilitating narrative skills in children and adolescents: A dynamic systems account incorporating eight narrative developmental stages. In Edy Veneziano and Ageliki Nicolopoulou (eds), *Narrative, Literacy and Other Skills: Studies in Intervention*. Amsterdam/Philadelphia: John Benjamins, pp. 193–219.

Norrthon, Stefan (2019). To stage an overlap: The longitudinal, collaborative and embodied process of staging eight lines in a professional theatre rehearsal process. *Journal of Pragmatics* 142: 171–184.

Ochs, Elinor (1992). Indexing gender. In Charles Goodwin and Alessandro Duranti (eds), *Rethinking Context: Language as an Interactive Phenomenon*. Cambridge: Cambridge University Press, pp. 335–358.

Oh, Youjeong (2015). The interactive nature of Korean TV drama. Flexible texts, discursive consumption, and social media. In Sangjoon Lee and Markus Nornes (eds), *Hallyu 2.0: The Korean Wave in the Age of Social Media*. Ann Arbor: University of Michigan Press, pp. 133–153.

Paltridge, Brian, Angela Thomas and Jianxin Liu (2011). Genre, performance and *Sex and the City*. In Roberta Piazza, Monika Bednarek and Fabio Rossi (eds), *Telecinematic Discourse: Approaches to the Language of Films and Television Series*. Amsterdam/Philadelphia: John Benjamins, pp. 249–262.

Patta, Yoda (1997). Questions for a research paper. Hatrack River: The Official Web Site of Orson Scott Card. <http://www.hatrack.com/research/interviews/yoda-patta.shtml> (last accessed 18 February 2020).

Phillipson, Robert (1992). *Linguistic Imperialism*. Oxford: Oxford University Press.

Piazza, Roberta, Monika Bednarek and Fabio Rossi (eds) (2011). *Telecinematic Discourse: Approaches to the Language of Films and Television Series*. Pragmatics & Beyond New Series 211. Amsterdam/Philadelphia: John Benjamins.

Pilkington, Adrian (1991). Poetic effects. In Roger D. Sell (ed.), *Literary Pragmatics*. London: Routledge, pp. 44–61.

Pilkington, Adrian (2000). *Poetic Effects: A Relevance Theory Perspective*. Pragmatics & Beyond New Series 75. Amsterdam/Philadelphia: John Benjamins.

Planalp, Sally (1998). Communicating emotion in everyday life: Cues, channels, and processes. In Peter A. Andersen and Laura K. Guerrero (eds), *Handbook of Communication and Emotion: Research, Theory, Application, and Contexts*. San Diego, CA: Academic Press, pp. 29–48.

Planalp, Sally (1999). *Communicating Emotion: Social, Moral, and Cultural Processes*. Cambridge: Cambridge University Press.

Planchenault, Gaëlle (2015). *Voices in the Media: Performing French Linguistic Otherness*. London: Bloomsbury Academic.

Planchenault, Gaëlle (2017). Doing dialects in dialogues: Regional, social and ethnic variation in fiction. In Miriam A. Locher and Andreas H. Jucker (eds), *Pragmatics of Fiction*. Handbooks of Pragmatics 12. Berlin/Boston: de Gruyter Mouton, pp. 265–296.

Quaglio, Paulo (2009). *Television Dialogue: The Sitcom* Friends *vs. Natural Conversation*. Studies in Corpus Linguistics 36. Amsterdam/Philadelphia: John Benjamins.

Queen, Robin (2004). 'Du hast jar keene Ahnung': African American English dubbed into German. *Journal of Sociolinguistics* 8(4): 515–537.

Radford, Colin and Michael Weston (1975) How can we be moved by the fate of Anna Karenina? *Aristotelian Society Supplementary Volume* 49(1): 67–94.

Rich, Motoko (2003). What else was lost in translation. *New York Times*, 21 September, Section 9, p. 1, <https://www.nytimes.com/2003/09/21/style/what-else-was-lost-in-translation.html?searchResultPosition=1> (last accessed 18 February 2020).

Richardson, Kay (2010). *Television Dramatic Dialogue: A Sociolinguistic Study*. New York: Oxford University Press.

Rimmon-Kenan, Shlomith (2002). *Narrative Fiction*. London/New York: Routledge.

Rossi, Fabio (2011). Discourse analysis of film dialogues: Italian comedy between linguistic realism and pragmatic non-realism. In Roberta Piazza, Monika Bednarek and Fabio Rossi (eds), *Telecinematic Discourse: Approaches to the Language of Films and Television Series*. Pragmatics & Beyond New Series 211. Amsterdam/Philadelphia: John Benjamins, pp. 21–46.

Rudanko, Juhani (2006). Aggravated impoliteness and two types of speaker intention in an episode in Shakespeare's *Timon of Athens*. *Journal of Pragmatics* 38(6): 829–841.
Schegloff, Emanuel (1997). 'Narrative analysis' thirty years later. *Journal of Narrative and Life History* 7: 97–106.
Schiffrin, Deborah (1996). Narrative as self-portrait: Sociolinguistic constructions of identity. *Language in Society* 25: 167–203.
Schubert, Christoph (2012). *Englische Textlinguistik: Eine Einführung*. 2nd edn. Berlin: Erich Schmidt.
Searle, John R. (1975). The logical status of fictional discourse. *New Literary History* 6(2): 319–332.
Semino, Elena (2007). Mind style 25 years on. *Style* 41(2): 153–203.
Senft, Gunter (2014). *Understanding Pragmatics*. London: Routledge.
Silverstein, Michael (1976). Shifters, categories and cultural description. In Keith H. Basso and Henry A. Selby (eds), *Meaning in Anthropology*. Albuquerque: University of New Mexico Press, pp. 11–55.
Silverstein, Michael (1985). Language and the culture of gender: At the intersection of structure, usage, and ideology. In Elizabeth Mertz and Richard J. Parmentier (eds), *Sociocultural and Psychological Perspectives*. London: Academic Press, pp. 219–259.
Sperber, Dan and Deirdre Wilson (1981). Irony and the use–mention distinction. In Peter Cole (ed.), *Radical Pragmatics*. New York: Academic Press, pp. 295–318.
Sperber, Dan and Deirdre Wilson (1986). *Relevance: Communication and Cognition*. Oxford: Basil Blackwell.
Sperber, Dan and Deirdre Wilson (1987). Précis of *Relevance: Communication and Cognition*. *Behavioral and Brain Sciences* 10: 697–754.
Sperber, Dan and Deirdre Wilson (1995). *Relevance: Communication and Cognition*. 2nd edn. Oxford: Basil Blackwell.
Stapleton, Karyn (2010). Swearing. In Miriam A. Locher and Sage L. Graham (eds), *Interpersonal Pragmatics*. Handbooks of Pragmatics 6. Berlin/New York: de Gruyter Mouton, pp. 289–305.
Stockwell, Peter and Sara Whiteley (eds) (2014). *The Cambridge Handbook of Stylistics*. Cambridge: Cambridge University Press.
Swales, John (1990). *Genre Analysis: English in Academic and Research Settings*. Cambridge: Cambridge University Press.
Taavitsainen, Irma and Gunnel Melchers (1999). Writing in nonstandard English: Introduction. In Irma Taavitsainen, Gunnel Melchers and Päivi Pahta (eds), *Writing in Nonstandard English*. Amsterdam/Philadelphia: John Benjamins, pp. 1–26.
Tannen, Deborah (1989). *Talking Voices: Repetition, Dialogue and Imagery in Conversational Discourse*. Cambridge: Cambridge University Press.
Toolan, Michael (2011). 'I don't know what they're saying half the time, but I'm hooked on the series': Incomprehensible dialogue and integrated multimodal characterisation in *The Wire*. In Roberta Piazza, Monika Bednarek

and Fabio Rossi (eds), *Telecinematic Discourse: Approaches to the Language of Films and Television Series*. Pragmatics & Beyond New Series 211. Amsterdam/Philadelphia: John Benjamins, pp. 161–183.

Tottie, Gunnel (2016). Planning what to say. *Uh* and *um* among the pragmatic markers. In Gunther Kaltenböck, Evelien Keizer and Arne Lohmann (eds), *Outside the Clause: Form and Function of Extra-clausal Constituents*. Amsterdam/Philadelphia: John Benjamins, pp. 97–122.

Van Dijk, Teun (1976). Pragmatics and poetics. In Teun van Dijk (ed.), *Pragmatics of Language and Literature*. Amsterdam: North Holland, pp. 23–57.

Vuille-dit-Bille, Clara (2018). Swearing and identity in J. K. Rowling's original and translated Harry Potter novels. MA seminar paper. University of Basel.

Watterson, Bill (2020). About Calvin and Hobbes: Character descriptions. <https://www.calvinandhobbes.com/about-calvin-and-hobbes/> (last accessed 18 February 2020).

Watts, Richard J. (2003). *Politeness*. Cambridge: Cambridge University Press.

Watts, Richard J. and Franz Andres Morrissey (2019). *Language, the Singer and the Song: The Sociolinguistics of Folk Performance*. Cambridge: Cambridge University Press.

Wiley, Terrence G. (2004). Language planning, language policy, and the English-Only Movement. In Edward Finegan and John R. Rickford (eds), *Language in the USA: Themes for the Twenty-first Century*. Cambridge: Cambridge University Press, pp. 319–338.

Wiley, Terrence G. (2014). Diversity, super-diversity, and monolingual language ideology in U.S.: Tolerance or intolerance? *Review of Research in Education* 38(1): 1–32.

Wilson, Deirdre and Dan Sperber (2004). Relevance theory. In Laurence R. Horn and Gregory Ward (eds), *The Handbook of Pragmatics*. Oxford: Blackwell, pp. 607–632.

Wilson, Deirdre and Dan Sperber (2012). *Meaning and Relevance*. Cambridge: Cambridge University Press.

Zillmann, Dolf (2011). Mechanisms of emotional reactivity to media entertainments. In Katrin Döveling, Christian Scheve and Elly A. Konijn (eds), *The Routledge Handbook of Emotions and Mass Media*. London/New York: Routledge, pp. 101–115.

Index

A Game of Thrones, 24, 25, 75
A Song of Ice and Fire, 75
accidental recipient, 44, 45, 48, 52, 56, 191, 231
activity type, 61, 63, 76, 153
Adam, Douglas, 148, 227
address terms, 102, 130, 140, 142, 145, 146, 162, 171, 187, 233
addressee recipient, 44, 45, 47, 48, 231
Adichie, Chimamanda Ngozi, 120
adjacency pair, 140, 145, 146
alienation effect, 99, 103, 116–19, 237
Allott, Miriam, 48–9
Amadeus, 70, 229
Americanah, 120
Andres Morrissey, Franz, 45, 203
Androutsopoulos, Jannis, 100
Anglo-American pragmatics, 7–8, 14
Animal Farm, 129–30, 132
animator, 49–50, 231
As You Like It, 222
asynchronous communication, 37–8, 136
Atonement, 93
attention signal, 140, 145–6
attributive language use, 215–16, 220, 222, 234
audience design, 42–3, 45, 82, 84, 87, 100, 146, 171
auditor, 42–3, 45, 52, 231
Austen, Jane, 28, 89, 116, 163, 232
Auster, Paul, 168
Austin, John, 6, 17

Bax, Stephen, 64–5, 67, 70, 74–5
Bednarek, Monika, 102, 121, 126–7, 131, 134, 149, 178, 195

Bell, Allan, 42–3, 45, 231
Beloved, 119
Biographia Literaria, 21
Blakemore, Diane, 200, 206, 223
Bleichenbacher, Lukas, 112–16
Blue in the Face, 168
Bride and Prejudice, 116
Brontë, Charlotte, 19–20, 24, 29, 31, 87
Bubel, Claudia, 58, 231
Bucholtz, Mary, 100, 121

Calvin and Hobbes, 174, 181–2, 190–1
camera work, 185, 188, 193
Catbird (poem), 221
Cham, Jorge, 172
Chapman, Siobhan, 14, 223, 238
characterisation cues, 94, 99, 109, 111, 116–19, 228–9, 232–3, 236–7
Chekhov, Anton, 71
Clark, Billy, 14, 208, 211–12, 215, 222–3, 238
Clark, Herbert, 8–10, 181
Cockney, 104, 107–8, 228
Cognitive Principle of Relevance, 197–8
Coixet, Isabel, 174, 183, 194
Coleridge, Samuel Taylor, 21, 22, 230
common ground, 70–2, 76, 81
communicative act, 39–42, 49–52, 56, 85, 199, 206, 220, 225
Communicative Principle of Relevance, 198–201, 206–7, 210, 213, 220
community of practice, 154, 170
composite signal (of emotions), 181–2, 190

Continental European pragmatics, 7, 235
Cooperative Principle, 208–9
core recipient, 44–5, 48–9, 191
Cressman, Dale L., 167, 169
cross-overs, 32
Culpeper, Jonathan, 14, 102–3, 172
Cummins, Chris, 14

Dayter, Daria, 84
deixis, 14, 89–90
descriptive language use, 216, 219
dialect, 102–4, 107–8, 112, 118, 120, 130, 228
dialogue, 3–4, 6, 11–12, 50, 77, 90, 96, 102, 108, 113, 115, 119, 125–38, 144, 146–8, 158, 161, 167, 233
diegesis, 9
discourse marker, 140, 142–4
display rules, 177
Dürscheid, Christa, 39
Dynel, Marta, 44, 56, 58, 76, 231

eavesdropper, 42–3, 45, 47, 54, 56, 213
elimination, 112–13
Emma, 163–5
emotion cues, 178–83, 185, 187–90, 193, 230
emotion talk, 178–82, 188, 192, 195
emotional talk, 178–82, 188, 192, 195
epic, 66, 70, 77, 87, 117
Erin Brockovich, 150, 154, 168–9, 188, 227
ethnic variety *see* ethnolect
ethnolect, 103–4, 130
evaluation, 80–2, 93–5, 128–30, 158, 232
evocation 112–14, 229, 232
explicature, 212–13
external focalisation, 92–3
extradiegetic, 8–9, 11, 36, 43–4, 46–8, 52, 54–6, 71–3, 135, 152, 169–71, 231
eye-dialect, 107–8

face, 153–8, 161, 165–6, 168
fan fiction, 3, 12, 24, 28–33, 66, 227
features of orality, 13, 126, 136–40, 143–4, 146–8, 229, 233, 237
Fforde, Jasper, 30, 34

fictional contract, 16, 21–2, 33, 67, 93, 95, 101, 118, 119, 129, 135, 147, 172–3, 190, 196, 225–33
film rating *see* movie rating
Finding Nemo, 88
focalisation, 92–3
foregrounding, 94
foreshadowing, 71, 95
Forman, Miloš, 229
frame of expectation, 61–7, 71–5, 150–4, 166, 225, 227

Games of Thrones, 34, 75, 117
genre, 4, 12, 19–25, 33, 61–78, 81, 84–8, 94, 96, 98, 102, 116, 147, 150, 162, 193, 226–8, 213, 236–7
genre schema, 64
Georgakopoulou, Alexandra, 83–4
George, Elizabeth, 85–6
Glassco, John, 221
Goffman, Erving, 42, 49–50, 52, 62, 154, 231
Goldfish, 37–8
gothic novel/fiction, 66
Gregory, Michael, 139
Grice, H. Paul, 208–9, 213–14

Hall, Kira, 100, 121
Hamilton, Heidi E., 128
Hamilton, Steve, 212, 222
Hamlet, 19, 131–4, 144–6
Harry Potter, 24, 25, 28, 32, 120, 130, 169
Haugh, Michael, 14
He's Just Not That Into You, 69, 74–5, 228
heterodiegetic, 92
highpoint story, 96
Hodson, Jane, 108, 121
Hoffmann, Christian R., 91–4, 97
homodiegetic, 92
House MD, 44–6, 58, 71–2, 76, 148
How I Met Your Mother, 53
Huang, Yan, 7, 14

identity construction, 83, 96, 99, 100, 106, 121, 152–8, 162, 166, 169–71, 177, 201, 213, 236
ideology, 7, 72, 100, 108, 112, 116, 119, 150–72, 229, 232–3, 236–8
idiolect, 103–4, 112

illocutionary force, 40–1
implicature, 102, 205–6, 209–14, 223
impoliteness, 7–8, 119, 147, 152, 165, 232
improvisation theatre, 6, 136–7, 229
I-narrator, 24, 30, 143–4, 212, 222
incidental recipient, 44–8, 56, 191, 231
indexicality, 74, 99–101, 108–9, 112, 117–19, 127, 147, 150, 152, 155, 163, 194, 228–9
Inside Out, 57
internal focalisation, 92–3
interpersonal pragmatics, 150, 172
intertextuality, 64, 84–8, 134, 236
intradiegetic, 8–11, 36, 43, 46–7, 52–6, 71–3, 158, 169–71, 231
irony, 128, 134, 197, 214–20, 222–3, 225, 234
'Itinerary' (poem), 38, 50, 57, 71

Jahn, Manfred, 70, 75, 77, 85, 92, 97, 127, 134
James, Henry, 113–14
Jane Eyre, 19–20, 24, 29–33, 86
Jemisin, N. K., 90
Johnstone, Barbara, 80–1, 97
Julius Caesar, 217, 219

Keats, John, 48–9
Kincaid, Nanci, 183, 194
Klapproth, Danièle, 78, 85–6, 97, 235
Klauk, Tobias, 19–20, 35, 84
Köppe, Tilmann, 19–20, 35, 84
Kozloff, Sarah, 125, 127, 130, 134, 149

Labov, William, 78–80, 83, 97, 231
Landert, Daniela, 92, 94–5, 97
Langlotz, Andreas, 174–5, 177–8, 183, 185, 190–2, 195
Levinson, Stephen C., 63, 76
Linde, Charlotte, 83
linguicism, 116, 119
Lippi-Green, Rosina L., 108, 116
literalness, 207–8
Locher, Miriam A., 65, 76, 117, 121, 154, 172, 183, 195
lonelygirl15, 26–7, 33, 93, 228
Lost in Translation, 114–15, 148
Lynskey, Dorian, 203
lyric, 66, 85, 202–5, 237

McEwan, Ian, 93
Machura, Stefan, 73, 76
Martin, George R., 75
Mayer-Schönberger, Viktor, 32, 35
Melchers, Gunnel, 109
Meloholic, 68, 228
Melville, Herman, 9–10, 89
meta recipient, 44–8, 56, 191, 231
meta-comment, 80, 114, 144, 166, 188
metaphor, 37, 94, 153, 183, 185, 197, 205, 207–15, 220, 222–3, 225, 234
mind style, 91–4
mise en scène, 175, 185, 188, 193
Moby Dick, 9, 89
Morrison, Toni, 119–20
movie rating, 167, 191
multilingualism, 72, 99, 102, 109, 116–17, 120
My Cousin Vinny, 109, 162
My Fair Lady, 106
My Life Without Me, 174, 183–91, 194, 226

narrative, 9, 23, 31, 33, 66, 70–1, 74, 77–99, 102, 125, 127–9, 131–3, 136, 138, 147, 149–50, 173–5, 179–80, 228, 231–2, 235, 237
narrator, 4, 9, 24, 30, 81, 86, 88–95, 102, 113–14, 119, 127, 130–1, 134–5, 143–4, 152, 173, 178, 180, 188–9, 212, 222, 230, 232

offline planning, 136, 138
Oh, 57
online planning, 135–9, 147, 229
orality, 13, 126, 136–48, 229, 233, 237
Orwell, George, 89, 129–31
ostensive communication, 198–9, 202–6, 220–1, 234
overhearer, 42–3, 48, 52, 156, 231

paradox of fiction, 175, 189–94
participation structure, 10, 12, 41–56, 58, 155–6, 158, 226, 231
Patta, Yoda, 32
Penny, Louise, 85–6
performed fiction, 4–6, 17, 21, 36, 51–7, 70, 74, 136–9, 147, 173–4, 178, 233, 235, 237

perlocutionary effect, 40–1
PhD Comics, 172
Pilkington, Adrian, 205, 223
Planalp, Sally, 175–6, 183, 189, 191–2, 195
Planchenault, Gaëlle, 161, 121
planner, 140–5
plot, 12, 50, 64, 66–74, 77, 85–6, 88, 91, 94, 96, 106, 109, 113–14, 116, 118, 126–34, 147, 150, 152, 159, 161–2, 166, 171, 231, 236
poetic effect, 197–207, 223, 237
politeness, 8, 13–14, 43, 103, 119, 150–72, 229, 232, 237
Pretending the Bed is a Raft (short story), 183, 194, 226
Pride and Prejudice, 89, 116
principal, 49–50, 52
Principles of Relevance, 197–201, 206–10, 213, 220
Pygmalion, 106–8, 118, 148, 162, 229

quasi-synchronous communication, 37–8, 136
Queen, Robin, 118

Radford, Colin, 190
red herring, 71
regional variation, 99–100, 103–4, 108, 118
relational work, 150–72, 177, 232
relevance theory, 197–223, 234
Rhys, Jean, 29–30, 86

Schiffrin, Deborah, 83, 100
Searle, John, 6, 17–18, 21, 39
Seeger, Pete, 202–5
Semino, Elena, 93
Senft, Gunter, 14
Shakespeare, William, 11, 15, 19, 24, 28, 34, 67, 108, 125, 131, 134, 144, 196, 217, 222, 227
Shannon, Elwood, 197
Shaw, George Bernard, 106–8, 162
showing mode, 127, 170, 178–80, 182, 185, 189, 193, 194, 230, 233
signalisation, 112–14
small story, 84, 96–7
sociolect, 102, 104, 108, 112, 130
song lyrics *see* lyric

Sperber, Dan, 197–201, 206, 208, 210–11, 214–16, 223, 235
spin-offs, 28–9, 32–3
spontaneous fiction, 4–6, 13, 21, 84
stance, 63, 82, 84, 94–7
Stapleton, Karyn, 167–9
Star Wars, 24, 117
Sterne, Laurence, 86–7
story schema, 84–6, 94–6
story world, 3, 9, 11–12, 28, 36, 71, 74, 77–8, 80, 82, 84, 88–99, 112, 117–19, 128–9, 148, 171, 194, 227, 236–8
storyline, 3, 26, 28, 33, 71, 77, 86, 88, 96, 166
strong communication, 197, 199–200, 202, 205–6, 220–1, 234
supradiegetic, 53–6, 231
swearing, 82, 150, 152, 154, 162, 167–71
synchronous communication, 37–8, 135–6

Taavitsainen, Irma, 109
taboo, 167, 169–70
target audience, 44, 57, 82, 85, 87, 100–1, 113, 115, 117, 119, 128, 167
telling mode, 127, 170, 178–82, 185, 189, 193–4, 230, 233
text type, 10, 16, 20, 23, 25, 61, 64–6, 74, 136, 147, 226, 233, 236
The American, 113–14
The Big Lebowski, 88, 101, 139–43, 148, 162, 170
The Eyre Affair, 30, 33–4
The Fifth Season. The Broken Earth: Book I, 90, 95
The Hitchhiker's Guide to the Galaxy, 148, 227
The Passion of the Christ, 117
The Tudors, 104–5, 117
The West Wing, 159
tiny story, 84, 96–7
To Hope (poem), 48–9
Tristram Shandy, 86–7

Van Dijk, Teun, 41
voice-over, 126, 134–5
voice-over narrator, 134–5

Watterson, Bill, 181
Watts, Richard J., 45, 153–4, 203, 238
We Shall Overcome (song lyrics), 202–6
weak communication, 197, 201, 202–6, 210, 220–1
Weaver, Warren, 197
Weston, Michael, 190

Wide Sargasso Sea, 29, 32, 86
Wilson, Deirdre, 197–201, 206, 208, 210–11, 214–16, 223, 235
Winter of the Wolf Moon, 212, 222
Wong, Jennifer, 37–9, 41, 50, 57, 71
Wong, Lena, 32, 35

zero focalisation, 92–3
Zillmann, Dolf, 190